the venture
imperative

the venture imperative

imperative

a new model for corporate innovation

HEIDI MASON
TIM ROHNER

HARVARD BUSINESS SCHOOL PRESS
Boston, Massachusetts

Requests for permission to use or reproduce material from this book should be
directed to permissions@hbsp.harvard.edu, or mailed to Permissions, Harvard
Business School Publishing, 60 Harvard Way, Boston, Massachusetts 02163.

Library of Congress Cataloging-in-Publication Data

Mason, Heidi, 1952-
   The venture imperative : a new model for corporate innovation / Heidi
Mason, Tim Rohner.
      p. cm.
Includes bibliographical references and index.
   ISBN 1-57851-335-9
   1. Venture capital. 2. Technological innovations—Finance. I.
Rohner, Tim, 1961- II. Title.
   HG4751 .M37 2002
   658.4'063—dc21

                                      2002001459

The paper used in this publication meets the requirements of the American National
Standard for Permanence of Paper for Publications and Documents in Libraries and
Archives Z39.48-1992.

To Peter, Alex, Tess, Jack, Charles, and Diane

—H.M.

To Janis, McKenna, Ted, and Cal

—T.R.

contents

preface

Why We Wrote It and Why You Should Read It

We wrote this book because we believe every company must venture if it is to be successful in the long run and in a technology-intensive world. The historical performance of corporate venturing as an industry is, well, not very good. Yet we've both seen some extraordinary and unique value created from corporate venturing programs: the kind of value that transforms companies and puts them on new growth curves. Unfortunately, the landscape is so littered with failures that the successes have been hard to notice.

Our perspectives on corporate venturing are from a practitioner's point of view—taking lessons from prior corporate venturing failures and successes as our road map. Heidi has spent the last twenty years in Silicon Valley as a start-up consultant and strategist working with the venture community, independent start-ups as well as corporate programs. Tim, who currently leads DiamondCluster International's digital strategy and ventures practice, has spent the last two decades as a senior strategy and technology partner with leading management consultancies, assisting and guiding big companies in their efforts to innovate. In addition, we have a "visceral" understanding of the venturing process, having started and dealt with the challenges of running multiple ventures of our own. This combined experience gives us a clear perspective on how corporate venturing can succeed, and why it fails.

The trigger for actually writing the book was the "dot-com" boom, when we saw how much money people were throwing at ventures—

good and bad, VC and corporate. It had all the makings of an ugly train wreck, and ultimately it was. The good news was that this age of exuberance and overindulgence motivated many companies to get some skin in the venturing game. The bad news was that in the end the skin had a lot of painful road rash that added to thirty-five years of accumulated error.

What this period of intense experimentation clearly showed was that venturing, done right, offered several things to the mature corporation that couldn't be obtained anywhere else: access to exceptional talent, the means to focus on important new opportunities that didn't fit into the established mold and culture, and the ability to experiment with different ways of organizing and operating that were more suitable to the issues at hand and future growth. This period also demonstrated that established corporations offered things to the fledgling start-ups that they couldn't obtain through any other method: access to rich resources, including deep domain experience and knowledge, technology, established brand, supplier, and customer bases.

This interesting codependency—each side getting what each needs and finds difficult to obtain in other ways—is at the crux of the matter and the argument for corporate venturing. But if the dual-value propositions for corporate venturing are so clear, why is the track record so abysmal? The list of post mortem causes is long, and we explore them throughout the book. But we can also learn a lot from the successful corporate venturing efforts that form the bright and often overlooked part of this history. Not surprisingly, business journalists find the failures better reading, and it's certainly easier to catalog and analyze problems than it is to define success. We believe that a careful examination and consideration of this history reveals a clear path for success—a new model for corporate venturing, one that lives up to its potential and is sustainable over time. That model, and how we formed it, is the backbone of the book.

But back to the difficulties of venturing. The problems of blending new ventures and big-company operation are significant. In the case of talent, how do you meld the opportunities of a small company—freedom of operation and upside pay for performance—with the constraints of a big company that strives to be fair to all employees? How do you take advantage of the big company's rich resources without suffering the same limitations that the company does—the constraints of the corporate culture and institutional knowledge that form the very basis of mainstream success?

The challenges in solving conundrums like this are significant, but the stakes are already high, and we think they're about to get much higher. Peter Drucker, for one, seems to agree. Assessing the impact of the information revolution on the corporation, Drucker sees more or less everything in flux. He indicates that the future success of a company hinges to a considerable degree on the ability to move from a traditional organizational structure to "confederation" models of strategic cooperation and alliance. According to Drucker, the time to prepare for this is now (2001), "especially in working with alliances, partners and joint ventures, and in defining new structures and new tasks for top management."[1] This certainly sounds to us like a call for new kinds of innovation in the face of inevitable decline, and a problem for which corporate venturing is at least a very good answer, and quite possibly the best answer.

In this struggle for change in an uncertain and rapidly evolving technological world, entrepreneurism and innovation are synonymous. Big companies must face the challenges head-on and create an environment that nurtures innovation without eroding what makes a big company strong. Our proposal is a structure we call the venture business office (VBO)—a "demilitarized zone" that connects the big company, the outside venture community, and start-ups, whether they emerge from inside or outside the corporate walls. The VBO is the logical conduit between these very different yet potentially synergistic worlds.

We think there is an opportunity to learn from the successes of venturing, and create tools, organizational structures, processes, and—most important—a point of view that will make venturing work for most companies that are willing to take the matter seriously—as one that may ultimately amount to corporate life or death. Based on the successful implementation of these methods and tools, all of which are within the reasonable reach of every enterprise today, corporate venturing will join the other corporate programs that foster innovation and transformation of the core business. It will work as radar for mergers and acquisitions, it will work as a commercialization function for research and development, it will work as a fast-cycle version of business development, and it will work as a core execution tool for corporate strategy groups. Corporate venturing is an essential mechanism and agent for change in the enterprise, one that uniquely insures its future.

Who Should Read It and How

This is a book for a broad spectrum of readers, from the curious to the committed. The curious are those that know little about venturing, or know a bit more and don't believe in it. The committed are those who see the light but aren't sure whether it's the other side of the tunnel or the train—and want some help. The job titles that fall into these categories are many, and they start at the top of the corporate hierarchy with the CEO and others involved with venturing such as the CFO, head of R&D, head of M&A or corporate development, head of the venturing group, and everyone in each of the organizations. Also, this book can be helpful to those building the ventures, with lessons on how to interact with corporate partners.

We have organized the book into three logical groups. Chapters 1–3 talk about the need for corporate venturing and why it is so hard to do well. Chapters 4 and 9 define the structure we call the venture business office and detail how it works and how strategic value is measured and captured. Chapters 5–8 provide the "bird's-eye view" of how to recognize a successful or failing venture at each major stage of development and prescribe what to do about it, whether you're investing, building, or triggering actions with the parent corporation. Gordon Bell, in addition to his ongoing support, was kind enough to articulate his view of the value and future of corporate venturing in the afterword. As appendixes, we've included useful reference material, including corporate venturing tools and templates for ready application.

Finally, you can't fit everything in a book. And if we did, you wouldn't read it. So we created a companion Web site at www.theventureimperative.com. There you'll find additional information on topics covered in the book, links to other readings, corporate venture groups, independent advisors, portions of the Bell-Mason Venture Development Framework, and a discussion thread if you have questions, comments, or stories to share.

acknowledgments

For those of you who haven't yet tackled the task of writing a book, we are here to report that, no matter what the subject, it really does "take a village." We'd like to take this opportunity to name some of those colleagues who so generously shared their time and talent in support of this project.

First, we want to thank all the folks at DiamondCluster International: Mel Bergstein, chairman, for supporting our work from the beginning and making the resources of the firm available to us; Chunka Mui, chief innovation officer and coauthor of *Unleashing the Killer App*; and Paul Carroll, editor of *Context* magazine and author of *Big Blues: The Unmaking of IBM*. We'd also like to thank Adam Gutstein, John Sviokla, Kevin Grieve, David Garnitz, Krishna Narayan, Patrick Gannon, Paul Blase, and Lance Murata, for their help and ideas. Of course, many Diamond Fellows provided great guidance and critical thinking, including David Reed, Gordon Bell, and Alan Kay, to name a few.

Mark Klopp, the managing director of the Eastman Ventures team, gave us an inspiring example of corporate venturing leadership, and patiently critiqued multiple drafts. Peter Christy, a Silicon Valley veteran, contributed patient insight and review throughout this process. Liz Arrington and Rosemary Remacle provided important contributions and commentary, as did Cathy Cook on marketing issues. Linda Yates, founder and former CEO of Strategos, provided active support and shared visions of bridging the worlds of start-ups and Global 1000 enterprises. Earlier in the development of these ideas, Saj-Nicole Joni collaborated with us and greatly encouraged our investigation of corporate venturing approaches. Randy Komisar, author of *The Monk and the Riddle*, was an ongoing source of guidance on the writing of this book, and a spirited debater to the thinking within—all of which has made the end result better. Other friends and colleagues also helped shape our thoughts and guide our delivery along the way, and to them we express our gratitude as well.

Through the wild mood swings of the Internet economy, we had ongoing support from Hollis Heimbouch, editorial director of Harvard Business School Press, who was never afraid of a contrarian's point of view; as was also true of Jacque Murphy, who seamlessly assumed Hollis's role as editor and majordomo on our project. Amanda Elkin shaped our manuscript into a real book, while Penny Stratton provided critical and intelligent copyediting. And we would have never gotten this project off the ground without the able assistance of Daniel Casse and The White House Writers Group.

And finally to all those who generously shared their corporate venturing experiences and gave us insider views, including those at Eastman Chemical, Cargill, Deere & Co., Motorola, General Motors, TRW, Boeing, British Telecom, CNA Insurance, McDonald's, Jeff Daley at Mitsubishi, and many others—we thank you.

Part I

laying the
foundation for
innovation

1
the venture imperative

a new model for corporate innovation

Now this is not the end. It is not even the beginning of the end.
But it is, perhaps, the end of the beginning.

WINSTON CHURCHILL

Venturing is an essential tool for every company that intends to be a leader in a world that is increasingly technology-driven. Indeed, corporations *should* routinely embark on new ventures. Unfortunately, venturing does not play this essential role today, for clear and even rational reasons. But the consequences of *not* venturing could be fatal to most companies in the long term. In fact, three points underscore the importance of venturing:

- Companies that are market leaders continually innovate and transform their businesses. But it is important to understand that innovation is one of the toughest activities for any business, especially a successful business, to achieve.

- To succeed at innovation, companies need ideas from inside and outside their organization. And they need a way to bring these ideas to fruition. Inside the corporation, innovation emanates from groups such as research and development, corporate development, and business development. Outside the corporation, new ventures are the main way new ideas are brought to life.

- Unfortunately, corporate venturing's track record is uneven. In this book, however, we present a new model for corporate venturing, distinct from private venturing models, that will greatly improve the odds of success.

Market Leaders Continually Innovate and Transform

In his book *The New Market Leaders*, Fred Wiersema argues that market leaders outperform their peers by two to ten times, as measured by sales and market value growth.[1] Two common characteristics of market leaders are their attention to new technologies and their focus on lead customers. They use these technologies and customers to innovate and even transform their businesses. Yet it appears that only one in eight companies are market leaders, and only very few of those have transformed themselves from one business into another.

Innovating has proved difficult for established companies. Large, tradition-laden corporations are often unable to transform themselves until they are already in decline. By that point it is often too late. Indeed, stories of well-known companies successfully transforming themselves through the application of new technology are rare. But this is not to say that it never happens.

In the 1970s, scientists at Corning's labs created the first low-loss fiber-optic cable, providing the company with the base to secure its position today as the leading producer of fiber-optic cabling (while at the same time introducing other successful business lines, including Corning cookware). Other companies, too, have been able to build on their past to secure their place in the future. GE, 3M, and Nokia, for example, have been able to transform themselves to serve new and growing markets by developing innovative products and delivering them to market.

But these companies stand out because they are the exception rather than the rule. Most established companies struggle with attempts to pursue corporate innovation—as demonstrated by failures at places as wide ranging as Apple Computer, Sears, and Rand McNally.

In a sense, these large companies are victims of their own success.

Their vast markets and revenues often paralyze them, leaving them unable to commit the time or resources to invest in risky endeavors. They are too busy succeeding at doing what they do now. A large company won't even consider developing a new product in a small market unless the product is projected to have high margins. As Clayton M. Christensen and Michael Overdorf have pointed out:

> For a $40 million company to grow 25%, for instance, it needs to find $10 million in new business the next year. But a $40 billion company needs to find $10 billion in new business to grow at the same rate. . . . One of the bittersweet results of success, in fact, is that as companies become large, they lose the ability to enter small, emerging markets.[2]

Therein lies the paradox: A large company will not pursue new markets unless the markets are large or extremely profitable—but new markets are usually small and low margin by definition. Yet, if a company fails to introduce new products or enter new markets, eventually the margins on its current products erode to nothing, as they become commodities. So not only must an innovation clear a high margin hurdle to be of interest to large companies, it must also satisfy a large base of established customers—customers who are often themselves locked into the status quo.

Seagate Technology is a clear example. In 1985, Seagate was prepared to build on its position as one of the most successful companies in the microelectronics industry. The company was one of the first in that sector to develop working prototypes of 3.5-inch hard disk drives, developing more than eighty such models with a low level of funding. But it shelved the new smaller drive, ceding first-mover advantage to an aggressive start-up, Connor Peripherals, which was founded by several former Seagate employees, among others.

Why did Seagate hold back? For one thing, its leading customers (including IBM) indicated that they were not interested in the new drives. For another, company analysis showed that the smaller drives would not match the margins on higher-capacity 5.25-inch drives. When laptops took off using these new drives, Seagate was left behind.[3] Seagate's experience is common. Consider IBM's struggle with the impact of PC operating systems, or Barnes & Noble's difficulty dealing with Amazon's challenge. Corporate managers, struggling to keep up with existing markets, are unable to see a potential future forest among today's trees.

PRAXAIR, INC.: A CLASSIC STORY
FROM LATE '90S CORPORATE VENTURING

The experience of Praxair, Inc., an industrial gas manufacturing and distribution company, is hardly unique. In the late 1990s, Praxair began to, well,
run out of gas. After decades of producing and delivering industrial gases
used in the manufacturing industry, the company struggled to grow the top
and bottom lines. That's when management looked to the Internet for
growth, and to defend the company's franchise. They conceived and created a new business to revolutionize the metal fabrication supply chain:
essentially, an Internet portal site with transactional capabilities, electroni-
cally connecting all the players in the metal fabrication industry.

It was a bold move. For one thing, it was a direct threat to the company's own core business, potentially offering products made by Praxair's
competitors. It would take Praxair into demanding new areas in which it
had no experience, such as brokering steel and finding contract labor. And
in an industry characterized by an old-boy network, competing electroni-
cally was a leap into the unknown.

Praxair management made it clear that the new venture was a priority.
Proven executive talent, including Praxair's own CFO, took the helm of the
new business. The company put its money where its mouth was, to the tune
of several million dollars. This new supply chain portal business appeared
to have everything. Everything, that is, except revenue. After less than a
year of red ink, the parent company pulled the plug on the venture.

Praxair's experience is common: A mature company tries to revitalize
itself by setting up a new technology-driven business, but then is unwilling
to invest the time and capital necessary to develop a new market, unable
to adjust to the demands of a new business, and unprepared to make the
long-term commitment that venturing demands.

These examples and so many others confirm something that most
corporate managers already understand: that managing a new innovation, especially one involving technology removed from a company's
core business, is an unmapped territory fraught with problems. And the
groups that manage these innovations within a corporation often clash

with the dominant organizational culture. They operate on a different timetable. They demand attention, but they also require more freedom than most corporate divisions do.

And yet, such corporate ventures may also be the most promising mechanism for corporate growth. In either a rising or declining economy, a company can find no better way to reignite an aging corporate strategy. There is no more direct way for any company to reach into the world of technology—including access to ideas, talent, and products. That is why businesses must learn to "do" innovation well. Their goal should not be merely to get lucky. The large, diversified company must learn how to create a structured innovation competency that is continually fueling new ideas, products, and businesses that are relevant to the company's overall industry. Ideally, innovation becomes a core element of corporate strategy to pursue both top- and bottom-line growth.

Innovation from Inside and Outside the Corporation

Few would argue that all innovative ideas could be generated and executed from within the four walls of an existing organization. But in today's networked world, accessing ideas and businesses from outside the organization is easier than ever. However, there is a bias against looking too far outside for ideas that have a fundamental impact on an organization's core strategy. The "not-invented-here" mind-set continues to permeate the culture of many long-standing companies.

Relying on Internal Groups for Innovation

Most organizations rely on several different groups to drive innovation, the most common being research and development (R&D), corporate development, and business development. R&D tends to focus on product development, often weighted toward longer-term products or their components. Corporate development tends to focus on merger and acquisition (M&A) and joint venture (JV) activities, especially large acquisitions or JVs that fundamentally influence the strategy of either a business unit or the corporation as a whole. Business development will generally be involved in building important strategic alliances; most have revenue-enhancement objectives at their core. Of course, so many variations of these groups exist that it defies discussion. But for our purposes, understanding the key types of innovative actions that an organization undertakes is sufficient. (See figure 1-1.)

Tapping External Ventures for Innovation

Technology, it is worth repeating, has made continuous innovation an inescapable mandate for a competitive business, particularly those that have been in traditional and relatively low-tech fields. To these businesses, the tech boom of the 1990s was an opportunity but also a dangerous threat. By now the story is familiar. Suddenly companies saw their business models imperiled by a networked economy in which geography, reputation, or closely held knowledge became far less important. New ventures without profits, even revenues in some cases, were receiving multibillion-dollar valuations on Wall Street, valuations that provided the capital to enable them to grow their businesses aggressively as they pursued the incumbents' market share and profits. Even executives who could see through the hype in much of the Internet boom also recognized that this new global communications vehicle had rewritten the rules of marketing, sales, distribution, and supply chains by making companies more transparent to other participants in their industry, and interactive with them. Old business models in manufacturing, retail, or professional services, which had thrived profitably for decades, now faced the threat of obsolescence. Suddenly, selling products from a storefront, or offering high-fee financial services in local markets, or distributing products by trucks to a loyal customer base—business models that had essentially existed since the Industrial Revolution—were at risk of being undermined by e-commerce, business-to-business auction sites, and Internet-based supply chains. No more could companies coast on previously reliable business formulas. New ventures, especially in technology, were exploiting new ways to interact with suppliers and customers.

During the 1990s, the most successful and path-breaking technology companies seemed to understand this formula intuitively. Although companies such as Dell, Intel, and Microsoft were rewriting the rules of the economy, they understood the precarious nature of resting on a single

FIGURE 1 - 1

Corporate Innovation Platform

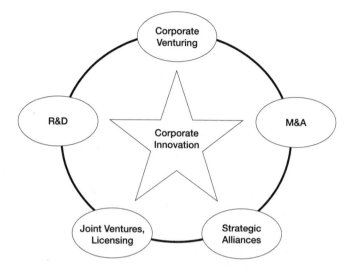

winning formula. Microsoft, Bill Gates has famously said, is always within two years of extinction. That is why many technology powerhouses were also the leading forces in corporate venturing. Their activities took various shapes and had many disparate purposes. Intel invested hundreds of millions of dollars across many companies, in each case helping fuel businesses that would later have a large appetite for Intel's chips. Lucent Technologies invested in or acquired different business lines, increasing their value and then spinning them off or taking them public. Microsoft made many investments that could be considered a form of corporate venturing. In some cases, such as its investment in WebTV, its strategy may merely have been to obtain promising technology that might one day prove to be a threat to its dominant software. Or perhaps Microsoft thought the technology could expand the customer base for its own software products.

For its part, Cisco Systems followed an unconventional form of corporate venturing, which might be called "external R&D." The company developed a tight formula for evaluating, acquiring, and integrating start-ups and growing technology firms. It has acquired more than sixty-five start-ups in the last decade.

Business analysts and corporate executives have pored over and celebrated these examples of corporate venturing. But to most companies desperate to enter the venturing world, they offer little instruction. Indeed, their problem is more fundamental. Technology is not yet central to their business, yet they recognize that if they were able to succeed with some ideas related to the Internet, it could advance their core strategy.

Eastman Chemical Company found itself in this position during the late 1990s (see the following sidebar). In many ways, Eastman typifies many companies that hoped venturing would help make them a leader in the use of technology to drive business innovation and create customer solutions—even with little involvement in information technology or communications. Eastman was certainly an innovative company. It had enjoyed many breakthroughs related to R&D in the chemical industry. But information technology remained largely a back-office function, used to process bills or produce financial statements. It was not, itself, an engine of innovation. All that changed when the company invested in a software application that would become indispensable to all its customers and suppliers. Suddenly, Eastman was leading a *technology* revolution within the very traditional confines of the chemical and shipping industries. For Eastman Chemical, corporate venturing became the door through which it could step into new, high-growth arenas related to its business but in which the company had little experience and few skills. For most companies with little experience in technology, this entry into new, profitable pursuits should be the real objective of venturing.

The mere need for innovations that can help a company enter new markets begs a critical question: Can a large, traditional, even hidebound corporation be the catalyst for new ideas? For much of the past three decades, the task of developing and introducing new technologies seemed to be the special province of small, privately held or newly public companies that were spry enough or lucky enough to win money from established venture capital firms in Silicon Valley, Boston, Austin, or other high-tech hubs. A large company seeking innovative products, the consensus held, could either acquire smaller companies that needed financial resources to bring innovations to market or they could make huge investments in research and development. But the beginning-to-end

EASTMAN CHEMICAL ADDS VENTURING TO THE MIX

At first glance, Eastman Chemical Corporation seemed like an unlikely candidate to blaze a pioneering new trail in corporate venturing. More than twenty-five hundred miles away from Silicon Valley by road and culturally a world apart, Eastman Chemical hadn't even moved forward with an e-commerce strategy or opened a dot-com storefront until 1999.

But CEO Earnest Deavenport understood the need for his company to create a venturing program. From his corporate perch in the eastern Tennessee town of Kingsport, Deavenport could see the potential of electronic commerce. And he believed that innovating would lead to growth, which was crucial to a company struggling to increase market share in a mature industry. At $4.59 billion, Eastman's revenue in 1999 was just slightly higher than it had been when it split off from Eastman Kodak five years earlier.

But Deavenport also understood that if Eastman was to venture successfully, he had to create a special environment in which the normal rules that had always served Eastman well would no longer apply. That environment would be alien to Eastman's culture, traditional practices, and many of its own vested interests. Creating it without dooming it to failure or fatally undermining the company's traditional strengths would require groundwork, planning, dexterity, and the right mix of people. The ventures group would need its own processes, allowing it to import the art that is essential to venturing and build the science that must go with it.

It's worth looking at the initial steps Eastman took as a brief primer to the way a company transforms itself:

- NUDGE CORPORATE THINKING. Deavenport laid the cornerstone by talking up his executive team, recommending books for them to read, and holding in-house seminars featuring outside experts on corporate investing and the Internet. He sought to determine which members of his senior executive team were paying attention to the new approach, tossing questions at them and keeping track of who seemed to get it and who didn't.

- PUT IN PLACE PEOPLE WITH COMMITMENT TO THE NEW VENTURE MISSION, AND GIVE THEM THE SCOPE TO ISOLATE IT FROM CORPORATE TRADITIONS THAT COULD THREATEN IT. One of Eastman's executives moved away from the corporate shadow in Kingsport and relocated to Silicon Valley, where he could be closer to new ventures and new thinking. He set up a venture business office, creating its own governance structure for himself and his employees.

- SPREAD EASTMAN'S BETS AND BUILD A PORTFOLIO OF OPTIONS. Many in the business world see corporate venturing as one thing and one thing only—undertaking new ventures and running them within the company. That's actually only a fraction of what corporate venturing needs to be. Deavenport recognized that Eastman could not succeed in the venturing game through one or two big investments, or by rushing into a solo start-up. The company was prepared to invest $20 million in its corporate venture capital program, and that meant it had to diversify to create a range of options and minimize risk. Incubating a new business from within the company or setting up a separate wholly owned enterprise could be only one part of Eastman's venturing program. What the company needed was a diverse portfolio—including venture investments, joint ventures, and industry partnerships.

- ENSURE THAT THE INVESTMENT PORTFOLIO IS STRATEGICALLY RELEVANT TO THE COMPANY'S CORE BUSINESS. Eastman had to build adjacent businesses that would be related to its proven strengths and experience, making the company more efficient and accelerating its core capabilities. Every investment involved a technology with the potential to improve the way Eastman did business. In that way, venture investments, joint ventures, incubations, and all other elements of the program would provide the company with additional strategic leverage, over and above their impact on return on investment.

Eastman's results reflected its thought-out approach. Through its new venture organization, the company soon began creating a hothouse of

task of carrying an innovation from concept to seed to product development all the way through to market development—that was outside the parameters of an established organization.

That model is no longer relevant. Our view is that the modern corporation's task is to use a variety of methods to harness creativity, to new projects. The company made equity investments in related enterprises such as exchanges, service providers, business process applications, and software infrastructure.

As well as equity investments, Eastman entered a joint venture to establish Asia's first large-scale online chemical exchange, and a partnership in an online exchange targeted at the $64 billion paint and coatings industry. And it launched a company that manages logistics for chemical buyers and sellers.

In the midst of these new ventures was Eastman's greatest gamble: its investment in webMethods, a fledgling start-up company that was trying to persuade corporations to get behind its XML software as a standard for integrating communication with customers and tracking orders and shipments. This integration software enables supply chain transparency, giving Eastman a rare bird's eye view of its trading partners' inventories—how much of any chemical a customer or supplier has in stock—facilitating pinpoint accuracy in inventory decisions.

In an industry where many suppliers still didn't use fax machines, introducing an online exchange required a leap of faith. But what helped push Eastman management toward webMethods was the realization that they might be creating not only an efficient, cost-saving customer interface, but possibly a new standard that they could license to every company in the chemical industry.

In the first two years after launching its corporate venture process, Eastman invested in about twenty ventures. Some, like webMethods, revolutionized the company's relationship with customers. Others revealed basic flaws at an early stage. But all the investments express common themes: a focus on enhancing tools and techniques for better delivery of the company's core business, developing new techniques for doing the things it does faster, better and cheaper. In fact, eighteen of the first twenty-two investments had an established strategic partnership and/or customer relationship/usage.

centralize it within the organization so it works in tandem with the company's larger strategic goals, and to create a platform that allows the innovation process to be continuous. Corporate venturing utilizes several techniques to innovate continuously—it's not just venture capital or spinning off businesses. (See figure 1-2.)

FIGURE 1 - 2

Corporate Venturing Tree

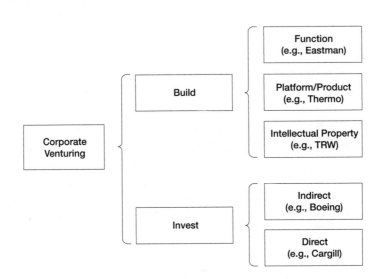

A New Model for Corporate Venturing

Given the critical role that new ventures play in driving innovation outside the corporation, it would seem that there must be a way for them to achieve a similar status inside the corporate environment. At the highest level, we believe that corporate venture groups must embrace three broad parameters. First, they must achieve both financial and strategic returns from these investments. Second, the returns must encompass both product and market opportunities. Third, businesses should come from inside and outside the company, as illustrated by figure 1-3. Of course, it's never that easy.

Corporate Venturing's Track Record Stinks

We begin with this unsettling observation: Most companies have tried some form of corporate venturing, and most companies have failed at it. So why do they venture? And why do they fail? They venture because it is an effective tool for innovating, and they fail because they don't know how to do it right. These answers beg another question: If corporate venturing is so hard to do well, why don't large, established

FIGURE 1 - 3

Different Levels of Corporate Venture Strategy

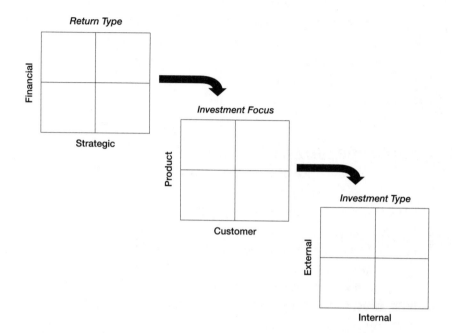

companies simply stick to their core businesses and acquire new capabilities once others have developed them? Quite simply, those that wait to buy innovation "off the shelf" will lose the opportunity to use breakthrough ideas in technology to revitalize their own core business and create competitive advantage. This may be the key argument for venturing, and it is why the venturing process itself needs to be part of a larger corporate strategy.

For most large companies, corporate venturing has been either an out-of-body or an all-too-familiar experience. Although many have observed the venturing world from the sidelines with a mix of puzzlement and envy, others have jumped in and pursued it with vigor. The practice soared during the 1990s—along with the Nasdaq Index, venture capital–backed start-ups, and corporate cash—as large and small companies seemed to race against each other to launch new businesses or set up funds that would fund new ventures to produce payback in both profits and innovation.

But when the Nasdaq began to fall to earth in April 2000, the outlook for new technology companies suddenly didn't seem so bright. The sound of new ventures crashing to the ground seemed to relieve large corporations of the pressure to respond to innovative new entrants to the market. And investor skittishness prompted corporate executives to ask themselves, Is this the time to venture or to stay at home and look after the knitting? Those who argue that corporate ventures are a costly

APPLE AND IBM: A CLASSIC STORY FROM
EARLY 1990s CORPORATE VENTURING

In 1992 Apple and IBM decided to join forces to create a new venture, Kaleida Labs. Kaleida was to spearhead the parent companies' multimedia efforts into a next-generation object-oriented multimedia operating system and player, to be used for everything from interactive TV set-top boxes, to handheld devices, to personal computers equipped with CD-ROM drives. As an independent venture, Kaleida was also in a position to drive cross-industry alliances to rally round its platform, and to create a powerful alternative to Microsoft and Macromedia, the leading competitors of the day. Press and analysts alike touted it as a hot company to watch.

Kaleida's team was as auspicious as its parentage: the original CEO was multimedia pioneer Nat Goldhaber, a former venture capitalist and a founder of Electronic Frontier Foundation. He had vision, experience, and a deep reach into the multimedia industry. Both founding companies put their money on the line: they funded their start-up more than amply, and they provided the "star" management team and employees with significant incentives and equity participation. Nevertheless, three years later, Kaleida lay in shambles. Its second CEO, Mike Braun, a twenty-year IBM veteran recruited in 1993 to get the company on track, announced in early 1995 that Kaleida was closing its doors. How could a venture with so much promise and support fall so far and fail so miserably?

In retrospect, it is never one thing that causes such failure. Rather, it is the confluence of timing and severity of many things. And in Kaleida's case, many of the root causes were typical of failed corporate ventures.

and high-risk adventure seemed not without evidence for their case—a case largely built on corporate venturing's mixed and often embarrassing history. Business magazines are filled with gleeful stories of companies that stumbled badly as they poured money into ultimately failed new enterprises in their hot pursuit of the Holy Grail of innovation and corporate transformation. But for these companies, was venturing a bad idea—or bad execution?

In terms of the development effort, Kaleida was a "big" complex idea, and no doubt more difficult to implement than originally forecast. Schedules were slipping. Early signs of slow performance, lack of application toolsets, and difficulties of use posed significant development challenges, but unfortunately, the hype around the product introduction remained high which further elevated expectations—making the market development effort even harder. Further complicating life for Kaleida were different, some would say incompatible, cultural styles of the parents, and the lack of singular focus and ruthless oversight which private venture capitalists would have brought. In particular, Apple's brand of cultural "Not-Invented-Here", its own inconsistent multimedia strategy, and its own management disarray—as well as competitive concern around Kaleida's independent business agenda and alliance targets—further foiled the already struggling start-up. In the heat of all this internal strife, the industry was moving: Macromedia, while not as technically all-encompassing and sophisticated, was gaining de facto market share and "standard" status, making the market development task for Kaleida even more difficult. The Internet was looming, and Kaleida needed to keep pace with a strategy for it.

Some would say the decision to pull the plug on Kaleida couldn't have come at a more inopportune time. It had a release in place to fix the previous product performance problems, it was beginning to make some headway signing up powerful alliances, it had some early customer support with pilots, and it had just announced a Netscape browser plug-in module. Application toolsets were beginning to come along.

But for Apple and IBM, it was too little, too late—another example of corporate venturing gone wrong.

Distinguishing between Private and Corporate Venturing

Of the trillions of dollars in market capitalization created during the boom and bubble of the late 1990s, how much did corporate venture capital create, compared with private venture capital? What is the most successful corporate venture in history? Why do investment dollars in private venture capital funds outnumber those in corporate venture capital funds by a margin of 5 to 1? In fact, why are the largest investors in private funds representatives of these corporate entities themselves? The answers to these questions in and of themselves indicate that the two forms of venturing are quite different.

What is important is not whether ideas from a corporate venture emerge *de novo* from an idea hatched and developed at company headquarters or from proprietary technology in which the company invested in Silicon Valley. Rather, what matters—and what makes corporate venture groups distinct from venture capital firms—is the ability to draw strategic value from the new enterprises that expand the parent company's horizons *and* the ability to send strategic value to the new enterprise to make them successful. A corporate venture group completely cut off from the corporation's influence is likely to be a third-tier venture capital firm. The goal of holistically organizing the venturing process within the corporation's heart and soul is to help drive and transform thinking—to absorb a large company's experience and industry knowledge and to deploy it through new enterprises. In the successful corporate ventures we have seen, the needs and insights of the parent company's business units have influenced both venture investing and building priorities.

None of this can work without a solid and explicit framework for how a corporate venture group operates. Some managers might think that is an odd criterion. After all, business innovation is associated with unstructured, out-of-the-box thinking and creative chaos. Indeed, venturing in all its forms—especially launching start-ups—is often viewed as an entrepreneurial art. Seasoned venture capitalists have always implied, or even boasted, that theirs is a craft rooted in creativity and unique judgment. As it happens, a recent paper published in the *Journal of Business Venturing* found that venture investors as a group are highly overconfident about their ability to make accurate investment decisions.[4]

But such evidence has not diminished the popular conception that successful venture capital investing demands an instinct for new ideas, an ability to recognize entrepreneurial talent in its most nascent form, and a network of contacts who share these talents.

While they have made much of their rare skills, members of the VC community have often denigrated the notion of corporate venturing. They have suggested that anything that involved corporate process would never be able to replicate the maneuverability needed to create a trailblazing business. Others point out, often correctly, that few corporations have the stamina to endure the volatility of venture investing.

An Integrated Model for Corporate Venturing

As illustrated by successful companies with widely differing definitions of their corporate venture groups, there is no single way to venture. Some focus on R&D, some focus on mergers and acquisitions, and some launch new businesses based on proprietary intellectual property. However, we believe there is a best way, one that combines and integrates the different approaches being undertaken. Few companies are doing it this way today, but those who are see strong results. By integrating the different approaches to venturing, a company achieves two key benefits: It builds a diversified portfolio that spreads risk, and it enables each approach to learn from the others. Cargill, for instance, pursues investments in external and internal ventures. Boeing Ventures does the same. With the experience of investing in external ventures, the teams have better criteria for making objective investment decisions on internal ventures. And by building ventures themselves, they are better equipped to understand the real issues external ventures face.

The question we have always posed to clients is whether those same qualities of successful venture capitalists (VCs) can ever be reproduced within a corporate environment. We believe they can—but only with a formal structure for the company to follow, against which it can assess its venturing performance. Corporations need the discipline of a venturing structure precisely because they are large, fragmented, and often tradition-bound. By contrast, most VC firms are relatively small (none, for example, have anywhere near a thousand employees), because the key partners in the firm monitor and tightly control the work of venture investing.

The formal structure we have in mind—and the one we have applied in dozens of corporations—does nothing to inhibit creative thinking inside a company. But it does force the corporation and its venture office to measure every aspect of its venture operations and use that data to constantly refine itself. That is easier to do in a VC environment without elaborate process because venture capitalists understand that a business's failure undermines their own compensation. That is to say, everyone in a VC fund has an enormous financial stake in making ventures succeed. In a corporation, however, where managers may feel somewhat removed from company profit centers, there is less commitment to making sure every aspect of the venture plan is on target. A formal structure for venturing effectively creates a set of milestones and action agendas that most VC firms tacitly understand.

But corporations also need a structure to allow a venture office to fit within a corporate organization. Simply leasing space to a handful of employees and asking them to fund and discover innovative ideas is not a realistic model for corporate venturing. Corporate ventures must have an established relationship with the senior management of a corporation, and they must create clear lines of communications with other business units. In addition, they need a unique but clearly stated compensation policy. And finally, they need to understand the rules for poaching ideas, people, and resources from other parts of the company. These rules help a venture earn and sustain credibility with top managers (who may be skeptical about the venture's ultimate value) while the organizational ties to the company give a venture legitimacy and access to resources that it might not otherwise enjoy.

Jim Clark, the legendary Silicon Valley entrepreneur and the founder of Silicon Graphics, Netscape, and Healtheon—and a man deeply rooted in the culture of VC firms—has cast doubt on the necessity of a formal structure for corporate venturing. "If you have a team that has done good stuff before, they can take even a mediocre idea and make a good company," he once said.[5] Yet his confidence in the ability of talented and experienced individuals to be the primary driving force of a venture overlooks a critical fact about corporations. Most do *not* have people with extensive experience launching new businesses. Many have never worked outside the corporate bubble, much less for a start-up. It is precisely this absence of experience that makes a formal structure for the corporate venturing process so necessary.

What are the key ingredients of a structured framework for corporate ventures? We suggest that any corporation should have a plan that meets the following four criteria:

1. Linkages between every venture, the corporate strategy, and the executives responsible for that strategy must be explicit and monitored. Accordingly, the strategic value of these ventures to the parent should be identifiable and measurable. Even Dell Ventures had difficulty with this connection as discussed in the box that follows.

2. Financing must be based on objective measures of progress against key milestones. Annual budgets and quarterly earnings are not the appropriate criteria for venture financing. These objective measures of progress, detailed later in this book, also form the backbone of governance between the venture and the corporate investor.

3. The team, not each individual, must be able to demonstrate substantial experience with three different skill groups: venture building, venture investing, and operating the core business of the parent. The weak link in this circle can obliterate the value of an entire corporate venturing effort.

4. Corporate venturing must be based on a portfolio of investments (either internal or external) and must set forth specific financial and strategic metrics and milestones. The time horizon to return will be at least twenty-four to thirty-six months (for early stage investments) before the first financial returns begin to accrue, although strategic value may be measurable in advance. Any new business takes time to build and to accrue revenues; corporate venturing is no different. Finally, the plan must articulate specific financial and strategic objectives in terms of investment, return, and time frames.

These criteria will help keep a venture program on course and connected with the parent corporation's strategic intent. But they also help the corporate venture process assume its place as a core competency. They provide a form of governance that ensures proper screening of projects, measurement of their results, and decision-making regarding their fate. If corporate

DELL VENTURES MISSES STRATEGIC VALUE

It would be easy to draw the conclusion that so-called old economy companies are unsuited for corporate venturing. Like most easy conclusions, it would be wrong. An equally dismal example of corporate venturing can be found among the most celebrated companies of the new economy. In 1999, Dell, the revolutionary computer manufacturer, was an early mover in a trend that was becoming increasingly common among growing companies: setting up a corporate venture fund to seed start-ups, in search of a window on technology and corporate synergy as well as big profits.

Founder Michael Dell sought to parlay his reputation, technological expertise, and big bankroll into corporate-venturing success, setting up a unit called Dell Ventures (DV). By the end of 2000, DV had made over 125 investments.

What a difference a year can make. After its whirlwind of activity, DV made only one investment in the first quarter of 2001. What caused the retrenchment? Although the firm's overall level of investment and returns are not publicly available, we can measure the initial track record of several companies in the portfolio. By 2001, Dell's investments in five companies that went public before the NASDAQ 2000–2001 dive had a cumulative worth of just $43.6 million, less than 25 percent of their initial value. Planned IPOs such as Garage.com never hit the road.

Of course, Dell's venture portfolio did not comprise the only technology investments to lose market value during that period. But the investments offer a particularly interesting lesson over and above the decline in dollar value: the apparent absence of a link between the investments and the company's overall business strategy. We see this strategic void frequently in many corporations' corporate venture funds. Consider Dell's investment in LivePerson in early 2000, a 9 percent stake in the New York company that allows proprietors of Web sites to conduct online conversations with customers at the point of sale. Not only did the value of the firm plummet—from $95 million to just over $10 million—when it went public, but even worse than that, Dell's own business units began using a competing product (from FaceTime Communications, in which Dell had no investment) rather than LivePerson. The result? The worst of all possible worlds—no return on investment capital and no strategic leverage or synergies.

FIGURE 1 - 4

Corporate Venture Group Interactions

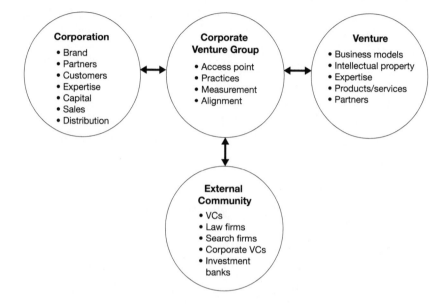

venturing follows a measurable and accountable path, it stands the best chance of becoming a fixture within the company's organization, acting as an engine to drive new growth opportunities, as illustrated by figure 1-4.

So if venturing is so crucial to corporate growth, why aren't more companies enthusiastically embracing it? Because many believe a number of myths that suggest venturing isn't for them. In other words, they have fallen prey to a *fear of venturing*, as we like to call it. In the next chapter, we try to bust the most prevailing myths about corporate venturing that prevent some otherwise innovative companies from even getting started.

The Venture Imperative: Key Lessons

- *Market leaders must innovate to stay ahead of the competition.* Leaders achieve above-industry average growth, margins, and valuations. To maintain leadership, they must continually innovate, or risk losing their advantage.

- *Corporate venturing permits companies to seize technology opportunities.* Companies with limited experience in technology can still profit from it through corporate venturing. The successful corporate venture will exploit new technology so that it becomes an important force for companies whose core business used technology only peripherally.

- *Corporate venturing is different from the work of venture capital firms.* Corporate ventures must focus on more than financial return as an objective. They must produce businesses that are relevant to the parent company's strategic intent and assets. Similarly, the corporate venture groups must use these assets to help the ventures themselves grow.

- *Corporate venturing integrates different innovation approaches.* Ideally, the corporate venture office manages a portfolio of activities that includes both incubation of new businesses and investments in existing but still maturing start-up enterprises. Corporate venture offices pursue both, depending on opportunities and the parent company's strategic needs.

- *A corporation must approach venturing not as an experiment but as a highly structured and ongoing process.* Whereas the art of venturing is sufficient for small VC firms, the complexities and scale of the corporate environment demand that the corporation establish explicit processes and criteria for venturing including ensuring the regular interaction between the parent and the start-up company.

2

the fear of venturing

shedding the misconceptions

The only thing we have to fear is fear itself.
FRANKLIN D. ROOSEVELT

If corporate venturing is a strategic necessity in our technology-driven economy, and if there are proven models to pursue it, then why aren't more companies engaging in corporate venturing, and doing so successfully?

Companies face two principal roadblocks to success in corporate venturing. One is structural: Large, established companies are well set up to guard against risks, not to take them. We will focus on that problem in chapter 3. The other roadblock is perceptual: Many corporations are misinformed about what corporate venturing is (and is *not*) and consequently never seriously address the subject. These misconceptions tend to fall into three different categories:

- *The idea that venturing is irrelevant to the business.* Some managers, for instance, believe that venturing is strictly for companies introducing disruptive technologies, and not for mature, brick-and-mortar companies.

- *The idea that venturing is too expensive, that it is difficult to measure and tough to capture.* Further, some managers believe, wrongly, that

R&D, corporate development, and business development can achieve the same results with less expense and risk. New ventures can capture value only through IPOs, which themselves depend on bull markets.

- *The idea that venturing is too risky.* The company may have tried it once unsuccessfully or managers may generally fear that new ventures fail too often to be a viable strategy. And some believe that corporate venturing burst along with the Internet bubble.

Unfortunately, these misconceptions paralyze most companies with the fear of failure, a mind-set that sends companies off in the wrong direction, right from the start. To avoid failure, then, companies come up with certain excuses, which have a basis in their misconceptions. Let's start by looking at some of the excuses that center around the mistaken idea that corporate venturing is irrelevant to some businesses.

Venturing Is Irrelevant to our Business

Excuse #1: Ventures Are Applicable Only to Disruptive Technologies

To many corporate managers, the words *corporate venturing* conjure visions of businesses engaging in edge-of-the-envelope technologies, taking their company out into a brave new world.

But a company that restricts its venturing efforts to solely disruptive businesses or innovations is actually setting up its venture program to carry a heavy burden with reduced prospects for success. Disruptive businesses and innovations represent a break from a company's ordinary way of doing business. They are *disruptive* because they

- draw the company well away from its established customer base, skills, or methods of operation;

- require unique skills to create, produce, or sell;

- are frequently characterized by the potential to cannibalize a company's own revenue base;

- and address smaller or less profitable markets.

While these types of new businesses may turn out to have high impact to the parent downstream, in the short term they are usually unfamiliar and antagonistic to the core business. They are the hardest to "pull off" on the outside: for example, completely new types of businesses often require the parallel changes in the current environment or development of new infrastructures to support them. A wide range of initiatives, however, rightly fall within the category of corporate venturing as 'continuous' ventures because they:

- build on existing corporate strengths;

- cross into immediately adjacent markets and areas of expertise;

- address customers' existing needs;

- and improve profitability in existing markets.

They are clearly less challenging than 'discontinuous' ventures within the corporate environment, and they are more likely to yield greater near term profit and strategic benefits.

Disruptive business models outside an established core competency pose a particularly perplexing and potentially costly challenge to large, established companies. As Joseph L. Bower and Clayton M. Christensen point out, "Most companies have well-conceived processes for identifying and tracking the progress of potentially sustaining [continuous] technologies, because they are important to serving and protecting current customers. But few have systematic processes in place to identify and track potentially disruptive [discontinuous] technologies."[1]

Eastman Chemical recognized that it faced big challenges when it decided to launch its corporate venture program, described in the preceding chapter. It began by first building a sustaining portfolio strategically relevant to the company's core chemical business and initially focused on extending the capabilities of its e-business initiatives and IT operations. For example, one of Eastman's strengths has always been logistics: an ability to move materials by land, sea, or air. Its venture investments built on this core capability—such as its equity investments in an online chemical exchange and a transportation management software company, as well as partnerships and joint ventures in targeted online exchanges and a logistics Web site relevant for the chemical industry.

Eastman recognized that the more discontinuous and disruptive a venture is, the more challenging it will be to manage. A company that overly weights its venture portfolio with discontinuous investments and businesses is comparable to an investor holding a high-beta, aggressive mutual fund. It can produce high returns but it can also suffer steep declines.

And that in turn sets up another risk: the risk of being canceled when the economy goes south. What's the first thing a company will cut in a cost crunch? An expensive, cutting-edge project with no immediate path to profitability has to be high on the short list. Discontinuous businesses or innovations have to compete within the company against more tangible efforts that can contribute immediately to the bottom line. During a downturn it's more important to show immediate results. When a project doesn't, it's easier to say, We can't afford it now. That's exactly what a number of companies, including several firms in the financial services sector, did begin to say about discontinuous ventures in 2000.

A company with a portfolio full of discontinuous projects may suddenly find itself unduly exposed, with nothing to show other than considerable forgone investment and reduced commitment to venture development. A *balanced* corporate venture investment program, encompassing both discontinuous and continuous businesses and technologies, will be far more likely to provide a constant renewal process that can span downturns as well as upturns.

None of these strategic considerations explicitly rule out discontinuous investments or business models as part of a balanced portfolio. But they do show that when companies pursue discontinuous projects, they must do so through a completely new organization fully protected within the parent company or existing outside its confines, or through minority investments in external businesses. The reasons are consistent from company to company:

- Discontinuous business models present difficulties for the average company, whose culture can handle only so much change at a time.

- They represent a target for established divisions within a company, which aren't likely to appreciate a new competitor for resources and attention.

- They find it harder to compete for funds, given their small initial customer base.

- To a greater degree than other corporate ventures, they require an approach to management, staffing, budgeting, and other areas that diverge radically from the predominant corporate culture.

Excuse #2: Venturing Isn't for Mature or Brick-and-Mortar Companies

Many executives in mature, brick-and-mortar companies tend to resist launching any kind of venture, either continuous or discontinuous. The reasoning goes that technology companies have lower barriers to entry and rapid product cycles and that therefore they are *forced* to innovate on a more regular basis, whereas mature brick-and-mortar companies have higher barriers to entry and longer product cycles and therefore *don't* need to innovate at the same rate (at least not as fast as their technology counterparts).

What they are really saying is that rapid innovation doesn't apply to them or that new technology doesn't apply to them. Unfortunately for them, technology now plays a crucial role in every business and will continue to gain importance from a competitive standpoint. It's interesting that most of the dot-com frenzy was aimed at using technology against these traditional companies. Substitute a few words and you'd be hearing the same excuses that businesses used at the dawn of other economic periods. When Henry Ford created the assembly line, how many companies resisted the new cost-efficient technique, believing that it didn't allow for the individual craftsmanship their own particular industry and company were known for?

The key to renewing the life cycle of a company is a willingness—in fact, an enthusiasm—for adapting to the realities of a new economic era. That applies whether the company is brick-and-mortar, manufacturing, or low-tech. It applies whether the company is pursuing new markets or existing ones.

Corporate venturing isn't for large brick-and-mortar companies? Tell that to Wal-Mart. With a million employees, more than twenty-five hundred stores, and more than a million customers a week, Wal-Mart nevertheless decided to launch its own e-commerce site, Walmart.com, which has a separate board of directors and management team, including a CEO and other top executives recruited from outside. This allowed the venture to develop the strength, in terms of business model, talent, and offering, necessary to survive on its own in a very short period of time. Since then, Wal-Mart fully acquired the venture and folded it into the company's main operations.

Corporate venturing is only for high-tech companies? Tell that to General Mills. In 2000, General Mills invested in an online market research company, MarketTools, which gives it the capacity to conduct three-quarters of its consumer surveys online (compared with one-tenth of them, as was the case in 1999). It will also yield a cost saving of 45 percent.[2]

Corporate venturing is only for companies addressing new markets? Tell that to United Parcel Service. UPS is investing aggressively in new transportation technologies to evolve its core business. In the spring of 2001, UPS planned to invest $10 million over the next year in technology related to biometrics, middleware integration, and supply-chain application software.[3]

Or tell it to Intel, which invests over a billion dollars a year on corporate ventures largely in businesses that create demand for its processing capabilities, or products that enable efficient manufacturing and production of its products. Or tell it to Cargill, Incorporated, an American icon since 1865, whose venture story is told in the accompanying sidebar.

There is only one kind of company that venturing isn't suited for: a company not committed to growth and renewal.

Venturing Is Too Expensive

Excuse #3: Value Is Difficult to Measure and Tough to Capture

Most Wall Street analysts do not value corporate venturing programs. Instead, they treat them like poorly run R&D departments—essentially cost centers that produce some immeasurable option value through unknown innovation. The problem is that corporate managers must then adopt the analysts' perspective, motivated in part by the Street's need to estimate future cash flows accurately. By fully discounting any expected value, they run no risk of a negative surprise. Positive

CARGILL eVENTURES

On the surface, there is nothing that would seem "new economy" about Cargill, Incorporated. The company, headquartered in Minneapolis, was founded in 1865 and initially made its reputation as a grain merchandiser. Over the years, Cargill has expanded into a vast array of agricultural-related businesses, including grains, soybeans, cotton, cocoa, and sugar. Cargill also has a sizable financial trading group. Today it has operations in fifty-seven countries and revenues in excess of $49 billion. And it is the largest privately held company in the United States.

Cargill is also among the most innovative companies when it comes to e-business and corporate venturing, which is all the more surprising given its lengthy, traditional brick-and-mortar history.

The seeds were sown in the mid-1990s, when Cargill's CIO made sure discretionary funds were available at the SBU level for experimentation. Cargill began to add extranet applications to its platform. By 1998–99, there was enough momentum inside the company, as it reorganized to deliver customer-driven solutions, and outside, as the Internet revolution continued to gather steam, to convene an e-commerce task force. The task force was charged with defining new ways to drive innovation at Cargill through the use of new technologies. One of its key responses to this mandate: corporate venturing.

Cargill eVentures was chartered in 1999 to further enhance the company's core businesses and strategic directions via new venture investing. Its vision: nothing less than the transformation of global supply chains, using technologies that create innovation and lower costs, ultimately benefiting Cargill, its partners, and its customers.

Today, Cargill eVentures has a substantial fund under management and a global perspective, with seventeen people spread across offices in the Silicon Valley, Minneapolis, and London. To date, it has invested in and nurtured more than a dozen new businesses. The Silicon Valley office focuses on networking with entrepreneurs, venture capitalists, and other technology companies, while the Minneapolis office maintains links with the company and networks with midwestern VCs and entrepreneurs. The team composition also reflects this combined external and internal focus. Several members have come from Cargill operational positions, and their domain expertise and internal network of contacts have proved extremely valuable in validating concepts. In addition, a few external people were hired to add technological depth to the team.

Jim Sayre, the CEO of Cargill eVentures, had the clear intention of merging Cargill's unique strengths with the best practices of venture capital and the corporate/industrial world. Through investments in start-up companies and internal incubations, Cargill eVentures has supported businesses that are applying new technologies to transform traditional business processes and create new business opportunities.

Incubations have focused on using technology to create online marketplaces and communications platforms to establish industrywide standards for electronic commerce. With a robust market share in a number of vertical industries, and a recognition of the power of electronic business to lower the cost of transactions and improve customer relationships, Cargill wanted to be involved in developing these solutions. The company launched businesses where the opportunity was not being addressed and where it could leverage its industry expertise and industry relationships. One such example is LevelSeas, conceived by Cargill and cofounded with BP and Shell, which pioneered collaborative chartering and management of oceangoing vessels for global shipping.

Cargill eVentures's investments in start-ups focus on early-stage investments in technologies that broadly benefit, or are consumed by, global Fortune 500 enterprises. Cargill looks for opportunities where it can act as a test bed for the product, helping to lend its industry or process knowledge to product development. In some cases, doing so involves the transfer of Cargill IP. Cargill eVentures maintains its active involvement through a board seat or observer status on each of its ventures' boards and also organizes "chief officer"-level roundtables across its portfolios so that executives can share ideas and best practices.

Cargill eVentures is equally innovative in the way it has structured itself within the Cargill family of businesses. Even though eVentures is wholly owned by Cargill and treated as a business unit, it has its own governance and compensation structure (including carried interest in the portfolio) that is distinct within the parent company. Its investment decision processes are equally optimized and speedy. The eVentures team is guided by its own rigorous investment standards and stage-gate systems, and a small "board" of four (comprising handpicked corporate officers and e-business leaders, with Cargill's CEO ex officio) to provide oversight. Performance is measured by a rate of financial return typical to any venture capital firm, but in the case of Cargill eVentures, these financial returns are the "table stakes." The ultimate goals for the firm—indeed, how its long-term impact will be most felt—is in its delivery of strategic value to the corporation, driving innovation internally and introducing new styles of doing business, both entrepreneurial and collaborative. "This is the true basis of our success as a unique change agent within the company," says Sayre.

Many corporate venturing groups find the roles they are chartered to play within their parent companies even more challenging than building a position in the outside venture community. With the blessing of the Cargill leadership, the eVentures group has addressed these challenges very creatively, by constructing multiple sources for return of value. For example, it offers the following:

- An entrepreneur-in-residence (EIR) program, a structure borrowed from the VC world. Cargill eVentures maintains this program for providing business planning and strategy assistance to those whose proposals it approves. Many business unit employees join eVentures during the early-stage period for fixed periods of time, returning to their business unit to help evangelize for the new product or service.

- Expert advice and counsel to SBUs on market intelligence, prospects, and portfolio companies

- Direct aid to each SBU in developing e-business strategy and partnering models

- Centralized review and vetting of all new technology-focused business plans and proposals within Cargill, which creates standards, maintains quality, and insinuates a venture point of view and entrepreneurial culture

- Pilots as a competitive edge, introducing new technologies and applications by actively bringing portfolio companies and SBUs together to do early testing and pilots. It continues to monitor results with the SBU and other partner pilots.

Creating new business is an ongoing process at Cargill. When the eVentures group executive team meets every Friday to review venture proposals, it always asks key questions to ensure that the new business fits within the larger strategic interests of the parent company: Could Cargill be a customer for this service or product? How could Cargill add value to the start-up company? How can Cargill's customers or partners benefit? How easily could this new business be sold within our business units? Cargill has learned how critical it is to keep ventures closely attuned to the needs and interests of each business unit. The result has been successful ventures that are highly complementary to the company's core businesses. Much of that success has come from relying on expertise already inside the company. "We figure that if Cargill is a logical user of one of our eVentures, it is likely others in the industry will have the same needs," says Sayre. "That allows us to spearhead industry leadership in new technology."

surprises are all right, especially when they are rationalized as a one-time event. In addition, because a corporate venture group often holds large stakes, it frequently has trouble unwinding the investment to maximize return in the timeframe and means most comfortable to a parent dealing with the pressure of reporting on a quarter to quarter basis.

This viewpoint misses the rationale for corporate venturing—creating strategic value. Cisco Systems is able to create value from its investments and acquisitions in new technology companies, using corporate venturing as a substitute for a portion of corporate R&D. How much would Cisco have needed to invest in R&D to accomplish the same level of innovation achieved by tapping into the collective capabilities of everyone who doesn't work for the company?

Agilent Technologies underscored this premise when it launched Agilent Ventures, its first venture fund—scheduled to invest $100 million a year—in early 2001. Just a little more than a year after it was spun off from Hewlett-Packard, Agilent made it clear why it was entering the venturing game. "We are not a huge fund, so we're going after [technologies] we think can bring us some strategic benefit, instead of primarily financial benefit," explained Agilent Ventures managing director Maximilian Schroeck.[4] Agilent was looking for potential investments in companies that provide the components underlying communications networks, especially early-stage optical networking and wireless start-ups.

The same strategic emphasis makes sense in the financial services sector. JPMorgan Chase, for example, views its venture arm, LabMorgan, as a vehicle to locate and develop technologies that will bolster its "e-finance" strategy. In late 2000, for example, LabMorgan invested in a New York start-up that gives wealthy customers an online overview of all of their holdings across financial institutions. The firm's strategy team determined that catering to people with high net worth would be pivotal to the firm's growth.[5]

For a large company, venturing—in the form of incubation—offers one of the most important strategic advantages of all: the opportunity for a venture to develop outside the bowels of the company, without distracting from the firm's immediate strategic focus. Sony offers an excellent case in point. In 1998, Sony Computer Entertainment America was focused on the development of console and CD-based games, especially those for its popular PlayStation 2. At the same time, a Sony team was in the final development stage of EverQuest, an online subscription game. More than anything else, EverQuest was a distraction to the core business. Unable to give it sufficient marketing attention, Sony decided to employ one of its favorite strategies: It spun EverQuest off as a separate company, Verant Interactive, rather than canceling the project.

Fortunately for Sony, it also retained an option to repurchase Verant, and the company was soon glad it had, for while Sony had been concentrating on growing its established markets, Verant had quietly been creating a new one. When EverQuest was launched the next spring, the new company's servers were jammed by subscribers—almost a quarter-million within six months—and they met year one customer goals in the first week after they launched!

Sony now had time for a new kind of game. Less than two years after Sony Computer Entertainment spun off EverQuest, another Sony Division—Sony Online—reeled it back in. In May 2000, it purchased Verant and folded its other online gaming businesses into this newly acquired group. The move bolstered sales and revenue. But the biggest advantage was strategic: Through its Verant venture, Sony established first-mover advantage in the new online subscription market.

Excuse #4: R&D Does the Same Thing at Lower Cost and Less Risk

If a company is already reluctant to venture because it believes venturing just isn't appropriate, fears about the cost of venturing can be even more of a deterrent. Some companies see venturing as a duplication of strategic measures they already budget for, principally R&D. But this just isn't the case. In fact, a recent study supported by the National Bureau of Economic Research has indicated that venture capital is up to ten times more effective in stimulating innovation than corporate R&D.[6]

Corporate venturing and R&D are not alternatives, however; they supplement each other. The importance of their interrelationship is proved by the examples of two of the largest R&D companies in the world. In late 2000, the pharmaceutical firms Merck and Lilly launched venture capital funds worth tens of millions of dollars each. If one industry is known for its dependence on R&D, it's the drug industry, where Merck, Lilly, and other firms spend hundreds of millions of dollars developing a single potential drug, with no guarantee it will even make it to market.

The two companies' decisions to launch venture funds— following the path set for more than a decade by the venture arms of firms such as GlaxoSmithKline (when it was SmithKline Beecham) and Johnson & Johnson—illustrate an important corporate message: R&D and corporate venturing work in tandem with each other, not in isolation.

SmithKline, through its internal venture unit, was an early investor in Synaptic Pharmaceutical, maker of drugs that modulate the nervous system; Corixa, which concentrates on treatments for cancer and infectious diseases; and Cogent Neuroscience, which develops drugs that target diseases of the brain and nervous system.

Like many industries, pharmaceutical companies have seen the built-in advantage to obtaining external research and development through venture investing. As an investor, a company can strategically tap into new technologies. At the same time, R&D through venturing minimizes the downside of failed projects conducted within the company. The same is true in the chemical business. Roger Mowen, Eastman Chemical's CIO and senior vice president of global customer services, knows that if one of his venture investments goes south, it won't dampen corporate morale the same way that closing an in-house project would. "I can more easily walk away and move on to the next one," Mowen says.[7]

But the R&D and corporate venturing functions do not have to overlap. Merck and Lilly established a mission for corporate venturing clearly distinct from their R&D arms. "We are separate from R&D," says

Per Lofberg, head of Merck Capital Ventures. "We are focused on investments that can help the business side of the business."[8]

Merck and Lilly gave their venture funds the mandate not to invest in new drug development but rather to focus on the commercialization and distribution of drugs over the Internet. Merck in particular was eager to take advantage of low valuations of Internet health care companies in the wake of the dot-com collapse.

At the same time, Merck decided to target companies that improve research processes, such as technologies that expedite distribution processes or companies that help physicians record and transmit patient information. The company decided that venturing was an effective way to pursue that form of R&D.

Excuse #5: Venturing Is Affordable Only in a Bull Market

The cost argument against venturing gathers steam during an economic downturn. But the strategy cannot be made to fit that neatly into the business cycle. "You can't just do it in good times," says Eastman Chemical's Mowen. "You have to have continuity over a number of years or else there is no point starting."[9] In fact, in the economic cooling at the turn of the century, the companies with the largest research and development budgets—IBM, Microsoft, and Intel—actually increased their spending in absolute or percentage of revenue terms. Venture funds, for example, are typically set up with minimum investment periods of five years. Over the course of five years, economic circumstances could change completely. Many corporate venture groups argue that a downturn is the best time to invest, not the worst, because then valuations are reasonable and the strong are surviving.

A slowdown may also offer an opportunity to grab an advantage over competitors who are busy retrenching. When Belgian movie theaters took a battering at the hands of cable and videos during the 1980s, that is exactly what movie exhibitor Bert Claeys did—grabbed an advantage. Most of the company's competitors simply reacted, by restructuring and downsizing—or went out of business. Claeys, however, spent time thinking about what was keeping people away from theaters. If customers wanted the comforts of home, then the company would give them those comforts in a theater. The result? A new kind of movie theater, called Kinepolis, characterized by stadium-sloped seating and wide spacing, as well as huge screens and leading-edge sound and visual systems. In its first year of operation, Kinepolis drove a 40 percent increase in Brussels's movie going market, capturing half of it.[10]

What drove this strategy? A slowdown in the industry. For Kinepolis, like many companies, innovation not only made sense during tough times, it helped bring on better times for an industry that had been taking a beating.

Of course, venturing during a downturn is considerably different from venturing during a boom. The pressure to show near-term results is greater. No one can ignore the market environment. But corporate venturing cannot be a stop-and-start activity. Companies must adjust their venturing activities and strategies based on the current financial and market environment. No corporate venturing program is going to be worth its weight unless it has inherent strategies for dealing with upturns and downturns. But that goes to the question of what *kind* of venture portfolio a company should have, with what *mix* of investments. In other words, rather than turn the tap on and off, a company must change the ratio of hot water to cold. They must adjust the level of risk, by reviewing

- the ratio of projects with immediate relevance to the company's core competencies compared to those meant to extend its range;

- the balance of ventures conducted in-house compared to those carried on outside the company;

- and the ratio of venture building to venture investment, the mix of alliances and partnerships compared to solo efforts.

In other words, the company must use *both* ends of the business cycle to corporate advantage.

Venturing Is Too Risky

Excuse #6: Corporate Venturing Burst Along with the Internet Bubble

After gaining considerable ground among corporate thinkers in the 1990s, corporate venturing encountered a new reason for resistance on

April 14, 2000. The Nasdaq fell 355.49 points, or 9.67 percent, to 3321.29, which brought it down to less than two-thirds of the record value it had enjoyed barely a month earlier. It would then decrease another 50 percent from that point less than a year later. This marked the puncturing of a market balloon that had been rising into the stratosphere for the previous 18 months.

Until that balloon burst, the pressure had clearly been on to innovate, to develop new technologies, products, and processes. Companies were viewing venturing as a vital corporate tool to secure a role in the "new" economy. In the minds of some corporate strategists and observers, the market decline changed all that. Suddenly, the argument that corporations had no choice but to race Silicon Valley start-ups to the outer edge of innovation no longer seemed so compelling. Suddenly, the temptation to sit back, cut costs, and wait to see what the future might bring didn't seem so much like whistling past the graveyard. And suddenly, the growth of corporate venturing, as measured by dramatic increases in corporate venture capital funds throughout the 1990s, looked like it might slow down or even sputter to a stop. Indeed, the speculative portion of the corporate venturing bubble had burst also.

The arguments are easy to understand. Why venture when you have less to gain? Why go out on a limb that had already collapsed underneath formerly menacing new competitors? When the Street is demanding results this quarter, why concentrate time and resources on something that might not yield quantifiable results until several quarters into the future—if then?

In mid-2000 Michael Mandel, economics editor of *Business Week*, made a disquieting forecast. In *The Coming Internet Depression*, he argued that "with a less formidable threat from well-funded startups, existing companies will be under less pressure to quickly adopt new innovations that might require painful restructuring . . . and they will have less reason to quickly adopt risky new innovations, because *their competition won't be doing it*" (italics added).[11]

Now, Mandel is no old-fashioned skeptic of the technology-based economy. Indeed, he forecast the potential of the Internet economy in its early stages. Thus his prediction was unsettling—and, as it turned out, prescient. Soon the Nasdaq plummeted. And within a year there was some data to back up his point. In the first quarter of 2001, for example, investment by venture capital firms declined for the second consecutive three-month period, tumbling more than 50 percent year-over-year (from $26.7 billion to $11.7 billion). Of course, the amount of venture capital raised does not depend solely on investor interest. It also depends on the amount of time VC firms must devote to addressing management and governance problems in their portfolio, compared to the amount of time they spend raising capital. But the decline in VC investment nonetheless raises a question: Can established corporations hope to rest on their laurels?

Investment patterns by corporate venture funds indicate that they don't seem to think so. Venture Economics estimates that, at the height of the "bubble," 16 to17 percent of all venture financing in 2000 came from corporations, up from just 2 percent in 1994. And, despite all the subsequent negativity, corporate VC is still 13.5 percent cumulative of total VC investments through the third quarter of 2001. Intel, for example, stated that it plans to invest roughly $1.3 billion in 2001, on a par with its venture investments the year before.

These companies recognized that the underlying reasons for venturing have not suddenly disappeared, as we still have a strongly technology-based economy. The rapid scaling curve introduced by new technologies still foments an unprecedented pace of growth. Large companies still face the daunting challenge of meeting this pace head on, and achieving that kind of growth and renewal or becoming irrelevant.

The level of investment still being made in corporate venturing in particular and in innovation in general makes it clear than any established company hoping to sleepwalk through a downturn runs the risk of being overtaken by wide-awake competitors—both established corporations and emerging start-ups. In fact, many corporate venture groups viewed the venture downdraft as an opportunity to find strong companies at good values.

What *has* disappeared is the panic. When start-ups were sprouting like wildfire from Silicon Valley to Boston's Route 128, large established corporations reacted out of fear. They set up corporate venture funds and launched their own start-ups as a defensive tool, behaving like an overpowered tennis player desperately batting the ball away rather than strategically aiming returns.

For established corporations, the tech boom served as a wake-up call. Then, the collapse of Internet stocks gave them the opportunity to prepare mentally for a new day—and adopt a new attitude to corporate venturing. The reality is that corporate venturing is not just a defensive tool. It is very much an offensive one as well—a response not just to fear but to opportunity.

Excuse #7: We Tried Corporate Venturing and It Didn't Work

Even when acknowledging the potential value of venturing, despite the upfront costs, some executives believe it is uniquely risky to them. Often their excuse is that they tried it once, and it didn't work out. The operative word is *once*.

Large companies often want to dip their toe in the water, pulling back when they feel a chill. Such an approach—based on one or two ventures or investments—often dooms a corporate program. In 1999, for example, the Fireman's Fund Insurance Company made substantial investments in two insurance e-businesses. When neither worked out, the firm closed its venture office.

Some companies seem to look at venture investments as a series of holes on a golf course, moving to the next hole only after they have sunk the last one. But venturing isn't like playing golf. In golf, sooner or later you're going to sink that shot. No individual venture is guaranteed to find the spot. Keep this in mind: Only one in ten venture investments is likely to be a runaway success. Two in ten will provide a normal return. The rest will fail. That means a company's first venture will have a 70 percent chance of being unsuccessful. These odds don't favor the out-of-the-blocks performance that endears subsequent investments from corporate parents.

Golfers equalize their odds by sporting a handicap. In venturing, the equalizer is called a portfolio, and venture capitalists have a reason for building one. While most investments may not pay off, the winners will more than cover the minimal losses on the failures. Investing small amounts in many risky ideas can generate some steady, spectacular returns even if individual investments don't. Silicon Valley does have something to teach big corporations about start-up businesses.

Look at it this way: Would any pharmaceutical company consider maintaining an R&D program that has only one research project? Pharmaceutical firms spread their R&D budget over dozens of potential products, trying to get as many as possible into the pipeline. They recognize that only a handful of their projects in development will even make it to market. Some will lose money, some will just cover costs, and the blockbusters will pay down the sunk costs and provide the margin of profit.

What makes sense for science and technology R&D also makes sense for business R&D. If a company's sole venture project goes down, not only is it left holding the bag for the losses, it is left without a venture program, faces a halt in momentum, and has no potential new businesses to which it can even channel what it has learned from the experience. In other words, if you make a wide range of investments, you're not taking on greater risk, you're essentially managing the risk.

Excuse #8: New Ventures Fail Too Often to Be Viable for Us

Perhaps the greatest challenge for some companies isn't the fear of failure so much as their definition of it. When Thomas Edison produced the first light bulb that worked, he explained that he had made more than two hundred attempts before developing the first successful bulb. "How did you feel about all of those mistakes?" a journalist asked him. "They weren't mistakes," he replied. "Every failure told me something that I was able to incorporate in the next attempt."

That is exactly the attitude a company needs when it is trying to introduce something new, different, and important. Corporate ventures provide the flexibility to experiment—to try things without fear of failure—to determine what may bear fruit and what may not. What some see as a failure, others see as an opportunity to learn—including to learn what doesn't work. In a big company, too often that's a way to damage a career.

Ventures provide the opportunity to experiment, to learn without the risk of catastrophic failure. That is especially true of corporate venture capital, with its multidimensional objectives over and above ROI. For that reason, even unsuccessful ventures yield greater benefits to a corporation than they would to a VC firm. When a venture goes down, corporations have more to sift through in the ashes. There is frequently something tangible, like technology or new methods, that a company can absorb back into the existing business, and always some lesson that it can apply to existing business units, future business units, overall operations, or strategic development. When comparing the assets and liabilities of corporations and VC firms in the field of venturing, that perhaps is the biggest corporate advantage: the opportunity to harvest and apply knowledge throughout the entire organization.

Moving Beyond the Excuses

Corporate venturing is a growth and innovation strategy. That is how companies—regardless of size or industry—need to view it. Corporate venturing, if structured correctly, creates a platform for organizations that makes the search for new and relevant business ideas a part of the company's day-to-day strategy. What links all the excuses we've discussed is the common but erroneous assumption that corporate venturing is a kind of experiment—a single investment in a promising lead. But corporate venturing, in our view, is much more like an embedded process. Over time, a well-structured corporate venture office will invest in and incubate dozens of business. Some will barely last beyond the concept stage. Others will be launched and spun out as independent businesses. All will extend the reach of the parent company's core strategy and give it advantages, expertise, and talent that it simply didn't possess before.

To begin that process, corporations must make two grand cultural and psychological leaps. First, they must get over their mistaken assumptions about corporate venturing, especially those based on the inappropriate excesses of the last few years. Much of the conventional wisdom—which leads to the excuses we've analyzed in this chapter—arises from experiments with venturing that had no process, no clear goals, and no structure that linked it with the firm's larger strategic purposes.

The second leap a company must make is to resist imposing its own traditional strengths and processes on the ventures it promotes. The unique characteristics that help establish and maintain a company's strength may also be features that undercut the freedom a corporate venture needs. As we mentioned at the beginning of this chapter, large corporations are good at guarding against risk. But when mixed with the other well-ingrained habits of a well-run corporation, that prudence can actually impede the flexibility that the corporate venture desperately needs. This is the tension between parent and offspring that every corporate venture process encounters. In the next chapter we examine this problem and highlight the behaviors that companies must avoid to prevent the crib death of an otherwise promising venture.

The Fear of Venturing: Key Lessons

- *Most of the reasons for not venturing are not valid.* For many large companies, corporate venturing is unfamiliar and uncertain territory. Misimpressions and "excuses" fuel corporate resistance. In fact, the temptation not to risk venturing can be irresistible—and dangerous. Coasting is the first sign of strategic exhaustion. Venturing, especially during a flat economy, is exactly what a company needs to do to create new opportunities.

- *Venturing means a portfolio, not a single bet.* No single success or failure should define a long-term corporate venturing program. Successful venturing requires a range of investments and start-up projects. A balanced corporate venturing portfolio is a mix of near and long term, strategic and financial benefits. Innovation need not be only "discontinuous." Some venture projects will be "continuous," extending a company's current businesses and capabilities to make it and its suppliers smarter, quicker and more cost-effective.

- *The type of business is irrelevant.* Don't believe that venturing is an activity solely for small entrepreneurs or sophisticated technology firms. Venturing can uncover new management or supply chain processes, automation and new technology applications, and new business models for every type of brick-and-mortar company.

- *Failure is a learning tool.* Only one in ten venture investments is likely to be a runaway success. Two in ten will provide a normal return. Corporations have the extra edge in salvaging and absorbing value even from ventures that don't make it. The greatest mistake is to close the doors on corporate venturing based on a couple of "misses."

3

battling corporate antibodies

prescriptions for success

The best defense is a good offense.

ANONYMOUS

Some would say that a corporate venture starts life like a child born with a silver spoon in its mouth. It has assets that independent start-ups can only envy, including physical and intellectual capital. A corporation that is venturing will typically have a network of business contacts and partners, deep knowledge of what is needed in its own industry space, and solid understanding of the competitive landscape. Better still, the corporate child's blessings frequently include a parent willing to sign a big check.

But over the course of more than two decades of consulting, we have realized that corporate ventures are at least twice as hard to launch as their independent counterparts. Why do big companies find it so daunting to do what small teams of entrepreneurs do all the time? What stands in the way of converting corporate resources into successful ventures? To understand the problems faced by a corporation that wants to fund and nurture new enterprises, consider the advantage that small entrepreneurs enjoy when they don't have to overcome an established history, culture, or code of policies. When they begin work on a venture, they start with something corporate managers view as a rare luxury: a clean slate. The entrepreneurial ventures are free to innovate, with no restrictions on the people to hire, the suppliers to contract, the businesses to cannibalize, or the markets to target. They don't need their new business to mesh with a parent company's existing business. They're united in strategy and execution. They face no conflicts with entrenched bureaucracies. They don't carry the weight of thick black binders full of corporate rules.

Corporate Culture: Protecting the Parent, Threatening the Offspring

New corporate ventures face the same challenges but lack the same opportunity to shape their own culture, policies, or even priorities. Institutionalized corporate "values," as Clay Christensen calls them, are among the things that make big companies great.[1] Ironically enough, however, these "values" are in diametric opposition to those required to start new ventures. It is in this context that good values turn into bad "antibodies" for fledgling ventures. So whereas corporate ventures begin life with a much higher degree of institutional security than independent start-ups, they often lack what they need most: a corporate atmosphere and attitude consistent with their needs.

Most corporate ventures, especially the unsuccessful ones, don't have much freedom. They must constantly negotiate with powerful corporate interests, cope with agonizingly slow decision-making processes, and juggle conflicting priorities. They must battle an internal environment that encourages everyone to mitigate risk constantly. Big successful companies remain big and successful because they have established a way of doing things that protects them from risk.

The result is a mind-set that is 180 degrees from the way a start-up looks at the world. Table 3-1 lists some generalizations about corporations and start-ups. Although most of you, our readers, have experienced or already know these things, the list puts in context the tensions every corporate venture must confront. At the very root of the differences is something quite simple: size.

TABLE 3 - 1

Cultural Differences Due to Size

	Start-up	New Venture	Growth	Mature
Size	Very small	Small	Medium	Large
Bureaucracy	None	Some	Significant	Stifling
Responsibility	High overlap	Low overlap	Specialization	Extensive specialization
Decision making	Founder	Founders	Small teams in each department	Everywhere and nowhere
Rules	None written	Few written	Entire manuals	Training courses
Administrative intensity	None	Increasing clerical and maintenance support	Increasing professional and staff support	Large, multiple departments
Internal systems	Nonexistent	Crude budget and information system	Control systems in place; budget, performance, reports	Extensive planning and financial systems with support
Task forces	None	Top leaders only	Some use of consultants	Pervasive

Source: Adapted from Richard L. Daft, *Organizational Theory and Design* (St. Paul, MN: West Publishing, 1992), which was based on information from Robert E. Quinn and Kim Cameron, "Organizational Life Cycles and Some Shifting Criteria of Effectiveness," *Management Science* 29 (1983): 31–51.

Large organizations must operate very differently than small organizations to get the business of the day done, because they need more people to accomplish the same tasks. From the strategy perspective, they must protect the franchise and extend it. New ventures are building a new franchise and aren't bound by the restrictions inherent in protecting and extending.

Why do these issues matter so much to the business success of corporate venturing? They matter because inside a corporation, the corporate culture is pervasive. That culture can unnaturally weigh a venture down rather than propel it aloft. Companies that build long track records do so on the foundation of inherited traits that preserve order and resist upheaval. But the same features that allow them to survive make it difficult for them to change. That's what gives birth to a paradox: What often prevents established companies from creating successful new ventures is not corporate weaknesses but corporate strengths.

Look at a company as a living organism. Like most organisms, it is protected by antibodies. In this case, the antibodies are practices, procedures, habits, and attitudes that help keep the parent corporation healthy. A corporation's antibodies help shield it from risk, maintain focus, preserve continuity, and uphold corporate harmony. But they do something else: They repel anything that is new and potentially threatening to the system they inhabit. While appearing to keep the corporate parent healthy, they also stunt its growth and prevent it from advancing to new stages of its life cycle. Because they have been shaped by the status quo and reflect its values, they defend the status quo like a mother hawk protecting her young. The antibodies will invariably perceive new ventures, which carry the threat or promise of potentially radical change, as a challenge to this corporate defense system.

Therefore, despite its track record at nourishing the kind of start-up ventures that corporations must build, the independent venture capital model has not been successfully transplanted into the corporate environment. The VC industry was spawned and flourished in response to the need for unique ways of funding and growing outside-the-envelope technologies, products, and companies. The venturing model has to take into account that these projects are risky, generating a big payoff from the big successes and failing in those attempts more often than not. It has to encourage the experimentation that is central to the success of a new business model. It has to be attractive to dynamic, entrepreneurial women and men with the creativity to shape a vision and the commitment to fulfill it. It has to combine capital with expertise and experience distinctly suited to creating new ventures.

While VC firms have made some bad bets, they have racked up a winning history of addressing unique needs—and seeding some big winners. This remarkable era in high-risk/high-reward venturing has generated many lessons—lessons that would be invaluable to any corporation. But corporate antibodies make the absorption of those lessons difficult. When you examine the most important elements that characterize start-up thinking and pave the way for start-up success, you can see that corporations cannot simply adopt these practices easily, automatically, or by fiat from the top.

Where Corporations and Corporate Venturing Collide

The fact is that in almost every aspect of their approach to business, the cultures of a venture and its parent corporation come in conflict. Corporations are enthusiastic about the potential benefits of a venture, but they are also wary that it may threaten the interests of the established business. Often these tensions escalate to a cold war, with corporate antibodies serving as an early warning and defense system to the top executives overseeing the venture operation. In these circumstances, there are always several familiar battlefronts.

A BULL IN THE CHINA SHOP: MERRILL LYNCH FINALLY THUNDERS INTO ONLINE TRADING

When Wall Street giant Merrill Lynch finally realized in the late 1990s that the online trading revolution was leaving it behind, its share price was suffering. In 1998, during the bull market, its stock dropped from $50 to $19.The company decided to begin online trading, but it chose not to devote one centralized core team to develop an alternative online business model. At first, the company pursued its technology strategy with a new chief technology officer and a group of senior executives, each of whom had other responsibilities. As a result, Merrill ended up with some 130 e-business development projects under way, none tied to a cohesive strategy, most populated with "fractional" resources from IT and other business units, none with start-up or consumer software experience.

It was only in February 1999—late in the online brokerage game—that Merrill, beset with continuous internal wars and culture clashes, gave up on building its online capability exclusively from the inside. It purchased a little-known investment company that had developed an online brokerage package. At that point, the company could lease space several blocks away from its downtown headquarters—important in establishing cultural as well as physical distance from the parent—and recruit senior, qualified personnel from the outside as well as inside and dedicate them full time to the effort. And it started behaving like a start-up.*

* "A Reluctant Success," *The Economist*, 9 June 2001, 79–80.

Talent

Perhaps the clearest impact of corporate antibodies is evident in an area central to any venture's success: the ability to hire, motivate, and retain the people it needs. The winning formula for start-ups begins with identifying people with the entrepreneurial traits required to get a business off the ground, and offering results-based incentives to sign them up and motivate them. But when a corporate venture tries that, it runs head-on into antibodies that say, "Don't take the best and brightest from our core business." Sometimes corporate antibodies unintentionally set up the opposite burden: The corporate parent installs in the new venture senior executives it considers among its best—people with years of corporate service and management success to their credit and experience or expertise in building and managing a start-up. Often these people are seasoned executives with a commitment to preserving corporate traditions rather than a willingness to test them. And even if they are willing to walk the tightrope of challenging corporate institutions, they rarely have a context for how to do so, or a model by which to lead.

Traditional ways of thinking often undercut a venture's ability to compensate prime talent. Risk takers aren't looking for safe pay; they're looking for risk pay, usually in the form of equity. Having a financial stake is one of the things that gets their juices flowing. But top management is bound to raise an understandable objection: "We're providing the initial investment, the intellectual property, the people, the distribution channels and the customers. Tell us again, why are we giving you enough equity to make you rich?" In an established organization, providing equity to a few participants in a select business also raises the issue of "inequity." It creates jealousy and antagonism among other employees. It wounds egos. It raises all the tensions that entrenched compensation policies have been designed to prevent.

In a new venture, everyone has to do everything, from participating in corporate strategy to wiring the network. The core team must manage, plan, and do. Instilling this hands-on attitude is one of the most critical tests a start-up must pass. It's central to survival, because of the crucial role cash plays in a start-up.

When the Internet-based health care management firm Healtheon conducted pitch meetings for its IPO, potential investors saw a small but telling illustration of the way entrepreneurs do things. Invariably, the

EXPERIENCED LEADERS—
WITH THE WRONG KIND OF EXPERIENCE

Senior executives who are rated by their corporation as top managers are often the most ill equipped to lead new ventures. This mismatch becomes apparent every time a new venture discovers that its original timetable and self-imposed deadline are unrealistic. In one project we worked on, an executive vice president of a mutual fund company was made CEO of the firm's new venture. The new venture intended to deliver to its customers online "life-enhancing" services, such as insurance and health care referrals. The plan tested well and had great promise as a new platform and partnership strategy for the parent. It also moved the company well beyond the scope of its current business. The new online venture had engaged the interest of the corporation's executive committee, which installed the CEO, sat on its board, and monitored its progress. Qualified outside consultants did the development, but the venture was managed by people, including the CEO, who had no start-up experience.

As so often happens with new ventures, specifications for the site began to change, upsetting delivery schedules and increasing the cash burn rate. The CEO's response was to threaten the team with unilateral shutdown if they missed another scheduled date. In the parent company, such a reaction was customary. It was even a good sign of disciplined management. Missing deadlines and failing to deliver projects on time and on budget are evidence of inadequate performance and often the basis for removal. The board, which comprised the parent's management hierarchy, sided with the CEO.

People experienced with start-ups, of course, see things differently. Because they are attacking new markets with innovative and unproven products and services, missing a deadline isn't necessarily a sign of incompetence.Schedule disruptions to preset are in most cases as unavoidable as they are predictable: components that haven't been integrated before won't perform as expected; customer testing reveals a desire for an additional feature; key partners prove less reliable than previously thought. In most start-up environments, adjusting schedules to meet new demands is simply an accepted and necessary part of product refinement and testing. Because a start-up must, almost by definition, react to a stream of new information, an incremental slip in schedule may well be worth the increase in value to the end product. For a new venture these critical calls to move back the schedule are usually the hallmark of leaders who have start-up, rather than exclusively corporate, experience.

slide projector supplied by the local hotel would break down. Instead of calling the business center to send someone to fix it, company founder Jim Clark simply tinkered with it himself until he got it to work.[2] In an established company, you wouldn't see the CEO repair the slide projector—but it's simply part of the culture of a start-up.

Roles

When you see a senior management team wearing many hats, you know that the same people who shaped the corporate vision are directly involved in bringing it to life. It guarantees that decision makers will rely on hands-on knowledge when forming their opinions. It inspires an esprit de corps needed to weather the challenges of birth. But when executives roll up their sleeves and work alongside the staff, more than morale improves. Senior executives who have first-hand experience with the nuts and bolts of a company's business help link strategy to implementation. In an independent start-up, no wall separates the two. One continually builds on the other. That's why in a start-up it's the rule rather than the exception to see the CEO assisting in customer interviewing, or driving the demo, or out in the field closing a sale. The real divining rod for venture success is flawless, lightning-fast execution combined with the ability to revise strategy on the run. That's possible only if the people who develop strategy and the people who execute it are joined at the hip—and usually it's merely the left and right hip of the same people.

Large corporations separate strategy and execution both physically and psychologically. Strategists and implementers are compartmentalized, with towering walls between them. The antibodies drive that: A big organization needs to delineate functions to ensure that all tasks are given undivided attention. As a result, decision makers can't get a feel for the impact their decisions will have at all levels of the company, and they sometimes stall when they need to shift gears quickly.

Risk

Because start-ups change course often and swiftly, they view uncertainty as a normal, managed risk. Many critical elements of the business model for a new enterprise can be determined only through active competition in the marketplace, not via analysis based on historical data.

But big corporations lack the dexterity to swing around quickly in midcourse. So how do they compensate? By demanding more up-front analysis—which is legitimate and accessible when you're talking about a new product or service in an existing line of business but wholly inappropriate when the business model and definitive use data don't yet exist. Corporate strategizing is a constant mission to eliminate risk. Sometimes it seems that the people in charge of corporate strategy aren't searching for a viable business plan so much as shopping for a bulletproof vest. That caution, often appropriate in a corporate setting, becomes an antibody ready to strike against corporate venturing.

To understand why, look at the environment in which most corporate decision makers operate. Most opportunities they evaluate have inherently lower risks and higher investment needs, as well as more predictable, incremental returns, than a start-up venture. Thus they have a different reference point. When corporate strategists and other corporate leaders cast their eyes on a proposed new venture, they're often looking for a work of analytical perfection that quantifies every element of the business plan and eliminates all risks. But in the search for a masterpiece, when do you stop analyzing and start executing?

Rules

The need to execute and adapt quickly discourages start-ups from yoking themselves to a thick, unchangeable rulebook. Thus they have flexibility to pursue opportunities throughout their operations. But large companies often have a stone tablet of corporate policies, a code designed to enable them to scale with consistency. Many of the most celebrated CEOs—even GE's Jack Welch, for instance—institute strict corporatewide policies that managers several rungs below violate at their peril. Whereas these policies create quality and consistency across a huge enterprise, they can be roadblocks that stop dead the progress of a corporate venture. The corporate goal is to create economies and leverage domain resources. Rigid policies may be necessary for large corporations that need to control the activities and expenditures of thousands or tens of thousands of employees. For corporate start-ups, these policies are nothing less than a bureaucratic straitjacket—created, unintentionally, by corporate antibodies.

Consider the case of one of our clients. In the process of launching a corporate venture, managers in other parts of the company thought they could provide some key services to their fledgling venture. One of the first capital expenditures the venture team needed to make was for laptop computers. They submitted their request to corporate procurement, dutifully completing lengthy forms and obtaining numerous levels of approval. This process made the first warning lights go off. In an independent venture, the team would have simply gone to, say, Dell's Web site, ordered the PCs, and received them within a few days at a highly competitive price. Instead, one member of the five-person venture team spent twelve hours working through the procurement process to get the right authorizations. Following corporate procedure led the venture team to buy standard hardware and software configurations that cost more than custom-configured Dells or Gateways would have—and delivery wasn't expected for six weeks! At this point, the whole team spent half a day convincing the parent organization that following corporate procurement policy would be detrimental to the venture. Their computer purchases were irrelevant to the parent's economics and it would kill the venture to follow these rules for every purchase. In the end, the venture team got an exemption for the PCs, but it cost them precious time and energy—penalties that independent start-ups with whom they compete will never endure. And they went on to engage in similar battles to contract for services, find office space, and even hire employees.

Performance

All new ventures struggle to prove their viability. Start-ups can't save their way to prosperity, and correspondingly, they do not have the option of refusing to invest in growth. Their early lives are challenged by steep market-development hurdles and irregular, unpredictable quarterly revenue and income progressions. Catering initially to small markets to establish entry, they're vulnerable to volatile demand and large swings on a small base. While no viable business should plan for losses as far as the eye can see, start-ups and the VCs who invest in them place their bets on the long view, with incremental checkpoints along the way to indicate whether they're still on the road to the goal. During the first years, new ventures' quarterly results are rarely decisive. Independent start-ups with experienced VCs as backers have the advantage of these funders' experience: a deep understanding of, singular focus on, and consistent track record with financing venture development.

Unfortunately, the start-up within a large company finds itself under even greater pressure in a less hospitable environment. Corporate ventures have parental financiers with other, more significant commitments and agendas, and limited, if not negative, track records with venturing. As a result, when the start-up posts erratic early revenues, which is natural, the parent most frequently doesn't understand, and corporate defense systems that work to limit losses kick into action.

Ventures suffer inappropriate comparisons in a corporate environment. Those lumpy revenues and necessary up-front costs compare badly with the steady performance of the corporation's established businesses. In fact, Wall Street rewards companies for their stability. How often do we see companies beating EPS expectations by a penny quarter after quarter? In the absence of new competition or a business slowdown, revenues stay within a consistent band, yielding steady income. New ventures don't, by definition, yet operate within that band—and thus they test the parent's tolerance.

Cannibalization

Every corporation that enables a venture to flourish eventually has to confront two critical questions:

- How much do you allow the venture to compete directly with you?

- How hard can you rock the boat by introducing established customers to unproven products and services?

These questions are inevitable when two mind-sets compete. Looking in at the corporate business model, start-ups—both corporate and independent—are focused on how to compete for customer dollars and how to build customer relationships. Looking out from their headquarters, corporations see the wolves racing toward them from the woods below. Corporate ventures creating new markets or revenue streams have to overcome a high hurdle: the value of current business. Current customers represent a revenue annuity stream that is often more profitable than new customers, since lower marketing, sales, and delivery costs are necessary. Corporate managers have to ask themselves if they are willing to accelerate a decline in the core business if a new venture stands to replace it, even though it might, for the foreseeable future, bring in far less revenue and profit.

The dilemma: Threaten an existing product while it still offers significant revenue to mine, or wait to develop a new market and find that a competitor has arrived first. The antibodies always perceive the danger in moving too soon—it's harder for a corporate defense system to sense the risk of moving too late. It issues warnings of "cannibalization" or of "undermining our customer base." Concerns about sacrificing first-mover advantage rarely seem to be taken as seriously.

It's always difficult to pull the trigger when one of your profitable products is in the line of fire. But failing to act swiftly can be the biggest risk of all. That's what one insurance company learned when it was considering incubating a venture to sell over the Internet. A potential uprising by the company's traditional brokers delayed a go-ahead decision for several months while management thought through the implications. The result? The company found itself left in the dust as competitors moved quickly into the space.

Brand

The parent company has reason to play defense with brand also. It takes years of business to develop a brand and investment of millions if not billions of marketing dollars to promote it. No wonder the parent corporation is reluctant to endanger that investment, and potentially sully the brand, by risking a high-visibility venture failure. It's one thing for a pair of twenty-somethings to burn more than $130 million in less than two years on a global business that fails, such as Boo.com, the high-fashion e-tailer.[3] But if Donna Karan or Armani did the same thing, what would be the impact on their brands?

So does the corporation lend its brand to make the venture successful and risk damage? Or does it withhold the brand to prevent damage and risk impeding the venture? The answer is nearly always the latter. Maneuvering around the brand issue is one of the corporate venture's greatest challenges: Ultimately, the right answer is in its business plan. For example, if the corporate venture is intended to provide products and services to other industry players and potential corporate competitors, as well as the parent, it must not be perceived as so closely coupled with the parent that the quality of its service to other customers and potential parental competitors might be compromised. In this case, the value of the parent's brand is in being one of the venture's first round of early customers, lining up with the value of other early reference customers in the form of volume sales and high-value customer relationships that propel the new venture forward.

Alternatively, providing the new venture with the identity and potency of the parent's brand exclusively can be a powerful weapon. And that may be what's required to launch the new venture with an immediate market advantage over other similar endeavors, and speed customer sales and adoptions. The downside of this approach is that it increases the level of exposure and risk to the parent and increases the precautions the parent must take. A new venture must take that downside seriously. If it chooses to use the parent's brand, it must expect the parent to demand additional levels of internal validation and scrutiny prior to the venture's public launch and throughout the market development process. After the venture is launched and on its way, it is more than likely that the parent will insist on an increased level of oversight to ensure that the venture stays closely aligned to serve the parent's present needs and strategic direction: a position that may not best serve—or may even be in opposition to—the venture's growth. And, of course, any use of the parent's brand name will require interaction with the whole legal, regulatory, communications, and investor relations superstructure. Borrowing the parent's brand name, in other words, extracts a high price from any start-up venture.

Failure

The mother of all antibodies is the reaction to failure. Long-established companies have spent decades perfecting processes and technologies, triaging products and services, and targeting profitable markets. As a result, they avoid failure and hence risk taking.

A corporation may try to open a door to risk taking by offering limited immunity, promising that an unsuccessful project won't freeze the manager's career track in suspended animation. But corporate managers have to ask themselves, "If I take a risk and end up with an unsuccessful project on my record, next time I'm up for a promotion how am I going to compare with a candidate who played it safe and kept his or her nose clean?" Looking ahead twenty years, a manager may be better off taking a risk today. But most people focus on their next promotion, not the one that might come around in a couple of decades.

We're not saying that failure doesn't carry a price. Rather, our point is that failure is defined differently in a start-up. Being wrong or guessing incorrectly is not seen as failure in the venture community. Rather, it is failure to heed the fundamentals of creating a new business: It is failure *not* to rapidly and constantly test assumptions, or *not* to incrementally refine, or *not* to correct the strategic course continually as you learn. New ventures embrace that attitude intuitively, and it's easy to understand why. After all, what precedent is there for the products and services that new ventures are creating? Usually none at all. What's the market? Usually it doesn't exist yet. In uncharted territory, no "right answer" has been established. Start-ups have the opportunity to create the right answer—through a combination of timing, circumstance, agility, and swiftness of response.

Established companies are used to being guided by precedent. They're used to being measured on the basis of a known quantity—established or mature markets. They're used to metrics that spell success or failure in unambiguous terms. Corporate antibodies have been shaped by this history of certainty. That makes it difficult for them to adjust to a competitive environment increasingly characterized by ambiguity. For every decision—from how to hire to what determines failure—large companies and small start-ups have views as different as night and day. If they were married, they would be in divorce court. Instead, they're in the trial phase of an uneasy relationship that is not as profitable or productive as it could be.

In summary, we can say that corporate antibodies send one loud and clear message to start-ups: *Above all, don't fail.* Other messages fall into specific categories:

Financial

- Don't have a negative impact on this quarter's earnings.
- Don't give away our equity.

Staff

- Don't take away our best people.
- Don't distract top management from our core business.

Strategic

- Don't partner with competitors.
- Don't cannibalize current revenues.
- Don't jeopardize current trading relationships.
- Don't damage our brand.

Operational

- Don't move ahead quickly without doing more analysis.
- Don't violate established corporate policies.

How to Find the Common Ground

So can corporate venturing be salvaged? Do antibodies prohibit large companies from launching their own venture programs and creating start-ups? Do they doom corporations to a life without innovation and renewal? In trying to shelter corporate ventures from a company's defense systems, the venture team must keep a couple of things in mind:

- Corporate antibodies are powerful for a good reason: They reflect the values, priorities, goals, and fears of people who make up the company today and also those who helped build it over the years. Thus it is possible to come to terms, address their values, incorporate their priorities, share their goals, and calm their fears. There is a potential meeting ground. The challenge is to adapt the venturing approach to corporate realities while prodding the corporation to adapt to a changing world.

- Because corporate antibodies are powerful, they usually can't be eliminated, but they can be mitigated. The path of venturing and innovation cannot head straight into the corporate defense systems. It has to go around them. A corporate environment cannot be overhauled overnight. But it can be opened to new ways of doing things. That requires both art and science.

The goal is to shape a venturing strategy that will protect a start-up from its parent's defense system, while allowing it access to corporate advantages. Corporate executives must implement a formal framework for corporate venturing, which we will describe in Part II of this book. But, like venturing itself, creating a haven for venturing within a corporation is also an art—one of adjusting strategic thinking and finding areas of clear common interest. Changing context for the antibodies can give corporate start-ups a chance to succeed. This does not require an all-at-once, radical reorientation in corporate thinking. What it does require is an adjustment in corporate thinking that undermines any changes in any circumstances.

Using Venturing to Attract and Retain the Best Talent

A good example of the adjustment in thinking has to do with staffing the venture. Sometimes the parent company tries to restrict whom the venture team can hire, particularly when those people already work at the parent company. In this case, a company has to change its thinking from *don't take our best people* to *create better opportunities so we can attract and retain better people.*

Such a shift doesn't have to undermine any established interests. Think about it: The best managers of an existing business are not necessarily the best people to start a new business. A new business needs entrepreneurs who take deliberate risks, such as launching a product to find out how the market will react. A new business needs people who work best in a hothouse atmosphere, people who can change direction at a moment's notice. There may be more people like that on the payroll than the parent company's management realizes. They may be failing to fulfill their potential, working in an environment that can't summon their entrepreneurial instincts. A new corporate venture can provide a vehicle for getting more out of the overall talent pool rather than diluting it.

Are there enough people like that in the organization to run a start-up? Do any of them have experience in doing so? The parent company management needs to realize that they may need to hire a number of people from outside to run the start-up. Venturing can be a magnet to attract and retain people with an entrepreneurial, risk-taking attitude and a flexible approach to problem solving.

Using Equity Instead of Cash

By resisting special equity arrangements for start-up ventures, a corporation is trying to protect the corporate culture that has helped it grow. But it also needs to attract the talented people who will take it to a new level and new directions. And it must motivate them to retain their edge, build on diverse skills, and make every dollar count. Salary and bonus simply don't meet the recruiting realities of start-ups, where the performance of top individuals has an inordinate impact on the success or failure of a venture. A significant portion of their total compensation must be tied to the long-term success of the venture, and the best way to do that is to use equity.

How *do* you rationalize giving away equity when the parent bears much of the risk and investment? Remember, the equity is worthless unless a viable business is built. If a management team succeeds in building a new business, shouldn't they be compensated handsomely? The corporate managers' response is usually something like "We made the investments in intellectual property, distribution channels, technology, customer relationships, and brand, and therefore we should own the company."

Such a view doesn't have to get in the way of distributing equity. It does call for fair compensation for the established company, and luckily a method exists, grounded in traditional business practice: The new venture should pay market value for corporate assets or, as is more frequently the case, the parent company should provide assets for equity. Eastman Chemical, for example, provided its logistics knowledge to Cendian, the start-up shipping company, in return for a large equity stake. Similarly, TRW licensed its technical knowledge about radio communication to help propel RF Micro Devices.

The same thinking holds when ownership is diluted by bringing in new investors. As additional investors are acquired and as key business milestones are met, the parent should be prepared to dilute its equity stakes. Without the support of other companies, Weirton Steel's Metalsite.net would not have returned anything near its actual gain of sixty times the original investment in five years.

Turning Competitors into Partners

The parent company's competitors may potentially be some of the venture's best suppliers or customers. Parent companies sometimes find it difficult to adjust to this idea. But think about it in a different context, and it doesn't seem at all radical. Companies have been partnering with competitors for decades, even in mature industries. It's called situational competition. Depending on the situation, a competitor can suddenly become a supplier or a customer. Take oil refining. Companies trade capacity when supply and demand imbalances occur. Given the high fixed costs associated with supply, having a significant excess capacity isn't economical. When demand fluctuates and exceeds supply, competitors buy from each other, turning a competitor-competitor relationship into a supplier-customer relationship.

Airlines do exactly the same thing. You get a chance to see it in action first-hand when American Airlines overbooks you on a flight and rebooks you with United. Book with United and you may end up being rebooked with American. Not only does situational competition allow companies to manage supply efficiently, it gives them an opportunity to pull in competitive intelligence. It allows every airline to know which routes and schedules have the greatest demand, and which don't.

Strategy as Innovation

Wall Street analysts hammer corporate chieftains to keep focused, stick to their knitting, and avoid getting distracted by ancillary issues. No doubt the atmosphere of controlled chaos in which entrepreneurs operate could be distracting to almost anyone exposed to it. Given the high rates of failures for new ventures, it follows that a great many urgent issues need to be addressed as these ships are sinking. It also follows that the more important the investment, from either a strategic or financial perspective, the more likely that the parent company's senior management is likely to get involved. And that kind of involvement is exactly what Wall Street doesn't want: It wants management to focus only on operating and growing the core business.

Growing the business is the strategy. And growing the business requires innovation. In a classic example, George Hatsopoulis, former chairman and CEO of Thermo Electron, has taken this strategy one step farther, creating a company that exists primarily to spin out new companies that are born of internal innovation. Not only was he not distracted by new ventures, he was in the business of creating them. And like any other core function in a business, a venture needs a capable leader who runs the day-to-day operations.

Testing, not Analysis

It's easy to understand the corporate commitment to rigorous analysis. Charting an industry's direction is critical, like the size and profitability of the market as it currently operates. But at what point do you start learning more by doing? Some things are not knowable through any amount of analysis. In 1995, if you had asked Barnes & Noble to forecast the potential market size for Internet book sales, the answer would have been quite different from what it is today. You would have had access to all the knowable data, including overall market size and breakdown between retail outlets and mail order. But it would have been futile to calculate the potential for channel cannibalization and incremental industry growth. Internet book sales depended on a massive change in both buying behavior and consumer technology penetration. The only way to analyze the potential was to test it. Critical elements of the business model for new ventures can become known only through experience in the marketplace, not analysis of it.

Market Testing New Businesses

Businesses, like the products and services they comprise, go through natural life cycles. When you consider the spare parts business, the product cycle of airplane manufacturing spans decades. An integrated circuit manufacturer deals in product cycles of roughly a year and half, whereas apparel manufacturers and toy manufacturers basically get one season. Especially with the external investment side of venturing, a company can gain first-hand exposure to the value of and constraints on new business models.

Reinventing Burdensome Rules

One size doesn't fit all. Corporate rules that guide and give coherence to one kind of business can become an overbearing bureaucracy that suffocates an early-stage venture. Just as different levels of management have different rules—and just as different divisions have different rules—so too must new ventures have different rules. These new rules should be viewed as experiments in streamlining cumbersome policies such as purchasing and hiring.

One client of ours had difficulty procuring consultant services in its ventures without going through a cumbersome qualification and bidding process that was standard in the core business. The parent used the new venture to develop a streamlined procurement process for professional services that eliminated nearly all the paperwork and took a third of the time and effort.

Building Stronger Customer and Supplier Relationships

Since new ventures set out to create new value for customers, a company's best partner may be its customer. Customers know what they need. How does a company use that relationship without jeopardizing it? By distinguishing between customers. Not all customers are interested in innovation. Some are, and that's all it takes. By setting up a collaborative innovation program in which only select customers can participate, companies can create the value and capture the insights that companies expect of new ventures.

Companies can actually use venturing as a tool to strengthen relationships with customers and suppliers by introducing them to new technologies and capabilities that deliver value to them. In one context, the new venture begins to function like the research and development arm for your customers and suppliers! Now that builds loyalty.

Treating Venturing as an R&D Budget

Companies find it easier to accept a start-up's bumpy cash flows if they recognize venturing for what it really is: business research and development. Business R&D is a cost center. The goal is to make it a profit center. All cost centers—traditional R&D, marketing, and technical infrastructure investments—have negative near-term earnings impacts but significant positive long-term earnings impact. Corporate start-ups can turn near-term costs into long-term benefits, such as new knowledge. The only real difference between start-ups and other cost centers is that start-ups can also generate long-term direct profits. The issue isn't just whether a new venture is having negative impact on income today. It's also a question of whether a company can see the potential upside tomorrow.

And it's good practice to limit the expense associated with venturing, just as companies limit the expense of R&D. Within a preset limit, the corporate venturing guys should be allowed to spend as they want, as long as progress is still tracking against the corporate venture plan. The corporate venture team must then manage the totality of investments and expenses within this budget.

Making Innovation Part of the Brand

The knee-jerk reaction of corporate defense systems is to *assume* that identification with new ventures will undermine brand, unless proven otherwise. But can a company prudently allow fear of giving birth to its own New Coke or Edsel to freeze it in its tracks? The Coca-Cola and Ford brands both survived their debacles. In an era when consumers and investors expect and even demand innovation, how long will companies be able to entrench brand *without* taking prudent and measurable risks? That too is part of building brand.

Venturing and innovation should be *core components* of the brand. The image of a company constantly trying to innovate by taking prudent risks in search of superior returns and market share is compelling. In fact, this proactive nature is a strong differentiator to customers and investors. During the height of the tech boom, much of Cisco Systems' reputation came from its unparalleled skill at acquiring and rapidly integrating new companies. Not only did Cisco take gambles on new ideas that could expand its reach, but it understood how to retain the pioneering spirit of these businesses while still including them in the corporate family.

WEIRTON STEELS ITSELF FOR CHANGE

Looking for new ways to grow in a mature industry, in 1996, Weirton Steel made a bold move. It launched an online exchange called Metalsite.net. Setting up an electronic steel market at the dawn of the Internet era was a radical step in a sector that had come to symbolize the old industrial economy. Weirton's CIO, a dogged change agent named Patrick Stewart, had pushed hard for the move. Like his namesake, the star of television's *Star Trek: The Next Generation*, Stewart was determined "to go bravely where no one else had dared go before." At Weirton, that included opening the exchange up to investing companies, including competitors, in order to make the venture financially and operationally viable.

Independent start-ups customarily view other companies—even competitors—as potential partners. Big corporations don't usually see it that way, particularly corporations like Weirton, where management was under stress and many were losing hope.

It's not surprising that a company that launches a new venture is reluctant to let competitors in on the ground floor. Corporate defense systems are designed to lock in equity, control, and revenue, rather than let them seep out. "This represents potential value, and we can't give part of it up at a ground floor price," some members of top management always seem to argue. "Let's develop the value and then sell some of the equity at a better price."

In Weirton's hard-fought and sometimes emotional internal debate over whether to share part of Metalsite.net, this standard argument could not counter one irrefutable piece of logic: A small piece of a big pie is better than a big piece of a tiny pie. The corporate antibodies were overcome, and investment was invited in.

The dissidents' initial fears were confirmed: Attracting plenty of eager investors, Weirton reduced its own stake in Metalsite.net to 25 percent. But Stewart's vision prevailed: A $5 million investment ballooned to a value of more than $300 million, according to published reports. That made it a lot easier for traditionalists to reconcile themselves to an untraditional move.

It took a combination of forces to drive change at Weirton: a CIO with missionary zeal, an embattled company in a tough industry, and an innovative idea and a need for capital and partnerships to exploit it.

The challenge is to identify the stages of developing a corporate venture and to follow an analytical framework that measures progress in each of these areas. In the next chapter, we will examine how a company can begin thinking about this process by creating the right environment for venturing, establishing a platform, and opening a venture office.

Battling Corporate Antibodies: Key Lessons

- *Corporations are filled with venture antibodies.* The successful corporate venture runs against the grain of the prevailing corporate culture. The parent company has a responsibility to create an environment in which the corporate culture does not smother the new venture in its crib.

- *Corporate goals are different from venture goals.* Accept that. In its planning, finances, and compensation, ventures must be allowed to create their own systems and own methods for conducting business.

- *No surprise: The right people are critical.* It is a business truism that people make the difference. Too often, corporations don't let the best people devote full-time to the venture. Or sometimes those who do have corporate experience are lost inside a start-up.

- *Parents and ventures will fight.* They ought to. After all, on issues of cannibalizing existing revenues, using brand, and introducing new (even competing) products, corporate and venture strategies will often collide.

- *Learn from the venture approach.* A corporation needs to do more than ignore a corporate venture that is running by its own rules. It must learn from the venture as a way of seeing new opportunities for growth, partnerships, and expansion.

- *It doesn't happen all at once.* Strategic corporate venturing goes through five distinct stages. At each one, the venture can be measured for progress, tweaked, changed, or canceled outright.

4

building the business
of building businesses

creating the VBO

Entrepreneurism is neither a science nor an art. It is a practice.

PETER DRUCKER

After many years of experimenting with different strategies for corporate venturing, we have learned that getting the corporate venturing *environment* right is the key to everything that follows. In this chapter, we demonstrate how to create that environment, beginning with the establishment of a new kind of corporate organization: the *venture business office* (VBO).

Many companies make the mistake of pursuing venturing with spirit and funding—but with no real structure to make venturing a permanent, integrated fixture of their business model. The VBO provides that structure. It is the platform, or centralized foundation, for the ongoing corporate venturing operation, requiring the same position and visibility as other mainstream strategic operations like R&D or corporate development. The VBO is able to leverage all the parent company's resources, relationships, and knowledge, but it is designed to operate just outside the reach of the corporate culture that may impede or prevent its success.

An effective VBO will achieve four critical goals:

- Protect new ventures from corporate antibodies.

- Launch and invest in new ventures while leveraging corporate assets to make them successful.

- Define, measure, and analyze financial and strategic return from these ventures.

- Link the internal corporation to the outside venture community.

To achieve these goals, the VBO demands a structure that shields it from the political, budgetary, and psychological environment of an established company. In this sense, the VBO is part oasis, part isolation unit. It operates significantly different than the traditional corporation. It requires different skills, different funding mechanisms, different criteria for "success," different culture, and even different compensation packages.

The good news is that the VBO can be built quickly, efficiently, and at modest cost, relative to other corporate growth mechanisms and offices. Like the ventures it nourishes, it must think big, start small, test often, and scale fast. And as with the ventures it invests in or builds, the VBO needs to observe and refine its strategy of operation as it modifies its own road map to the future.

Unfocused? Frenetic? Seemingly all over the map? Yes, at times, the VBO appears guilty of all these charges. Nothing more irritates the prevailing corporate culture of a successful company—which is one of the reasons why so many venturing initiatives get shut down after a first milestone "failure," and why a separate environment needs to be created for venturing needs.

A proven structure to manage venturing will safeguard against this understandable corporate reflex. This chapter describes the venture business office, and how it ensures four essential ingredients of successful corporate venturing:

- *Governance:* providing the right balance of corporate control and VBO latitude for decision making

- *People:* lining up venture experienced management, a proven board of advisors, and valuable partners inside and outside the corporation

- *Portfolio:* investing based on a diversified, risk-balanced strategic plan

- *Practice:* creating a continuous pipeline of ideas, quality management for investing and building, financial and strategic performance metrics, and continuous tracking of results

See Appendix A at the end of the book for more details on the structure of the venture business office.

Governance: Balancing Control and Latitude

Well-structured governance gives a VBO the latitude it needs to build a venture portfolio, while providing the parent corporation with the confidence and sense of security it needs to venture into a world it does not know.

Corporate management must crisply define the rules of governance at the outset in the business plan of the VBO in order to achieve these two goals. These rules define who will make critical decisions, and how. Building checks and balances into the decision-making structure will ensure that the goals are met. Without the proper balance, confidence in the corporate venturing program can quickly erode.

It is not surprising, then, that governance can become the first and biggest sticking point in getting a VBO off the ground. The natural corporate inclination is to insist on tight control. The natural attitude of the venture team is not to weigh down the potential for innovative brilliance with unnecessary process and bureaucracy.

Too much corporate control can create a VBO that is simply a reproduction of the corporate hierarchy: investing in and building ventures that fit within the current flows of the business (not threatening, but not necessarily innovative either), or choking innovative ventures off from the kind of corporate advantages the VBO is chartered to provide. Too little control can lead to ventures where $20 million is poured into what is merely an idea—or worse yet, one with no relevance to the corporation's strategic goals or strengths. We have seen companies follow both courses, with inevitable results: either gridlock or a short-circuited venturing program.

Rules

For the VBO to work, corporate management must define governance—the "operating manual" for decision-making roles and responsibilities—according to prevailing venture development practices, characteristics, and milestones, and the CEO and executive committee must actively "bless" it. Interestingly enough, the incremental checkpoints inherent in this venture process—from new venture proposals and funding to ongoing portfolio and venture management and exit strategies—present opportunities for the parent to exert control over the VBO if necessary. In this way, the parent corporation doesn't cede control to the VBO. Rather, the VBO redefines that shared control according to venture terms, and it provides the corporation with a new language and method for maintaining control and setting expectations. This begins with VBO funding and extends to govern all aspects of the interface with the corporation's core businesses and other growth offices.

Funding

In establishing rules of the road regarding VBO funding, the corporation must keep the goal of the operation in mind. A company's venturing program is a high-level, corporate mission, not just a collection of projects across various business units. And it is important that VBO funding be driven at the corporate level, not exclusively by individual strategic business units (SBUs). We don't mean that SBUs should be excluded from active financial participation. But some corporations have required their corporate venturing groups in effect to go hat in hand to the SBUs to finance every investment or build. The latter process not only jeopardizes the VBO's ability to make timely investment commitments to prospective portfolio companies, but also begins to limit the horizon on innovation—which partially defeats the corporate venturing purpose.

In many successful cases we've seen, funding is negotiated by the

VBO leaders and advisors, the CEO, and the executive committee (which considers the form of SBU participation, as well as integration with other growth office budgets). The VBO's "fund" may then be allocated as an annual budget, with a targeted total for a three- to five-year period, subject to reevaluation at given checkpoints.

Typically, the VBO management "draws down" against that allocation for individual investments and tracks its operating expenses according to standard corporate practice. Several factors usually determine the level of VBO autonomy: the VBO management's experience and track record, the size and scope of the investment being sought, and the corporate parent's economic health and appetite for venturing. The intention is to streamline the decision process to emulate venture-development techniques and timelines on the outside.

What are guidelines for how large or small an initial fund should be? We've seen funds as small as $15 million to start, though many funds start at the $100 million mark or more, in an attempt to get "critical mass" with a broadly diversified portfolio over this three- to five-year time frame. Indeed, companies as diverse as Bertelsmann AG, Qualcomm, and Deloitte Consulting created funds of several hundred million dollars in 2000 alone. But three factors should drive the size of the fund: the experience of the venture team (more experience warrants larger funds), the number of investments needed to diversify the portfolio and provide adequate strategic coverage, and the average size of the investment, which itself usually depends on the stage of investment (later stages often require larger investments). In our $15 million example, this fund covered a dozen investments over an eighteen-month time frame. We've also seen a seasoned team put $100 million to work in the first year.

But a corporate venturing arm needn't match the size of funds or individual investments of established private VC firms to participate in deals and add value to prospective portfolio companies. Financial support is always valued, certainly, but corporate venturing groups bring more than money to the table. In fact, their money isn't what's usually valued. They bring access to the parent company and its industry infrastructure, which provide strategic business leverage and focus—and which can greatly surpass the value of investment dollars.

A recurring pattern we have seen in over half a dozen clients during their first year of operation is three investments in outside ventures to every one investment in an internal venture, most often falling in the range of $1 million to $5 million for each. Funding should be expected to increase in year 2 and beyond, given the performance of the VBO, the health of the parent corporation, and the disposition of the economy. Based on these anticipated investments, the VBO can typically expect to see initial returns begin within eighteen to twenty-four months. It is not uncommon for some of these same investments to take five or more years to produce returns in a VC fund.

Resources

Unlike the issue of funding, the question of control and allocation of resources is not usually a source of immediate controversy; rather, it grows in importance over time. Frequently, the VBO—like SBUs and other corporate departments—is required to utilize the corporate infrastructure for all its administrative services (including procurement, legal, human resources, and banking.) But a VBO, like a venture itself, needs to move quickly and at minimal cost. One of the critical ingredients of the success of any VBO is its ability to obtain maximum cost efficiency and operating speed. Frequently, it finds early on that corporate services slow it down. That's especially likely when you consider that a VBO is likely to be one of the smallest units seeking internal services. Like most businesses, a corporate department will seek to satisfy its biggest clients first—leaving smaller operations like a VBO far back in the queue.

From a corporate standpoint, management must recognize the likely pace and volume of services that a VBO will require, even in its first year of operation. And true to the venture culture, required turnaround will be measured in hours, not days or weeks. To avoid disputes, it is crucial that the rules of the road be established before the venturing program gets into gear.

People: Getting the Right Management, Advisors, and Partners

A vibrant corporate venture program is first and foremost nourished by a handful of people near the top of the parent organization—people who act as a streamlined investment committee, who can proselytize, run interference, and apply not-so-subtle pressure when their colleagues get nervous and want to pull the plug. The VBO must have these friends in high places, high-powered support in overcoming typical corporate misperceptions about who should do the work, where they should come from, where they should focus, and how they should be compensated.

The first challenge is recognizing what the venture needs and who can do it. When companies pick teams for important projects, they understandably look for people with proven track records as managers. But ventures don't simply need managers; they need *doers* who also know how to manage. When it comes to finding the right people to own and operate the venturing process, corporations seem to make two consistent mistakes. First, they undervalue (or even ignore) the critical need for substantive start-up experience, which almost never exists in a large established organization. And second, they overvalue big-company skills and past experience in technology, engineering, finance, and marketing. The result? Few managers and venture team members are recruited from the outside, where most of the start-up talent is.

The Leadership Trio

A successful VBO demands a wide spectrum of talents and strengths that begin with three key people: the VBO managing director, venture executive officer, and the parent corporation's CEO or proxy.

VBO Managing Director. The VBO managing director is the equivalent of the CEO of the venture business office—its primary evangelist both within the corporation and on the outside, and the executive officer on whose desk the VBO buck stops.

Where is one most likely to find a qualified managing director? In the parent corporation, usually at the high end of middle management. A change agent at heart, he or she has spent time in the corporation and is savvy about how to maneuver in it; knows the people, infrastructure and political landscape; and has both informal and formal connections. This person must be as comfortable doing the work as managing the work.

The managing director is responsible for building the infrastructure of relationships inside the corporation that will be key to leveraging corporate capabilities and achieving recognition of VBO value delivery, while also building a position of strength and collaboration in the outside venturing community. The managing director must also be able to hire and lead a VBO team that is "lean and mean"—a small group of roughly six professionals drawn from inside and outside the company, skilled in such functions as deal sourcing and filtering, due diligence, portfolio strategy development, venture building and management, venture finance, and high-level business development.

Venturing Executive Officer (VEO). The VBO and its managing director need a venture executive officer, a champion within the parent organization who is both highly placed and well rooted in the daily operational aspects of running the corporation. An executive officer who often reports to the CEO, the VEO should be someone who is "sold" on the concept and practice of the VBO, who sees its potential for mainstream impact on the corporation's core business and strategic path, and who has the ability to influence the actions of the core business (more on this later).

Like the managing director, the VEO combines the best elements of an innovator with a genuine concern for the company's long-term viability. In some ways, the best VEO is a contradiction in terms—a company veteran who is wired into the power structures of the corporation but nonetheless a steward for change.

The VEO acts as chief missionary and "muscle" where needed, and works with the VBO managing director on the strategy and plan until they are ready for executive committee review. Simultaneously, the VEO is the first line of defense inside the company against corporate antibodies, providing advice, counsel, and influence to ensure the VBO gets what it needs to function on a day-to-day basis. Outside the company, she or he greases the skids for networking, partnering, and deal making. The VEO is also responsible, given agreement with the CEO, for assuring the development of a board of advisors.

Who are potential candidates for VEO? The corporation's CIO (given the technology heavy nature of many new ventures), the head of corporate business development or corporate strategy, the CFO (given that ventures are often viewed as small M&A deals), or the head of R&D (given the strong intellectual property nature of this function).

CEO of the Parent Corporation. As the corporate executive most visible both inside and outside the organization, the CEO of the parent corporation completes the triumvirate that is vital to the success of the corporate venturing program. As the business and cultural leader for the corporation, the CEO must be the active chief ambassador of the VBO and its strategy, both on the inside to the corporate troops and board of directors, and to all the outside constituencies—customers, partners, vendors, other CEOs, media, analysts, and Wall Street. The CEO is responsible for articulating an integrated vision of corporate venturing as a path to increased competitive advantage and growth. He or she must indicate—and be ultimately responsible for—where and how those results will be realized.

The Board of Advisors

The venture community has long understood the potency of advisory boards and boards of directors in building new businesses. Consider Siebel Systems, for example, a relatively young yet highly successful sales automation and customer relationship management company: Siebel began life with financial services entrepreneur Charles Schwab and the dean of the Stanford Business School on its board. New, independent ventures are always short of the full complement of capabilities and experienced talent they need at any given point in time, and the VBO is no different. It requires appropriate and high-powered oversight, structured in a way to serve its needs best. This oversight is uniquely provided by a VBO board of advisors, which is similar to a board of directors but does not have the burden of legal and fiduciary responsibility. (See Appendix B at the end of the book.)

All too often, corporations fail to establish a board of advisors. Or perhaps they retain outsiders, but then they exclude them from VBO meetings with the corporation's senior decision makers. Oftentimes they assume that they can build these functions without high-level outside venturing assistance. Or they assume that their venturing program is narrowly enough defined that it doesn't require such a high-powered board—or that bringing in outsiders to the corporation's "inner sanctum" will introduce a potential breach of confidentiality. Some companies agree with the concept of the VBO board of advisors, but they don't see it as a priority, preferring instead to wait until after the VBO has a successful venture or two under its belt. To demur over the formation of the VBO's board of advisors and operate without this blend of inside and outside expertise is to put at risk valuable time, resources, individual portfolio company development, and perhaps the success of the venture business office itself.

Not only does an advisory board help fill in the skill and experience gaps, but most importantly it brings unbiased objectivity. To provide seasoned advice and counsel, the VBO team recruits senior individuals—from inside and outside the corporation—who have expertise in areas the team lacks. Board members from outside the corporation bring, first and foremost, venture-development understanding as well as complementary industry or functional expertise and reflected credibility. Outside advisors also bring the powerful asset of their established networks—"black books" of key contacts in the exclusive venture community "club" and other related areas. Board members from inside the corporation bring authority and respect, strategic, political, and operational understanding, powerful internal networks, access to resources and domain expertise, and access to other corporate partners, customers, and industry players.

The board need not be large—half a dozen experts is sufficient to start—nor should its membership remain static. Like an external venture board, it should reflect—and change with—the needs of the VBO as it grows and matures over time. Here is what the VBO advisory board might look like and how one company implemented the structure (see the sidebar, "The Eastman Chemical VBO Structure"):

- CEO of parent

- VEO from parent

- VBO managing director

- Optional: CFO, chief of strategy, chief of business development, chief of R&D

- Three or more outsiders: venture capitalist, venture consultant, entrepreneur

THE EASTMAN CHEMICAL VBO STRUCTURE

The Eastman Ventures division of Eastman Chemical is a prime example of a successful VBO management structure.

Eastman CEO Earnie Deavenport, a visionary mentioned earlier in the book, was an early "convert" to the possibilities of the Internet and Web-enabled businesses, as well as to the partnerships and new alliances that were evolving from this base.

CIO Roger Mowen had twenty-seven years with Eastman in various business, marketing, and sales roles, including the vice president of global customer services. He had a unique perspective for a traditional company veteran of so many years—a rare ability to see the world from the company's point of view and the company from an outsider's. His was a new and revolutionary role, with responsibility for both the new business vision of IT at Eastman and the strategy for its implementation, within the larger context of business expansion and transformational operations.

Vice President of New Business Development Fred Buehler had also held numerous management positions in sales and marketing and corporate development within Eastman. As vice president of e-Business, he led the effort to establish Eastman's leadership in the use of e-commerce. Now his responsibilities focused on extending Eastman's business beyond its traditional base, to include advanced digital business and services development and new venture investing and incubation, ensuring the linkages and synergies among all these functions to Eastman core businesses and operations.

Managing Director Mark Klopp had, at thirty-seven, spent his entire career with Eastman. He was passionate about the company, and he had a fundamental understanding of its strategy, culture, and assets. Having just spent a year as executive assistant to the CEO, he knew the company's politics from the highest levels. He also had an entrepreneurial spirit and urgency about the Internet explosion and its effects on traditional businesses. Klopp relocated to Silicon Valley, absorbing the start-up culture of the high-tech world.

An **Eastman Board of Advisors** was formed as this new organization came into being, including three recognized expert "outsiders" with specialties in the areas of venture development, digital strategy development, and Business Week Global 1000 business strategy.

Within 18 months, the Eastman team had built one of the most successful in the new breed of venture business offices, with a portfolio of over a dozen investments, including three start-ups in development and a forward-looking plan for more.

VBO Compensation

Establishing the VBO compensation plan is almost always an area of conflict. Venture management generally seeks compensation based on analogs in the VC and the independent venture community: incentives for small, core teams based on "sweat equity"—high risk with potential high reward. However, large, publicly traded corporations have mature and often complex compensation structures, created over time to support thousands of employees. Compensation is a less risky cash salary, enhanced with employee stock plans.

Therein lies the conflict. If the VBO leaders and recruits aren't rewarded in a way roughly comparable to the outside venture world, the parent corporation is essentially training them to leave. But if the corporation creates a compensation structure heavily weighted toward sweat equity, it will not be consistent with its mainstream HR structures and operations. Disgruntled employees will ask, "Why them and not me?" A corporation serious about pursuing a corporate venturing program must address the issue head-on. Hesitating to acknowledge and resolve the conflict will not make it go away, rather just allow it to fester.

Another corporate venturing client who evaluated this issue extensively for six months found yet another valid conflict. Managers were concerned that having a financial interest in seeing individual ventures succeed might actually compromise the parent organization's strategic interests. For instance, if a new venture were contracting for manufacturing services from the parent and the venture team found a better deal with one of the parent's competitors, they may have the incentive to source from a competitor. Doing so would be in their financial interest but not at all in their strategic interest.

So how do we address this issue? We are still at the front end of establishing standards for corporate venturing compensation packages. Today, VBO and related compensation structures are typically a blend of elements and benefits from the corporate and venturing worlds. While there are variations, our experience has been that many corporations have moved to "carried-interest" models that are standard in the outside venture community. In this way, corporate venturing units receive carried-interest percentages in the portfolios they develop to augment cash compensation and other benefits packages. The "carry" totals up to 20 percent allocated to VBO team members and others it wishes to motivate, with some 3 to 5 percent typically held in reserve for later use. The typical vesting period mirrors that on the outside, at three to four years.

For venture building, the lines are much simpler: If a VBO team member joins a venture that is spun out from the corporation for independent development, he or she takes on greater risk and is awarded with market-competitive "sweat equity" and salary appropriate to the job being assumed (like most ventures on the outside).

Progressive corporations understand the need to attract SBUs and other corporate functionaries to collaborate with the VBO and its portfolio companies. One client takes an extremely innovative approach, allowing the VBO to distribute portfolio company equity, on a discretionary basis, back to participating SBUs—which in turn can allocate or reward employees that go above and beyond the call of duty to help these fledgling ventures. Companies can also use more traditional discretionary cash bonuses and/or awards of additional employee stock options in the parent corporation. Not surprisingly, all the top compensation firms have practices that address this need.

The Web of Relationships: Outside and Inside the Corporation

For the VBO to deliver on its goals, it must build a network of support, both inside the corporation and outside the corporation, in the venture community. The VBO always has these two worlds as its primary constituents, and it depends equally on each for its ultimate success. Interestingly, both the inside and outside worlds bring both customers (e.g., SBUs, new ventures) and suppliers (e.g., finance, VCs) to the VBO, as shown in figure 4-1.

External Networks. A network of outside contacts provides access to expertise and resources the VBO cannot find within its parent's walls. This external network, properly constructed, yields access to innovative technologies, products, and services; venture talent pools; venture capitalists' deal flows; specialized support services such as legal, accounting, marketing, design, search, and investment banking—an elaborate venturing infrastructure built and fine-tuned over the last thirty years. Breaking into this "club" is not only crucial to successful venturing, but

FIGURE 4 - 1

Web of Relationships

also vital for learning—and it is notoriously difficult. Adding to the challenge: Many corporations don't know how to recruit for or measure this specialized business development skill in their VBO team, and they often underrate it because it is carried out by word of mouth and personal contact.

The VBO goes out into the venturing world as a collaborator and partner, with the potential to bring unique value to VCs and start-ups alike. It brings domain expertise and industry infrastructure understanding, along with access to SBUs' other touch points within the corporation, and corporate business partners—capabilities most VCs crave. Indeed, the VBO's formal access points are part of its appeal to the venture community, which looks to the VBO to make these connections more efficient and effective.

Internal Networks. The VBO must identify and cultivate strong relationships with the decision makers, the influencers, and—most important—the early adopters or change leaders within the entire organization. This is one of the reasons it is important to have some corporate insiders in the VBO. The VBO will have informal relationships with many of these contacts already, given the years of corporate citizenship of the VEO and VBO managing director. The challenge is to make clear the lines of access and accountability within the existing corporate organization, to support the venturing effort at a functional and formal level. Such clarity is critical for everything from timely access to specialists, to quick action on contracts and funding decisions, to database access, to protection against standard operating procedure.

Portfolio: Mapping the Corporate Venture Strategy

Some corporations would like to invest in or build one venture at a time, embarking on the next venture only if the first one is successful. But consider what that means to the future of the corporate venturing program. Only one in ten ventures will be a runaway success, and only two in ten will provide a normal return. The rest will not provide adequate returns. So a first venture has a 70 percent chance of being unsuccessful. Following this logic, if the first venture is the sole basis for building a venturing program, the odds are the venture program will not be built.

That's why venture capitalists don't raise a fund to make just one big bet—they fund a collection of them at different stages of development. They build a portfolio because they know that while most of their investments won't pay off, the winners will more than cover the losers.

Corporations need to adopt the same attitude. Indeed, they need to take it a step farther; shaping a portfolio that is diversified between building and investing in new ventures. Both building and investing are required to provide a diversified source of deals, create a balanced portfolio of risks versus returns, build a rich complement of near- and long-term bets (eighteen months to five or more years), and ensure that strategic and financial value are delivered back into the corporation.

There are many different vehicles and approaches to building and investing, all of which offer many alternatives to hedging risk and diversifying the portfolio. Building ventures requires intense core team effort and significant resources, as well as ongoing funding until partners or other investors are brought on. A company can invest in many smaller bets with less overall commitment of time and resources.

The venturing world has defined and documented the ways in which to measure an investment's financial value, including increase in valuation relative to its own performance and comparable endeavors as it matures; return on investment at the venture's IPO, merger, or acquisition; increase in price per share in the public market; and internal rate of return aggregated across the portfolio. Corporate venturing involves one additional element: the financial value of an application to a parent corporation's business (for example, the net financial impact of investments that accelerate the rate of online orders or enhance their profitability).

However, the strategic value of the VBO portfolio should be more compelling to the parent corporation than its financial value. Even in the failure of a corporate venture investment or build, a company can often salvage value from what has been developed or learned.

Strategic return, though, is much harder to measure on an ad hoc basis. After all, venture funds have an investment cycle of approximately five years. A public corporation, on the other hand, has to report results quarterly. (We'll talk more about the need for building appropriate performance measurement systems for the VBO in chapter 9.)

For all these reasons, a company must approach venturing as a reasoned and well-defined exercise in building the rationale and logic behind what ideas it will pursue, in what order, and how. Focusing the playing field for corporate venturing in this way begins with creating a "strategic investment map."

In practical terms, a vision requires knowing what building blocks—what skills and assets—are available for creating a new business, and how strong or weak those skills and assets are. From these skills and assets will be constructed an investment map—a document that explicitly demonstrates, by category, how the building blocks can be put together to make new businesses. The map provides an "aerial view" of the corporate venturing effort, showing where the parent is strong or weak. It identifies which categories are the best choices for leveraging assets in service of corporate ventures, and it provides a guide to analyzing ideas and selecting those that fit into the parent's overall strategy.

In the pages that follow we will outline how to create an investment map, and how to decide which "box" opportunities to go after. Many corporate venturing offices go off track here. They don't narrow their range of opportunities based on where they can apply corporate assets and unique capabilities. Portfolios without a clear focus and path are frequently all over the place—fragments of inspiration that may ultimately be far afield from the parent's real interests. Portfolios without this strategic focus also begin to drift away from what fuels the VBO's value propositions to corporate strategists and stakeholders on the inside and the venture community on the outside.

Unearthing Assets in Your Own Backyard

The VBO must start by understanding the parent's current business, priorities, and strategic directions—beginning with an inventory of corporate assets and unique strengths that can be gold for helping or launching start-ups. The good news is that most large companies actually hold most of the essential ingredients for creative new ideas—loads of customers, huge databases, and decades of expertise. Indeed, some of the most valuable corporate assets are the very things a company takes for granted. But management tends to view these tangible and intangible assets as liabilities, much the way an accountant would. Corporate venture teams must bring a new lens to their own business. They must identify and value every corporate asset that fledgling corporate ventures can use. They can begin by collecting data in five categories:

- *Balance sheet assets:* may include inventory, vehicles, machinery, and facilities.

- *Information:* may include customer data, purchasing information, and product profitability data.

- *Technology:* may include customized product configuration software, patented engineered product designs, and proprietary product-testing equipment.

- *Methods:* may include patented manufacturing processes, custom software development techniques, and custom relationship selling.

- *Skills:* may include vertical industry experts, management skills, and customer service.

The next step is to create an inventory for each of these categories for every business unit on the organization chart. Assets are likely to be found in the following groups:

- *Research and development* is a gold mine of potential assets to leverage in start-ups. Companies with sophisticated R&D groups have tremendous intellectual property to contribute to new corporate ventures—particularly built ventures.

- *Marketing and sales* can provide four assets that are crucial to a start-up: brand power, market intelligence, sales channels and value chain partners, and customer bases.

- *Manufacturing and sourcing* can, among other things, supply key inputs or leverage buying power or preferential treatment for contract manufacturing.

- *Distribution and logistics* offers high-level systems to manage assets (a clear advantage corporate ventures have over independent start-ups).

- *Information technology* has software development tools and methods, including relationships with software developers and firms, and legacy systems information.

- *Customer service* offers sophisticated models for responding to inbound customer requests. An area where new ventures do not expect to invest much money or time, customer service can be a significant differentiator in the market.

Remember that internal network we talked about earlier in the chapter? If you're involved in a venture business office, start using it. Talk to the leaders of the SBUs and other key corporate areas to discern the direction of their businesses; their priorities, concerns, and challenges; and their corporate and industry vision for the future (near- and long-term).

A VBO should use the external network and other research to profile the marketplaces of potential interest and form a vision of future innovations: What is the structure of these marketplaces and value chains? How do they interact? What enabling technologies and applications are driving them? Who are the chief innovators and investors? In what areas does the VBO potentially apply its parent's strategic power to make venture bets, where financial and strategic advantage can be ultimately realized?

In nearly every corporation, much of this analysis is already done. If not, a corporation can use one of several credible mechanisms or methodologies that help with this process: The management consulting firm Strategos, anchored by Gary Hamel, offers techniques called "Journey

Mapping" and "Silicon Valley Inside" to the Global 1000. The Doblin Group, led by Larry Keeley, has perfected an approach called the Innovation Landscape Program. Bain & Company's approach is chronicled in a book by senior strategist Chris Zook. Called *Profit from the Core*, the book introduces the notion of defining core and adjacent business/industry areas. DiamondCluster International has built a specialized practice around the tenets of Fred Wiersema's *New Market Leadership*.[1]

Mapping Strategy to Ventures

A picture is always worth a thousand words. Displaying the landscape of a particular market in a graphical diagram is an effective way to determine levels of integration, from component and systems vendors through to end-use consumption, and also to show how categories relate to one another. It makes it easy to locate specific vendors, ventures, and prospects on the map, and to see where specific portfolio company investing and building have been initiated.

Figure 4-2 illustrates the result of Eastman Ventures's strategic mapping process. It was not an accident that they targeted internet-based businesses first. Eastman Chemical's IT group was already building an industry-leading e-business platform. Eastman Ventures would augment this effort with investments in new technologies and new product and service concepts that could serve to reduce cost structures further. Plus, establishing this focus and relationship to the venturing group ensured an ongoing channel to relay innovation from the outside back into the company.

As the figure indicates, Eastman was able to use its interest in XML integration to invest in webMethods. XML may seem like a peculiar investment for a chemical company, until you consider that webMethods connects suppliers and customers over the Web, a capability Eastman requires. In fact, Eastman's return is compounded because its own customers and suppliers need the software to facilitate connectivity, thus creating an opportunity for Eastman to introduce its own value chain—perhaps even the chemical industry as a whole—to webMethods. Eastman got a double payoff: It improved its customer and supplier connectivity while steering its investment in webMethods to be a success through proliferation of its technology. With customers and suppliers needing

FIGURE 4 - 2

Eastman Ventures's Strategic Investment Map

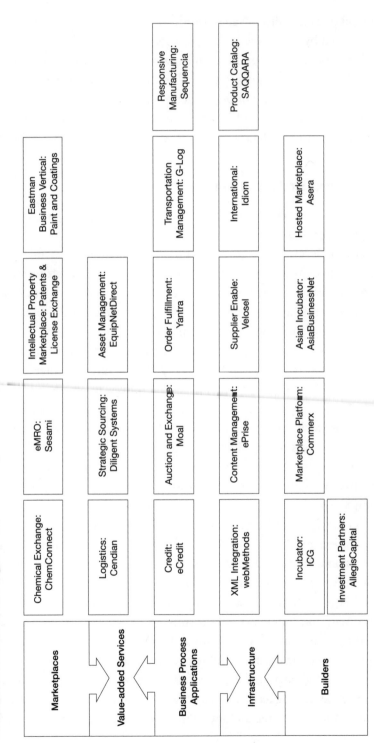

Source: Eastman Ventures.

connections to their own customers and suppliers, Eastman's webMethods investment demonstrates "viral marketing" at its finest. Eastman derives benefits as a consumer, as a business partner, and as an investor.

Practices: Generating Ideas and Tracking Progress

Given the need to hedge their bets, venture capitalists rarely constrain their choices early in the process of generating leads and deal flow. The goal is to build a broad base of ideas and venture proposals that they can quickly sift through, categorize, and develop incrementally. Corporate venturing should be no different in this regard. It too requires an external network to tap into the vein of deal flow.

A wealth of ideas float around every company. Most never see the light of day. The difference between a company that derives benefit from those ideas and one that does not is the existence of a formalized and focused mechanism to promote the creation and exploration of those ideas. One of the VBO's most important roles is to build and maintain a pipeline of ideas.

How does such a pipeline work? It should be as wide as possible at the entry point, to allow as many ideas to flow as possible. But it must consistently narrow, so the VBO can focus on proposals that address strategic and financial priorities. It must subject every idea or suggestion to a three-part examination, asking these questions:

- What strategic value would this idea bring to our business?

- What value would this bring to our portfolio?

- What is the intrinsic value of the venture?

Figure 4-3 shows how these questions can serve as progressively narrower filters for ideas in the pipeline.

The pipeline will bring ideas in from all directions. Some ideas will be interesting additions or changes to the product line, and the VBO team should direct them back inside the company. Some will not be unique or create enough value, and the VBO team should eliminate these from the pipeline. Some of the ideas, though, could form the basis for ventures that could incrementally help transform the corporation. The VBO team should fit those ideas into one or more of the categories developed through the investment map.

FIGURE 4 - 3

Opportunity Filters

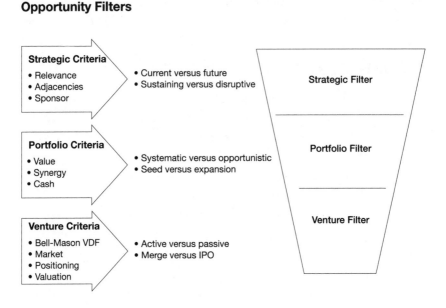

Nokia Ventures Organization (NVO) helped its parent, the Finnish mobile phone company, pursue nascent ideas that were not part of the company's existing business units. Its pipeline of ideas was full because NVO's express purpose was to look beyond the immediate business of the company for new potential business.[2]

The pipeline of ideas is also a powerful tool for retaining talent, countering employee frustration at a lack of challenge, responsiveness, or innovation in a large company.

Codifying Best Practices

The codification of venturing best practices gives the venture development process structure—which in turn makes it repeatable and scalable, critical elements for any corporation. It provides a "transplantable," adaptable framework to guide those in the corporation who are less experienced in venturing. A venture development framework provides a blueprint for calibration points and milestones, a way for the new venture team to use best practices while learning and internalizing these rules of the road. Such a framework is necessary to gauge the progress of venture investing and building objectively and consistently.

While venturing will always be something of an art, we can specify, and often standardize, the fundamental operations of the VBO for planning, implementation, and measurement. Examples of techniques to make these activities more structured are highlighted below:

- *Screening:* the use of software to standardize specific venture evaluation criteria.

- *Due diligence:* the use of an experts network to provide objective perspectives on value.

- *Deal construction:* the use of standard terms and conditions templates to limit variability.

- *Common language:* the set of standard definitions, e.g., concept stage plans, to ensure alignment around key decision points and to facilitate communication and interaction.

- *Governance structure:* the use of explicit agreement which covers criteria and processes for interaction to serve as a foundation for identifying and resolving issues.

You Get What You Measure

Performance measurement, especially during early stages of development, is extremely tricky. Most corporate managers are accustomed to using relatively unambiguous performance measures such as revenues, costs, profits, grow rates, market share, and market value. However, these measures can be misleading or simply don't work for new ventures or new venture programs. Similar to software development projects, incremental measures of progress (i.e., the leading indicators of performance) must be managed. We will talk more about this in chapter 9.

Once the corporate venture program is running, the team must agree on a system of measurement to determine progress and measure success. Most major corporate projects, such as the launch of a new product, are rigorously planned and controlled from the top. Implemented over a period of years, they involve drawn-out approval processes ensuring that nothing is left to chance, and that all units move together in lockstep.

Independent ventures, on the other hand, are often planned on the fly and seem to be controlled by nobody. An implementation period of years is a luxury they do not have; approval processes can take place on the elevator at the end of a long day; and units race to push forward their own mission regardless of whether all the necessary building blocks have been put in place.

Neither of these organizational models is right for a corporate venturing program. Unlike traditional major corporate projects, a corporate venture must have the opportunity for experimentation. So changes to the business plan—even the basic strategy and business model—must be accepted and even expected. Unlike many independent ventures of the past, the corporate venture must yield to a visibly manageable process. That is why the venture team must agree on explicit performance milestones.

Evaluating Progress: The Bell-Mason Venture Development Framework

To facilitate the science of venturing, we need a formal "operating manual" and tool set. In our corporate venturing practices, we use the Bell-Mason Venture Development Framework (VDF), which was created by Gordon Bell, legendary technologist and father of Digital Equipment Corporation's VAX family of computers, and Heidi Mason, veteran Silicon Valley start-up specialist and coauthor of this book. We will refer to the Bell-Mason VDF throughout this book.

The Bell-MasonVDF offers an objective means to chart the course and evaluate the progress of early-stage ventures. Originally based on direct access to hundreds of ventures over a five-year period, it has been used commercially for over fifteen years. It has been specifically adapted (since 1995) for Internet-related ventures and corporate ventures and is continually updated. It has been licensed around the globe by consultancies, VCs and other venture investors, corporations and governments alike. (See Appendix C for more details.) The premise behind its development is that you shouldn't have to understand the technology to ask the right business questions. The means for determining progress can be stated thus: "Look for the evidence of milestones achieved and incremental performance, and of doing the right things at the right time."

SUMMARY OF VBO "MUST-HAVES" AND "RED FLAGS"

VBO "MUST-HAVES": ELEMENTS ESSENTIAL TO HAVE IN PLACE

- VBO context, strategy and positioning, based on:
  - parent corporation's core capabilities and businesses
  - strategic investment map for venturing
  - external positioning in venture community
  - external positioning in industry
- Platform specified:
  - Governance structure: investment and operational decision-making roles and responsibilities; ongoing interface with parent (executive committee and SBU)
  - VBO team, managing director, VEO, and CEO; advisors, partners
  - Portfolio strategy and creation of initial investment opportunity map
  - VBO practices (sources of IP and deal flow, screening and due diligence, venture development building and investing, portfolio management, corporate business process connect points and integration, strategic and financial performance measurement and tracking)
- VBO's structure and first business plan (emphasis on first twelve to twenty-four months) approved by CEO/executive committee
- VBO performance hurdles (financial, strategic, and horizon for delivery) approved by CEO/executive committee
- VBO funding approved by CEO/executive committee; signatory levels set for individual investment decisions
- VBO governance structure/venture investment decision process approved by CEO/executive committee
- VBO compensation plans approved
- Managing director and initial team in place (job descriptions written and blessed by HR; includes ability to recruit outside) and being managed according to specific objectives

- VEO committed (for a minimum of one year)

- Board of advisors approved; advisors signed, especially outsiders

- Venture community infrastructure and relationships mapped; meetings in process

- Internal corporate infrastructure and relationships mapped; champions identified

- Online screening system up and running; VBO deal flow database framework in place

- Venture development best practices in place

- First deals starting into VBO pipeline (investing and building), tracked and managed according to VBO process

- Process and VBO plan metrics being tracked; architecture incrementally updated and refined (ongoing; formally once a quarter)

VBO "RED FLAGS": FACTORS THAT DEMAND IMMEDIATE ACTION

- No VBO!

- CEO is ambivalent or skeptical about venturing activity

- Creation of VBO dependent on success of first deal

- Haphazard, ad hoc investing and building across SBUs and in other areas: no corporate investment strategy or expertise; no integration

- Corporate venture unit is really service only to SBUs (they drive all the deals); no centralized portfolio strategy

- VBO in place, but no real business plan

- No VEO

- No board of advisors or outside influence

- Selection of unqualified team (VEO, managing director, VBO team)

- No (outside) venture-development framework adopted and customized for corporate use

- Separation of build and investment strategies and structures; venture expertise and structure not shared

- No systematic tracking/measuring performance of investments, builds, and VBO itself

- No formalized governance structure; no authority base to get attention/get needs met across corporation

- Corporate contribution/performance hurdles not defined, or defined according to ROI only, or horizon for return is inappropriately short (e.g., less than three years)

- No in-house business unit champions; no plan/no support for how to get them

- No traction with outside venture community (starting with limited or no access)

- Inconsistent corporate-level commitment to VBO funding

- Corporation doesn't approve VBO compensation packages; HR ties up new job descriptions/classifications

- VBO must use parent's recruiting system and suppliers

- Corporation unwilling to consider innovative incentive compensation packages

- VBO promises but can't deliver access to other corporate resources and SBUs

- VBO doesn't play active, ongoing role in managing portfolio company/SBU relationships

- VBO has to use internal corporate resources and corporate partners to meet its needs; can't go outside without significant political battles

- Screening is bottleneck and driven by personality rather than criteria

- Can't get access to quality deal flow (sees only "B" ventures and players)

The Bell-Mason approach is a rule-based system, documenting and embedding venture development "best practices." It includes four key elements:

1. *Twelve dimensions* or categories of analysis that can characterize any venture: platform, product/service, delivery, business plan, marketing, business development/sales, CEO, team, board, cash, financing, control/operations. While all actions in these dimensions relate to each other as the venture develops, the venture team must analyze progress in each dimension independently to reliably define and calibrate it. (See figure 4-4.)

2. *Four well-defined stages of development*, which chronicle the evolution of the venture (as a whole and per dimension) over time: Venture Vision, Alpha Offering, Beta Offering, and Market Calibration and Expansion. The specific activities and milestones within the twelve dimensions change over these four stages. Best-practice milestones to be achieved by the end of each stage are a prerequisite preparation for the next stage. We will explore each of these stages in detail in the next four chapters of this book.

3. *Quantification of a venture's progress*, in each stage, via key milestones and incremental performance measures. Taken as a whole, this element of the Bell-Mason VDF provides a stage-by-stage road map of venture development, achieved through prescriptive, detailed checklists for each stage to provide a guiding path forward with over 1,600 best practices in total, and diagnostic analysis provided at transition points between stages of development, offering pinpoint comparison between the venture's status versus the ideal best practices at that stage. This analysis is especially useful for investors doing due diligence or providing board-level advice and counsel, or as an internal review for a venture's team at end stage.

4. *Spider graphs*, or Kiviat diagrams, that depict the ideal state of venture evolution across the four stages, and provide a means to compare the real venture against the ideal. A picture is yet again worth a thousand words: The Bell-Mason spider graph (see figure 4-5) provides clear, simple, and visual illustration of the ideal state of evolution for a venture at each stage of development. It reflects the meeting of all

FIGURE 4 - 4

Twelve Dimensions of the Bell-Mason Model

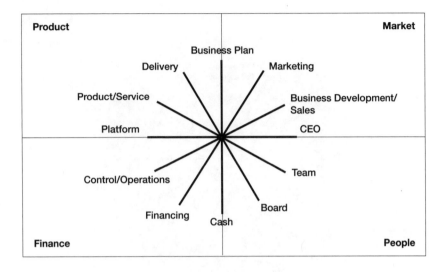

"best-practice" milestones and actions required to transition to the next stage, and it symbolizes what territory must be covered within each dimension to ensure lockstep progress. The graph plots the actual state of a venture against those ideal states, which are derived from the 1,600 underlying best practices.

You may think it seems odd to use such a seemingly complex chart for a corporate venture that by its nature, will be unstructured, experimental, and always shifting. We believe that such careful charting offers three key benefits that even most stand-alone, start-up companies sorely lack.

- It promotes synchronization by providing a visual tool for companies to track progress across all twelve dimensions of a corporate venture. The spider graph illustrations show how a company, quite typically, may have made tremendous strides in some areas but entirely neglected others. For example, engineers and marketers will typically want to move quickly to lead the venture. But it is dangerous to have any one component get too far ahead. The diagram helps remind the venture where more work needs to be done to keep the process in balance.

FIGURE 4 - 5

Ideal States for the Bell-Mason Model

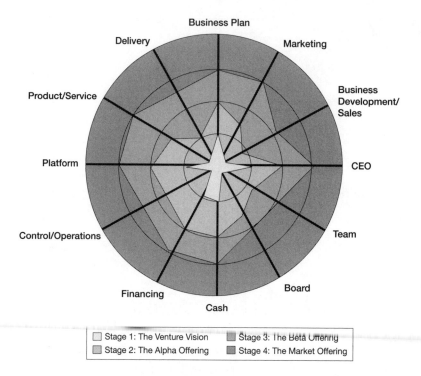

Stage 1: The Venture Vision   Stage 3: The Beta Offering
Stage 2: The Alpha Offering   Stage 4: The Market Offering

- It disseminates whatever has been learned from each stage by giving management an across-the-board view of progress being made in all sectors of the venture. The steady stream of checklists, milestones, and questions embedded in the Bell-Mason VDF creates a path of independent learning for everyone involved.

- It provides a basis for control, by measuring all fronts on a periodic, harmonized basis. Within a large corporation, this is a key asset. Parent companies are naturally uneasy about the venture in their midst. The Bell-Mason VDF helps create a highly accountable structure—one in which measurements are taken, plans are committed to, processes are documented, and communication with the board is regular. It achieves this control not with a set of restricting rules, but via the pointed series of milestones, targets, and questions that force the venture to focus on key issues and act in response to them.

Above all, this venture methodology creates a smarter, more efficient investing and building process for corporations. (See Appendix D.)

A Note about Part II

The application of the venture road map as part of a formalized corporate venture process may seem at odds with the unstructured, creative leaps that inspire innovative start-ups to be formed and funded. This is our way of warning you: The next part of the book may seem like arduous corporate planning rather than exciting entrepreneurial risk taking. You may think structured methods rather than free-flowing art dominate the discussion. Reading the chapters will not help you come up with new ideas—you will become familiar with a tested framework for turning ideas into reality. We will describe a model for constantly pursuing progress and continually measuring it. But most of all, we will show you a set of guidelines, questions, and next steps that make successful corporate venturing possible.

The next four chapters will provide an in-depth look at the stages of venture development, from the first stage, Venture Vision, through the fourth stage, Market Calibration and Expansion. These stages trace the evolution of ventures from idea to sustainable, scalable business. This bird's-eye view of venture development provides the guiding light for the VBO's operation.

Building the Business of Building Businesses:
Key Lessons

- *The venturing group needs to create a separate space.* The corporation must establish a separate organization, the venture business office or VBO, within the company where the standard corporate rules are redefined for venture success. It cannot be just another department, office, or company division.

- *The venture must build* and *invest.* Corporate venturing must do both as a method of diversifying its portfolio and managing risk and as a method for truly learning how to venture.

- *The venturing group must have a platform.* A platform, unlike a project, creates a sustainable basis for new ideas on a continuing basis. The parent company should evaluate the success of this platform, not simply the first pilots or investments it makes.

- *The company must create an investment map.* Companies need to collect information about their own internal strengths and assets to examine the kinds of business opportunities their VBO ought to pursue.

- *The venture needs the right kind of governance.* The operating manual for decision making between parent and venturing office puts the parent in control and allows the VBO to operate according to best venturing practices and clock rate. The governance can protect the venture from ad hoc corporate antibodies.

- *The right people are essential.* Every corporate venture needs friends and supporters within the parent company: the evangelist who can define and lead the corporate venturing office; the corporate revolutionary who is loyal to the company but an activist for change and therefore a VBO champion; and finally the ambassador, who is always the CEO of the parent company. No corporate venture office can succeed unless it has the blessing and support of the parent CEO. Similarly, the people inside the VBO must ideally be skilled in start-ups, loyal to the parent company, and advocates for the cause.

- *The right portfolio is essential, too.* Because the failure rate of new ventures is so high, the VBO must assemble a portfolio with an eye to both financial risk and the parent company's ability to leverage its assets.

- *Formalized practices are a must.* A VBO must have more than a spirit. It needs a set of formalized practices that stretch from the architecture of the platform to the development plan, to the consumer value that any new venture would create, to the core team's day-to-day responsibilities.

- *A system of measurement will help determine progress and measure success.* Well before the first venture is off the ground, a system of measuring the progress of the program that uses criteria such as those found in the Bell-Mason VDF should be in place.

a shaky foundation for venturing

In this case we recount one corporation's efforts to build a venture business office, and then we use the Bell-Mason Venture Development Framework to analyze the venture program's progress. (See Appendix D at the end of the book for more details about this process.) The analyses show a confusion of goals, governance, resources, and disciplined business planning. Figure 4-6 visually captures the good and the bad for this VBO.

Context

Let's look at how one of the world's greatest high-technology industrial organizations tackled the challenge of venturing. ACE, an enterprise with a storied seventy-five-year history, is the quintessential American success story in every respect: huge, profitable, market dominant, and a technological leader. This company had survived a massive industry consolidation and experienced a relatively low impact from the dot-com frenzy of the late 1990s except for the attrition of some key engineering talent. As with every successful company, however, the ride was bumpy. And recently, a combination of events that included everything from loss of market share in core businesses to extremely high attrition rates among the brightest engineers to a lagging stock price had left top management looking for routes out of the doldrums.

The annual corporate strategy-planning process, which sought ways to grow the top and bottom line, identified a three-part investment model to gain some quick wins and position the company for longer-term returns (that is, different risk-return and time horizon profiles). These were what the company called Stay-in-Business investments for near-term operational efficiencies, Return-on-Investment for medium-term new service businesses that complement the core products business, and Option-Creating investments for longer-term initiatives that leverage core capabilities and assets in wholly new directions.

FIGURE 4 - 6

Diagnostic of ACE Venture Business Office

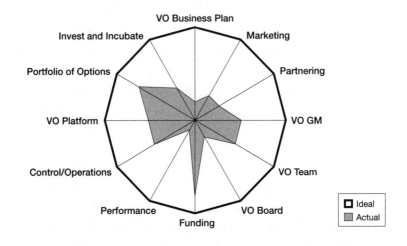

The engineer attrition problem had actually begun to affect the core business and, more important, the future of the core business. Significant R&D programs had to be aborted because of the loss of key people. Start-ups with similar business objectives, but with quite different environments, were raiding the ranks. Attrition rates exceeded 50 percent in certain areas, with entire teams leaving for the same start-up venture. The option-creating investments were intended to offer a competitive alternative to the independent start-up world.

The option-creating investments required special handling, however, because of the huge risks associated with the huge returns. Essentially, they have an equal chance of being a write-off or of returning 100 times the original investment. This third category requires a start-up-friendly environment because it needs an entirely new and different management approach than ACE's traditional, risk-averse businesses.

On the surface, ACE Ventures got off to an uneven start. On the positive side, the company did one very important thing: getting the CEO's attention and commitment. Six months after the strategic planning effort that identified the basic investment approach, the CEO assembled the top hundred managers in the company at the corporate headquarters to announce the creation of a several hundred million–dollar fund to be invested over five years in these option-creating initiatives. He also announced the formation of the venture business office, which would invest this fund in promising internal ideas for new businesses. The event was held in an atmosphere of great fanfare, with big banners, video screens, binders, T-shirts—everything the marketing folks could dream up. Given ACE's heritage in the high-technology industry, a huge number of big-ticket ideas were expected. And indeed, several hundred ideas did flow into the new organization within the first few days.

Over a year later, though, not a single investment had been made. In fact, the VBO managers had not even evaluated most of the ideas that were submitted, and they had killed all the ideas that they had evaluated. It turned out that none of the managers had any significant experience in starting a new venture from the ground up, let alone doing that same feat inside a behemoth corporation like ACE. Worse yet, the managers didn't even realize that they weren't executing—they didn't know what they didn't know.

Let's look under the surface to understand the core issues more deeply. Perhaps the best explanation is that starting the VBO is *exactly* like starting an individual new venture itself—building a business to build businesses. And ACE had violated many of the basic tenets of starting a new business. Unfortunately, from ACE's perspective, the managers believed they were doing all the right things. An extreme bias existed not to invest in the infrastructure and environment to produce and nurture ideas—or even individual ideas themselves—until they could be reasonably sure they would see some kind of return.

Clearly, the corporate venture program was off track from the start. Let's look at how ACE Ventures measured up in terms of governance, people, portfolio, and practices, the four elements of a VBO's platform.

VBO Plan

ACE exhibited the best and worst with regard to their funding strategy. Corporate allocated several hundred million dollars over a five year period to fund early stage ideas coming out of the company. This is best practice in that it shields the VBO from quarterly earnings pressures. On the flipside, the VBO folks had no strategy for how to spend that money other than opportunistically. This is worst practice because there is no approved strategy for where the money should be spent, so every individual venture will undergo "strategic" scrutiny before funding.

Nowhere did ACE define or measure strategic and financial value. Had they done this, they would have developed insights into customer behavior, competitive actions, supplier behavior, and the strategic application of technology that would provide invaluable information to ACE as they communicate progress back to the parent. For instance, if ACE were to implement its messaging technology in an intranet architecture, not only would the company prove the value proposition, but it would realize significant cost saving benefits, coming out ahead of competitors in its core business.

To complicate matters, ACE Ventures covered only the building of businesses. A separate group reporting to the CFO handled all venture investment. And all investments were made in other venture funds, with no direct investments in any new ventures. Essentially, then, the investments were purely a financial play, with little strategic value that would help either the ACE Ventures or the core business.

VBO Portfolio

Without the strategic investment framework, the ideas that came to ACE Ventures were all over the map. Because the VBO had no set of guiding principles for investment, the evaluation and funding decisions were difficult to make, and—more important—priorities were difficult to set. As a consequence, new business ideas developed at ACE ranged from a clever and flexible piece of messaging technology developed for an engineering application to a new type of integrated circuit for network routing to an interesting approach for leveraging purchasing power and using excess machine capacity.

VBO People

The leader of ACE's VBO, who came from the outside, certainly had the ability to drive discontinuous change, but he was just learning the ACE culture and needed to be cautious taking action until he established credibility with the executive management team.

The recruiting model created a dilemma at ACE. First, the company had difficulty attracting people to individual new ventures, because they were at such an early stage that ACE didn't want to create a new company with separate equity or significant funding—and yet still needed people from the outside to develop the business. Second, the right people from outside did not want to go to work for either a wholly owned ACE subsidiary or a venture with only a couple months' worth of funding. The company finally came up with a solution, an entrepreneurs-in-residence program, which mirrored practices that are common in the venture capital business. People were hired into the VBO with the expectation of moving to individual ventures while others were permanent employees of the VBO.

Finally, people need to know their specific accountabilities and responsibilities or job descriptions—who will source ideas, who will evaluate them, and who will seek funding for them. ACE, however, didn't specify these accountabilities, which led to confusion. Other than having a Web site for collecting ideas (which is a good idea) and a mentor to shepherd the idea (which is also a good idea), no set procedure existed to take an individual idea to market. It's also not clear what criteria the VBO used to evaluate ideas and who was making those decisions. All this confusion exacerbated an already chaotic process. The problem is that people make up job descriptions without these definitions and that adds uncertainty to an already uncertain picture.

VBO Practices

The VBO received several engineer-developed business plans for evaluation. Not surprisingly, the engineers did a superb job explaining the technology and a terrible job describing the business opportunity. Rather than helping the engineers, however, the team assumed there was an inadequate business need and sent the plans back. By the time ACE recognized that the engineers' plans did indeed reflect a need, several promising ventures had died.

Generally, ACE Ventures had a poor tracking system for the early stage ideas, so it couldn't determine what kind of progress it was making toward building its pipeline. A simple pipeline tracking report would have indicated that many ideas were at the front end of the process and only a few at the back end, even after a fair amount of time had passed. Thus the company would have been able to apply more resources in the front end to evaluate and nurture ideas more quickly.

Part II

a guide for venturing

5
stage 1

the venture vision:
validating the concept

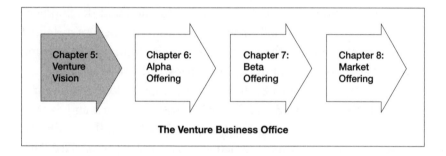

| Chapter 5: Venture Vision | Chapter 6: Alpha Offering | Chapter 7: Beta Offering | Chapter 8: Market Offering |

The Venture Business Office

The best way to predict the future is to invent it.

ALAN KAY

In this chapter we describe how raw ideas are shaped to become the foundation of a new venture, how a corporation makes its influence felt on a new venture, and the specific role of the venture business office in the venture vision stage of the venture development process. By the end of this stage, the venture will have completed:

- the first business plan (really, the plan for the plan)

- the outline of the business platform that will continuously generate new offerings

- the top-level description of the first product or service

- the initial "segment-of-one" interviews with prospective customers and other market research to understand customer needs and form value propositions

- the recruiting of the first members of the core venture team

How long does it take to reach these first venture milestones? In the outside venture community, the time frame for the Venture Vision Stage can be breathtakingly short, anywhere from a few days to a couple of months, plus the process is extremely fluid and informal. Such a compressed timetable and informal environment are the first things that distinguish the new venture strategy from traditional business strategy. But that's not all. Ventures are highly dynamic exploration-and-development "operations" in fundamentally new areas of business. They are sustained by oftentimes dramatic change, and best understood by the ongoing testing of assumptions and strategies in that volatile environment.

By contrast, traditional business strategy moves along a more predictable path of extension and growth, within mature and better-defined environments. In fact, most corporations lay out the details of a new business strategy before any actual market testing takes place. This type of detailed planning method makes sense for an established business that builds on known quantities and recognizable goals. It is also necessary if a new product or service is to vie for its share of corporate attention and budget, as well as manage the significant integration effort with other mainstream corporate programs, products, and services.

New ventures, however, are entirely different—they have no history, no legacy of existing products and services, no business base they must work within. The precise forecasts and predefined action steps of the traditional business are replaced by a general process open to discovery and change, driven by the constant influx of new information and refined analysis. The Venture Vision Stage certainly has its challenges; see table 5-1 for a brief description of them.

Stage 1: The Venture Vision

The objectives of this stage are simple: put a plan together that outlines the product and why it's different, the market and why it's attractive, the

TABLE 5 - 1

Stage One Challenges

Challenges	Circumstances and Context
Quantifying the market problem and the corresponding value proposition	You want *real customers* to measure the problem and the value of your solution. Entrepreneurs often think they know more than the market.
Differentiating the offering	The tendency is to dismiss the competition, or often to suggest there is none.
Defending against the competition	The tendency is to forget that there will be a competitive response. So where will it come from and how will the venture defend against it?
Defining a realistic business model	Obviously, the bias is to overestimate revenues and underestimate costs—both one-time and operating. After all, if you can't define a workable business model at this stage, the venture is dead.
Thinking big and starting small	One of these is always easy, the other is always hard. If you've got a big idea, it's hard to find a small starting point and vice versa.
Knowing adoption barriers	Adoption barriers are negative and entrepreneurs aren't. Rarely are the market entry problems given enough thought at this early stage.

team and why they are qualified, and a high-level business model and how much money is needed. The key capabilities the venture needs to demonstrate success at this stage include:

1. The ability to define the value proposition from the customer's perspective. This means having intimate relationships with potential customers to get the inside view—not "guesstimating" from the outside.

2. The ability to differentiate your product from the competition's, current and future. Taking a customer's perspective is, once again, important. Venture teams may assume they don't really have competition because they have a superior technology in their product. However, a customer is typically more interested in solving a problem at the lowest cost. Technological elegance is meaningless.

3. The ability to define a realistic business model. This requires the understanding of: the cost of developing and building a product, the cost of selling the product, and the price for which the product can be sold.

4. The ability to simultaneously think big, but start small. This requires visionary thinking to get the long view, but micro thinking to get the starting point.

5. The ability to know customers' objections to adopting your offering. This is closely related to point 1. Again, it means having intimate relationships with potential customers to get the inside view.

The Business Plan

The first step in the first stage can quickly descend into chaos. Thus we believe that from the earliest stages of a venture, managers must commit themselves to a written business plan. The definition of a business plan, as we will explain, is different in a new venture setting. Yet in many ways it becomes more crucial to a fledgling venture than to a traditional corporate initiative. The business plan, constantly subject to revision, becomes the organizing tool of the entire venture team—the place where objectives are listed and shifts in strategy are noted and announced. Questions the venture team must ask about the business plan at this stage include the following:

• Do we have a business plan that summarizes, in under ten pages, our vision, mission, and unique platform, our first product or service, and a relative time frame for delivery?

• Do we have a polished "elevator pitch" and "power presentation" that the entire senior team has mastered?

Can there really be such a thing as a ten-page business plan? What purpose can it have? In most traditional businesses, a business plan is the document used to gain initial support, funding, and budget approval. Once approvals are in hand, the business plan is quickly dispensed with and the work of running the business takes over. The initial plan, which may have taken months to develop, sits undisturbed on a shelf somewhere.

Venture business plans differ from a traditional corporate business plan in many important dimensions (see table 5-2). The business plan the venture needs at this first stage is much more pliable—more like the "plan for the plan." At later stages, as the team gathers more information, a more detailed and structured plan will emerge. But during the first weeks of the venture, the venture team needs, as a rallying point, a unifying, written document that *outlines* the venture and its possibilities. It should be brief and to the point as it will be continually refined, even during this stage. It is really a kind of "missionary" sales document, describing a compelling, initial vision and competitive differentiation for the venture that is a starting point for attracting "believers" and winning support. It should crisply communicate the "big idea." And it should focus on the logic of the path to implementation and launch, often within the next twelve months.

In our experience, the best Stage 1 plans have eight essential elements:

1. *Executive summary.* This brief synopsis of the plan should be no more than a page or two, highlighting the salient, compelling points around the venture's unique vision, positioning, and strategy. What's the venture in business to do, for whom, and why? What about it is

TABLE 5 - 2

The Traditional Business Plan versus the Venture Business Plan

Traditional Business Plan	Venture Business Plan
Months in development; used for a major funding pitch.	Prepared quickly so that the business plan does not become a project in itself.
Details the full development and life of the venture.	Captures the big idea and outlines implementation over the next twelve months.
Most often proposes an extension of an existing business line.	Describes a new product or service that reaches into new, previously unexplored markets.
Fits into an annual corporate budgeting process; is designed to navigate the existing preferences of the corporation.	One of many plans emerging from a Venture Business Office. No references to internal politics.
Becomes obsolete once funding is in place.	Remains an ongoing guide for future stages of venture development.
Involves large amounts of top-down research and expense analysis.	Focuses on the basic logic of the idea; existing quantitative analysis is qualified by one-on-one customer interviewing and infrastructure analysis.
Engages outside analysts and experts who are not involved in the venture to contribute to the plan. "Plan by committee."	Prepared by the leaders of the venture. "The person who writes the plan owns the business."

innovative, competitively unique, defensible? How will it be accomplished? Who will be on the team, and who will be key partners? What's required? (*Note:* The executive summary should be simple and clear enough to stand on its own, as it is the venture's first piece of "collateral"—a first introduction and presales tool.)

2. *Outline of the venture's uniqueness.* This part of the plan describes the venture's vision, positioning and competitive differentiation, with key distinguishing elements, such as the nature of the product or service, technology, marketing, and sales approach. It should include a high-level description of strategic connection between the venture and the corporation.

3. *Platform and first product/service concept.* The plan must be able to outline the venture's first product/service, the platform required to deliver it (and subsequent products/services), and—"front to back"— what is needed to launch it, including corporate resources. It should also note any "missing pieces" and areas requiring more exploration.

4. *The value proposition.* With the venture's first product/service offering, which customers will benefit and by how much? What problem is solved, what outcome hasn't before been attainable? What is the customer's perception of urgency for the value delivered?

5. *Gross estimates of target markets and delivery channels.* Which groups of customers will buy this service or product, and in what priority order (segmentation)? What are the channels by which the venture will reach each group? Emphasis is on segments targeted for launch.

6. *Initial business model.* The business plan should strive to create a preliminary "straw man" business model, delineating unit cost, pricing, and rate of revenue generation. This model should help answer questions such as the following: Is this a services company? An enterprise software vendor? Are channels direct or indirect? Can you sell the service/product for more than it costs to make and deliver it? at what projected rate?

7. *Partners.* This section describes or identifies the candidate vendors and alliances that will play an essential role in development, delivery, marketing, and sales of the new venture's product or service.

8. *Resource estimates.* Based on "like kind" models and the team's current knowledge of the development and delivery, what will be the venture's requirements for money, people and other resources? When? This section is the bare bones of what will eventually be the financing strategy plan.

A business plan that sketches out these eight elements takes a relatively brief time to prepare, and it summarizes areas that functional leaders on the team should already be exploring. The most important points here are that the plan does not lock the venture on a narrow path, and that it doesn't have to be "right." It is a first draft, which lays out the venture's *assumptions and logic*, its platform and products, and ideas around its launch. Indeed, the assumptions and logic will be tested and refined at each subsequent stage as more information is revealed. Finally, this business plan is the starting point for setting expectations and achieving vital consensus among the venture leaders about their purpose and priorities.

While the venture team is developing the first business plan, it is also perfecting the oral version of the "elevator pitch": a short (one-minute), succinct description of the venture and its objectives, which summarizes the key points and invites further interest. This elevator pitch—so called because it should be brief enough to be delivered to a prospective investor during an elevator ride to the fortieth floor—is a critical planning and marketing tool.

Far too often, new business ideas are so subtle or so complex that even the venture's most passionate supporter cannot convey the essence of the business in a handful of sharp sound bites. Even if no one is asking to hear the elevator pitch at this juncture, it will become an indispensable communication tool in every stage of marketing and fundraising. Equally important, the elevator pitch creates a common lyric for the venture team. Since group cohesion is essential at every stage, establishing and refining the common pitch—and disseminating it throughout the organization and the parent company—is a very important team-building and message-unifying activity.

The venture also needs a brief, powerful way to convey the venture's uniqueness and value in a presentation format: a "power" presentation. The team should be able to cover the entire presentation in as little as a half hour to forty-five minutes, leaving the remainder of an hour's meeting for discussion (the period that really reveals where you stand). We aim for eight to ten slides in such a presentation, but most start-up teams are doing well if they can limit themselves to twelve to fifteen slides. The venture's elevator pitch and power presentation become the core tools for selling itself to investors, influencers, partners, recruits, advisors, customers, suppliers . . . virtually every constituency the venture will need to "sign up." The elevator pitch and power presentation are essential in the corporate environment as well, serving the venture team and venture business office alike as they target and identify internal resources, undertake due diligence, and begin early "missionary persuasion."

Garage Technology Ventures is a unique early-stage investment banking firm in Silicon Valley founded by Guy Kawasaki, an Apple Fellow, start-up veteran, and serial author on entrepreneurism. Garage Technology Ventures has produced some excellent lists of suggestions for effective elevator speeches and venture presentations. (See the accompanying sidebar.)

The Platform

Corporate ventures differ from most other corporate initiatives in that they must describe a platform for ongoing activity. The goal of every corporation should not be merely to launch a one-time service or business. The goal should be to create a product or set of products that bring with them applications for numerous other businesses, many of them developed by outsiders or even competitors. The venture leaders must make sure that they have a vision for the platform rather than merely an idea for an interesting product. Questions the venture leaders should ask themselves about the platform at this stage include the following:

- Do we have a fundamental, defensible, and measurably unique basis for the platform and the first product or service?

- Do we have a written description of a relatively concrete product/ service concept? Is it self-sustaining, with future generations that we can bring rapidly to market? Do we have a tangible example of the customer interface or the product itself (e.g., a prototype)?

GARAGE.COM'S SUGGESTIONS FOR AN EFFECTIVE ELEVATOR PITCH AND POWER PRESENTATION

THE ELEVATOR PITCH

- This forty-five-second pitch is the purest distilled essence of your business plan.
- Make it short—give a 40,000-foot view of the situation.
- Avoid M.B.A. Speak/Geek Speak—use plain English.
- Concentrate on the following:
    - What is the burning problem?
    - How big is the opportunity? (Need to get the pulse racing here.)
    - What is your unique solution? (Provide relief— and do not get tangled up on the how!)
    - So what are the benefits? (Increase expectations.)
    - What is your company's mission statement? (Make it customer-centric, not product-centric.)
    - Call to action—"I want you to invest x million dollars in my company—How about you/we continue this conversation?"

THE POWER PRESENTATION

Focus on the 10 percent that matters and keep the total number of slides to twelve:

1. Title—how much money?
2. Elevator pitch (see above)
3. Problem and market size
4. Your solution
5. Your solution, continued
6. Technologies—barriers to entry
7. Competition
8. Marketing and leverage points
9. How do you make money—how much?
10. Management team
11. Status—what have you done so far?
12. Recap—call to action

Source: Bill Joos, Garage Technology Ventures, 2001.

- If our venture platform has a technology component, have we fully described it, including the degree of integration required?

- Do we have a simple platform/product/service development plan with resources and schedule, to be fleshed out and refined in the next stage?

We always look for ventures that have a top-level description of a unique platform that will enable the development and launch of its first product or service, but will also be the base for an ongoing stream of new products and services. Think of the platform as the "engine" for the venture, delineating the truly unique and differentiating components (e.g., new technology, process, brand of corporate parent or partner, custom integration). The description should also itemize everything that's required "front to back" to build and deliver (which will include the beginnings of a logical argument for make versus buy versus partner, specialized development know-how). The platform is, in fact, one of the key differences between a venture, which looks to create a sustainable, continually renewable new business, and a single product/service offering.

For example, eBay built a technology platform that enabled auctions for inexpensive collectibles, such as Pez dispensers, but quickly extended to anything that could be sold, including automobiles. This isn't surprising. Successful platforms are self-renewing. In the software world, for instance, a venture is typically pressured to have a second product or service ready to go within a few months of the launch of the first product or service. The underlying platform enables the rapid development and deployment of those subsequent products/services.

The full potential of a platform may take time to emerge. Even so, good "platform architects" and market strategists will already be looking ahead, gauging which subsequent products and services the platform might support. The reasoning is simple: If you can anticipate downstream demands, it's often more efficient to build "hooks" for them into the platform architecture the first time around, rather than try to "back fit" (in some cases, "force fit"!) later. But, as with all other elements of new venture development, the keys are balance and strategic decision trade-offs.

In 1995, Amazon.com used technology to change the book buying experience radically—to make it fast, easy, and enjoyable—compared to the retail store experience. This same technology also revolutionized buying in several other categories, from music to toys.

Other examples of successful platforms abound. Home telephone lines are platforms for services that range from voice communication to voice mail to electronic mail to video conferencing. Similarly, turbine technology produced applications as diverse as airplane engines and power plants. A company that has invested in a fleet of airplanes effectively has a platform that can be used to carry passengers, cargo, or U.S. mail, or to handle special delivery services.

In most cases, however, a venture's platform involves some type of proprietary intellectual property that has the potential—sometimes unrecognized—to create more and more value down the line. Venture leaders have a responsibility to question whether an idea's unique qualities make it viable in the market. At Praxair, the corporate venture team imagined that its ability to sell industrial gas to customers would quickly open up the possibilities of selling a wide variety of products and services—from steel to welders—over the same Web-based network.

A test of any platform concept is whether it can be summarized in writing. This is not just a good organization tool. The drafting of a written description typically works as a good filter of the concept, the assumptions driving its development and the logic of its construction. Missing pieces or areas that require additional understanding or exploration become much more apparent when in writing.

The definition of the platform becomes more detailed at this stage if the platform has a technological component. Venture leaders need not only describe the technology involved but also must ask how it will fit with other existing technologies, either with technology from the parent company or with technology suppliers or customers already use. If the venture is providing a Web-based service, how will it link, if at all, to services on the parent company's Web site? If the venture involves collecting data from customers on an ongoing basis, now is when an understanding of that technology is needed.

The venture's developers get to the notion of platform most often by focusing on the description of the first product or service that will launch the venture. This description is a simple definition that outlines what it is and what it does, and how. (A simple, functional block diagram is a good start). The simple product/service description also needs to specify the top features, functions, and benefits that will make the platform desirable to the target customers. It is also a starting point for competitive analysis. Ultimately, the first product/service stands as the unique entry point for the new venture itself.

Finally, venture leaders need a development plan and a schedule. Although the schedule helps drive the development, this initial plan and schedule constitute not so much a rigid timeline as a framework for identifying and estimating the duration of the tasks ahead. Like other aspects of the venture, the schedule is subject to testing and correction throughout its cycle. Here is a simple rule: If you haven't done it before, you can't schedule it with any degree of accuracy. And here's another: Incremental milestones and checkpoints mitigate big "all or nothing" risks. The continual, incremental, and efficient absorption of these experiences into the overall planning cycles make for superior development.

The best guidance for setting a start-up development timetable is to use the tool known as the Schedule Fantasy Factor (the name comes from Gordon Bell, our colleague and technology venture pioneer):

- Break an overall schedule into multiple major and minor milestones and assign a time frame for development to each.

- At each incremental milestone, measure the actual time it has taken to complete the task and compare it to the forecast time.

- Take the difference and apply it across the entire schedule.

- When the next milestone is reached, readjust it if necessary, for better or worse.

We have often seen companies make the mistaken assumption that after they miss a deadline they can reach the next milestone by doubling their productivity and workload. It's easy to understand how the pressures of a start-up can lead the team and its advisors down this path: They are dealing with the competitive urgency of getting to market, concern over increased consumption of funds that slips in schedule bring, the delay brought to other venture programs dependent on development's progress, and the like. But more often than not, artificially compressing the venture's schedule and doubling up the milestone requirements is a recipe for failure. Obviously, a missed deadline may be a by-product of an ineffective or inexperienced team, but more often it indicates development complexities that not even the most experienced of start-up teams could have projected.

Lastly, pictures are worth thousands of words. Nothing communicates the essence of the business to potential customers, investors, and employees like a product prototype. For a web-based business, this might be a dozen "screens" that the customer would encounter trying to execute a basic transaction. For a semiconductor company, this might be an artist's rendition of a finished chip. This exercise proves invaluable to the team in forcing consensus and specificity in their thinking. Clearly, this prototype or demo will have a short life as it is revised based on market feedback and the alpha offering is developed in the next stage. But it is the first tangible manifestation of the big vision that is described in the business plan.

The Market

Venture managers must begin thinking about the market when the venture is still an underdeveloped idea. Using our approach, they begin to understand their possible customers and create a strategy to reach them. The team should consider the following questions about the market at this stage:

- Have we identified the initial sets of customers ?

- Do we have a compelling value proposition for each of the customer groups? Have we identified key customer segments?

- Do we have a simple outline of a market plan?

- Have we developed a preliminary sales approach and distribution strategy?

Any successful venture team will begin thinking about potential customers and their needs at the outset. With a team of two to three people, it is crucial that marketing's perspective of the customer opportunity helps drive development's outline of the first product or service. This importance is particularly obvious when the team envisions and prioritizes the first key features of the product/service. Too often, a venture team becomes so enamored by technology—an online version of an existing service, for example—that they never consider how technology might change individual customers—or indeed, to what degree individual customers will even appreciate its value. Understanding how these individual customers will respond to a new product helps determine the right sets of product capabilities and focuses efforts on perfecting them.

This view marks a significant departure from many corporate marketing practices. In large corporations, marketing departments can rely on reams of existing demographic and sales data to determine how product extensions will fare in various markets. This exercise is expensive but useful. A quantitative understanding of group behavior can provide, for instance, the size of a total possible market for a given product or service.

The problem with traditional marketing is that it interprets and extrapolates from historical customer and group behavior. When Bank of America or Procter & Gamble or General Motors begin early-phase marketing of a new product concept, they already have a national market in mind. They therefore rely on storehouses of existing demographic data and regional buying patterns. These companies are less interested in how individual customers might or might not use a product because their focus is on a national launch of a product that, even if it does poorly, will be tried by millions. They think about customers and their needs in the aggregate, not as individuals.

Corporate ventures cannot pursue such costly national or global marketing analyses. In fact, because their ideas are so bold, they must conduct testing earlier and at a much more granular, customer-by-customer level.

Instead of broad-scale telesurveys and focus groups, new-venture marketing relies on intense, one-on-one interviewing—what we call "segment-of-one" marketing. Members of the venture team conduct approximately five to fifteen in-depth interviews during this first stage, starting with people who might be ideal customers, and including those who influence them. (Figure 5-1 summarizes the types of topic areas to be covered in building interview questions). Ideally, these interviews can be extrapolated to yield an understanding of the aggregate target market.

In a sense, they develop an understanding of the market in the reverse order from their large corporate counterparts. The goal is to understand the habits and predispositions of a small number of potential customers to achieve a *qualitative* perspective of the entire market of potential customers. Segment-of-one marketing permits a venture's team to understand the "whole" customer, and to refine its positioning and product or service value propositions in the process. Appendix E offers a customer/application profile template for capturing this vital information.

Segment-of-one marketing interviews should be carried out by the most senior members of the venture team, ideally those who understand the vision and strategy of the venture, its future product or service, and the underlying requirements. These senior people must be involved because, during this stage, they are the ones who must take the customers' reservations, nuances, and revelations and adjust the business plan accordingly. Often, we augment the internal effort with interviews by external venture marketing specialists. For something as important

FIGURE 5 - 1

Customer Interview Structure

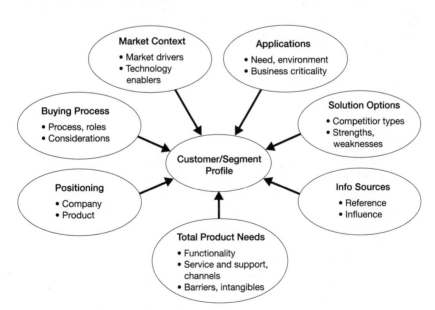

Source: © 2001 Liz Arrington, Affiliate, Sevin Rosen Funds and Bell-Mason Group.

as target customer profiling and identification, senior-level experience and outside objectivity serve as additional testing and reduce risk. A guide for this critical segmentation analysis and research process, which begins with the venture and continues throughout its development, is in Appendix F.

We've found that the venture team will always learn something vital during this interview process. Consider the case of a new venture team who described their first product/service as an enterprise "portal," tailored to provide a central platform for internal corporate communication as well as a pipeline for funneling in relevant outside information. They saw themselves as an enterprise software and Web-hosting company, and they had sketched out a business model that positioned them as application vendors. Segment-of-one interviewing revealed, however, that their prospective customers would be likely to see them as a tool vendor, not as a "plug, play and customize" enterprise application vendor. These results had enormous implications for every aspect of the new venture, including its basic business model.

Here's another example. A new Internet venture planned to deliver software that could optimize bandwidth for customers and emphasized the cost-reduction benefits of this unique approach. But in this case, segment-of-one interviewing revealed that their case for typical cost reduction was weak, and that it didn't highlight the software's unique capabilities. However, interviewers noted that in an entirely different area, these same customers had clear demands for how critical applications performed. By connecting the venture's unique ability to optimize bandwidth to the performance of strategic applications—valued by the customer and not easily attainable any other way—the team was able to see a way to increase the value of its first service and create a new, sustaining vision for the venture itself. Once they made this adjustment, prospective customers immediately responded. And again, the implications for most aspects of the venture—development, partnering strategies, pricing, marketing and sales, customer support—were significant.

In general, the vast majority of customers are not interested in a product or service simply because the technology is amazing. They are interested in services that solve their problems. Take personal digital assistants (PDAs) as an example. We are all accustomed to seeing PalmPilots and similar devices in the hands of many executives and people on the go. Yet the idea for the PDA is not new—it's been around for years. One of the first digital assistants was Apple's Newton. With its gee-whiz capabilities, Apple had high hopes for the product—and the "evangelistic" marketing machine—to facilitate high-exposure campaigns on its behalf. But Apple neglected to monitor the degree to which it would have to realistically change the way people thought and worked in order to build constituencies of happy customers. The Newton's handwriting-recognition software was cumbersome and impractical. Consumers, it turned out, liked the *idea* and the *promise* of a portable data storage device, but had little patience for the reality of learning a complex handwriting-recognition system or dealing with inadequate power sources or bulky devices. The Newton didn't make it, nor did the dozens of pocket organizers that followed. The problem was not an absence of demand, but rather the difficulty of designing these organizers in such a way as to fit true user preferences.

A man named Jeff Hawkins designed the PalmPilot a few years later. And instead of packing it with an overabundance of elegant features, Hawkins focused on the fundamentals of how his device would fit into the daily lives of users—of which he considered himself one. He designed a robust but limited set of the most fundamental features—schedule management, contact tracking, and reminders. He even considered the "comfort factor"—a truly important (and truly low-tech) issue that matters to every user. To make sure he got it right, Hawkins didn't just conduct a focus group or fiddle with a prototype for a couple of days. He carved a block of wood the size of the new device, then latched it onto his belt and carried it around for a year. This type of micro-market testing exemplifies the kind of approach a new venture needs to take.

Of course, identifying customers and understanding what they want is one thing. The task of the venture's marketing operation is to map out systematically how to reach them. Indeed, at this stage of the venture, the leaders need to be mapping out a simple marketing plan that traces how a new product or service can reach customers—and why. Most marketing plans assume that customers will gravitate to a new product based on familiarity with the brand or their demographic profile. A new venture cannot make these assumptions, however. Even ventures that leverage a corporate parent's brand need to prove themselves in a new context. Instead, the team must develop profiles of its likely customers and create a strategy to reach them.

This simple outline will evolve to become the first draft of a marketing plan in the next stage of venture development.

The Team

Every venture and every platform it produces reflects its founder's vision. But that is rarely sufficient to implement a venture strategy. During this stage, the task of the venture's leader is to start recruiting a qualified, full-time core team dedicated to the venture and able to move it forward rapidly. Any new business can recruit and hire talent, but a new venture must also understand the unique role of its employees, their relationship to the parent company, and their ability to interact in a start-up environment. During this stage, the founder(s) must assemble a core group of senior people who understand the demands of a start-up. Questions the venture founder(s) should ask themselves about the team during this stage include:

- Do we have a CEO who has demonstrated the skills to lead a venture?

- Do the two to three people currently on board have the critical experience and expertise to drive the venture forward through the next stages?

- Do we have evidence that the CEO and other team members function together as an integrated team?

The CEO. Because of a venture's small size and need for quick execution, the CEO of the venture takes on a more vital role than at the parent company. He or she must exhibit a number of qualities, all of them hard to find in a single person. The most important attributes are vision, passion and commitment to the venture, comfort with ambiguity, and start-up experience and expertise. These attributes serve the CEO well in winning the necessary support from the parent company and creating a compelling case to attract funders, recruiters, partners, and customers. "Selling" the venture with a missionary's zeal is the CEO's constant occupation through every stage of the venture.

The CEO's start-up experience and expertise are vital. A CEO without experience in this unique environment faces enormous hurdles. Ideally, the CEO has managed an early-stage team of a new venture or worked directly in the specific environment, such as having led a Web-based business in a related industry or domain. Corporations tend to place a "proven manager" at the helm of a new venture, rather than hiring someone who has managed the frenetic pace of a start-up. When they do so, it's a red flag of trouble ahead.

Of course, the CEO cannot act alone. He or she will need a team, with at least two or three senior-level members who have deep experience in the product or service area, knowledge of the parent company and potential partners, and confidence to drive the process. During this stage, what matters most is a team that can meet the initial elements of the business. An experienced sales manager is less important at this stage. Instead, the venture ought to be looking for people who can validate the initial design and business proposition, and think about marketing strategy and business development. Their ability to work closely as a team is, of course, indispensable.

Hiring. In the corporate world, the search for talent is tough, but with the right incentives, big business can almost always secure what it needs. In many cases, companies deliberately seek to hire internally so they can place someone at the helm of a venture who is already familiar with the corporate culture.

But in the venture world, at least half the people needed are not even a part of the corporation. And those easily found in the corporation likely have little or no start-up venture experience. Hence we find yet another case of counterintuition for corporate parents: No corporation has all the talent and experience a venture needs—you can't get it all from inside. And for many corporations, this realization is an early painful experience in venturing. It is the first in a series of challenges to the parent's culture and organization.

Outsider knowledge is key to venturing, because venturing is focused on doing things in ways that the corporation does not. A venture needs support from outside sources, and these vendors can bring much-needed expertise in areas such as market research (think of segment-of-one studies); specialized developers, designers, and engineers; and experts in venturing itself. For example, the venture capital firm Accel Partners and retail giant Wal-Mart Stores aggressively recruited outsiders for their joint venture, Walmart.com. The venture's CEO, Board, and key executive staff members were recruited from outside both organizations.

Though the team is vital to the ultimate success of the venture, the lack of a complete team is, at this stage, not an insurmountable problem—and not unusual, since the venture is merely a ten-page document without significant funding.

Advisors. At this point, when the conception of the venture is still emerging, it is not realistic to begin recruiting the kind of senior advisors the venture will eventually need. But it is not too early to begin thinking about the type of advisors the venture will need down the road, and to start drawing up "wish lists"—and even to start testing ideas with the individuals who might serve in this capacity.

The Financing

The issue of money hangs over every corporate venture, even during this early stage when no great investments are needed. Still, venture leaders need to be providing projections about financial demands and devising a way to meet them. Questions they should ask themselves about financing during this stage include the following:

- Have the founders been able to raise enough cash to support the needs of this stage, e.g., market research costs?

- Do we have the support of at least three reputable, known outside sources?

- Have we secured financing for the next stage?

How much money does a corporate venture need during this early Vision Stage? Many corporations find the answer to that question a mystery, which is why they are reluctant to commit funds to new ventures.

At the Vision Stage, their reluctance is reasonable. The venture does not yet have customers, partners, or an alpha offering. The work has focused on conceptualization and definition. That is why we believe that spending at this level ought to be extremely limited—usually less than 1 percent of the expected first-year expenses. Most venture leaders will find that outside the parent company they can drum up little interest in committing significant amounts of money for the vision.

But that is not to say that developing outside relationships is not important. Indeed, even without a financial commitment, creating alliances and friendships with recognized business leaders is an important priority for a venture during this first stage. Influential and knowledgeable industry figures might become investors at a later stage. The venture's goal during this stage is to whet their appetite.

It is the CEO's job to secure funding—perhaps as much as $5 million—for the next stage, when more people will be needed and the alpha version of the product or service will be constructed. But the leader of the venture will recognize that the better defined the platform and initial product, the more likely funding will follow.

There is one advantage of working on a limited budget throughout this stage: The absence of large funding works to filter out those who do not maintain a genuine interest in the venture. The demand for sweat equity is simply a part of a corporate venture, and it helps build commitment and enthusiasm through the first several uncertain weeks.

The VBO's Role in the Vision Stage

What can the venture business office do during this Vision Stage, when the new venture remains a series of ideas? The most important tasks involve creating a broader vision for new ventures that looks beyond the first product or service. The VBO should also be fostering a strategy of new ventures that has clear links to the overall strategy of the corporate parent. At the same time, it should act to protect its ventures from corporate interference, striking the right balance between insulation and input.

Specifically, the VBO has a series of discrete tasks to accomplish during the new venture's Vision Stage:

- Making sure its screening and filtering system for new venture ideas is up and running, and that the ventures it pursues fall within the strategic investment map we discussed in chapter 4. VBO leaders will also determine how to balance investments in promising companies with building new enterprises themselves.

SUMMARY OF "MUST-HAVES" AND "RED FLAGS"

VISION STAGE "MUST-HAVES": ESSENTIAL ELEMENTS TO HAVE IN PLACE

- Simple definition of the venture based on its initial platform, spelling out what makes it unique; essential elements that will have to be created, purchased, or partnered for; and a map demonstrating how the venture links to the parent in terms of strategic advantages and synergies

- Initial one-on-one interviews with prospective customers to determine market segmentation

- Outline of service/product possibilities, with prospective customers and potential value propositions

- First draft of a platform/service delivery approach, based on customer analysis

- Outline of development plan, listing requirements, schedules, and incremental milestones

- First venture business plan (approximately ten-page placeholder, to be refined and expanded) delineating prospective requirements and benefits to be delivered to the parent

- First draft of how the product or service will look and feel to the customer. For a web-based business this might include the basic transaction flow and examples of how the customer interface might look

- Initial team: venture manager/leader; business development and Web development heads (virtual team members, subcontractors or otherwise); venture executive officer or highly placed corporate sponsor; beginnings of board of directors and/or advisory board

- "Angel" funding from parent, based on itemization of resources required (especially enough resources to get through the next stage—the alpha offering)

- Governance in place to guide venture portfolio in general and this venture in particular

VISION STAGE "RED FLAGS": FACTORS THAT DEMAND IMMEDIATE ACTION

- Point product, product extension, or feature set masquerading as a platform, or enabling technology masquerading as an application

- No in-depth discussions with representative customers to determine whole context, needs, wants, tendencies, buying motivations (such as senior-level segment-of-one interviewing)
- A venture manager with project leader skills rather than venture CEO skills
- A venture team that is incomplete and inexperienced (especially in marketing, partnering, Web development, and new venturing in general)
- A project description masquerading as a venture plan (marked by a view limited to product/service definition rather than the integrated, cross-functional perspectives required to run a full business)
- No "mapping" to the parent (i.e., no case made for strategic importance to the parent, no view to downstream value contributed, no understanding of immediate resources from the parent that could provide "unfair advantage" to the developing venture; no organized view of dependencies)
- No commitment from the parent (no financial commitment, no sponsorship or ownership, ad hoc and unpredictable governance, no commitment to future initiatives pending results of first and only venture)

- Enlisting appropriate domain experts within and outside the corporation for due diligence and venture team assistance
- Facilitating access to other corporate resources as appropriate to this stage, and identifying potential SBU partners and other corporate assets to enhance the venture's proposition and plan
- Making sure the base criteria and milestones in which the VBO has an interest are met
- Organizing funding for the venture for the next stage

Notable Differences between Corporate and Independent Ventures

Throughout this section of the book, we are focusing our comments exclusively on corporate ventures as distinct from independent ventures.

Or in other words, ventures with substantial corporate representation on the board or with significant amounts of corporate funding and support. A corporate venture and an independent venture differ significantly, and these differences manifest themselves even at this early stage:

- *Breadth and depth of the business plan.* Because of the venture team's experiences, the corporation's requirements, resources available, and time allowed, the corporate venture team will often draw up an initial business plan that is more detailed than one that their external counterparts would produce. The process for developing this plan is deliberately more formal because the corporate venture has to explain why it deserves to operate outside many of the normal rules of the company The independent venture creates a business plan largely to raise money. Its format and the process for developing it are irrelevant if it succeeds in attracting investment.

- *Experience and commitment of the venture team.* At this stage, corporate ventures rarely have a team in place that will actually take the concept all the way to market. Most are simply working on a project basis until management decides to move forward—and only then will the venture's real managers come on board. In independent ventures, the founders are frequently the same core team that takes the project to market.

- *Emphasis on product versus market.* Corporate ventures often spend more time analyzing their potential market, whereas independent ventures often seem more focused on the product definition. Again, the emphasis appears to be highly correlated with the type of people involved at these early stages. Corporations want to understand market potential (and reduce perception of market risk) before they invest; independent ventures want to understand product viability and innovation implications before they move.

Corporate Assets Available to the VBO

Platform. While developing a platform at this stage of the venture, many of the corporation's basic assets will prove indispensable: for example, access to existing corporate platforms and products, software code, manufacturing and delivery expertise, customer service organizations—

even industry clout. And clearly, intellectual property, brand name, and product reputation are advantages that, used wisely, can give a new venture an enormous boost.

Market. Throughout the marketing process in this stage, the new venture can benefit from the corporation's existing base of market research and analysis, customer databases, infrastructure for program development, channel linkages and understanding, industry positioning, and infrastructure influence. In some cases, some slice of the corporation's current customer base may even represent the target customer of the new venture, speeding access and understanding of this set for segment-of-one interviewing and platform/product specification. Equally relevant could be the corporation's other marketing partners and affiliates.

Team. Corporations can offer a start-up team an enormous store of industry expertise and domain talent. Having access to the best of these people—as advisors, consultants, even team members to complement the rest of start up team—hastens the quality development of the new venture, and adds to its value. The key to engaging the right individuals is objectively determining and balancing the mix of talents and experience according to the venture's specific *team* needs in this stage. The ideal construction is a core team who are recruited and committed based on these special venture requirements, and have access inside and outside the corporation to the types of assistance they need in building the venture. It is also important to get cross-functional skills (e.g., marketing, finance, technology) infused now—otherwise, poor decisions with important downstream ramifications are inevitably made and will need to be fixed in later stages.

Financing. The parent company initially can provide both hard and soft dollars for a new venture. The hard dollars come in the form of start-up money, or funds simply to carry out a single piece of research that would help define the first product. Soft money can come in the form of overhead relief, computers and other equipment, domain expert consultants, accounting and payroll assistance, administrative staff, and so on. Access to such funding is one of the clear advantages that a corporate venture has over an independent cousin.

Common Mistakes: VBO Beware

Platform: The flip side of access to corporate advantages is the strings that are so often attached. Sometimes all the standard corporate antibodies are unleashed at the venture, such as slow and multitiered decision making on asset use, or analysis paralysis. Many corporations, uncertain of the future success of an unproven venture, are hesitant to lend their technology, product, and brand name for fear of damage to the "corporate jewels," even though these assets would prove an invaluable boost to a new product or service.

Marketing. The downside of corporate involvement in marketing is that the venture may find a certain type of customer/market information crucial and instructive, whereas the corporation finds it too detailed and insufficient for decision making and risk reduction. The new venture's marketing is ideally rich in qualitative analyses (e.g., segment-of-one interviewing, customer/application profiles) and relies on them to extract existing quantitative facts and figures as validation for its next steps. At this stage a venture has no sales contracts or early customer commitments. The absence of these things will frustrate a corporate parent accustomed to seeing projections based on statistical market surveys and focus group data. Without such data, the parent company may be inclined to make poor assumptions about the need for a service or product—or push the venture to provide more statistical analysis and broad-based sampling. But providing such data is counterproductive to the venture's needs and priorities at this stage, and ultimately not even compelling as the proof points the corporation seeks.

The Team. As we indicated earlier, the start-up might be imbalanced if too many insiders oversee or participate in the management of the venture. A similar danger arises when the venture team resists the involvement of outside advisors skilled in venture development. If the corporation is "loaning" its best people to the venture, most will remain in their primary jobs and devote only a fraction of their time to the new concern. As a result, the team may be spread across several locations. Ventures, even those that rely on outside hires and consultants, perform better with centralized, dedicated, full-time team members. Another downside of the corporate partnership, which seems to go hand in hand with resistance to outside employees, is the hesitancy to seek start-up expertise and help. Too often, corporations incorrectly assume that the talents and experience they have built running large, successful businesses are equally applicable to start-ups—or that they can learn it quickly enough. As we pointed out earlier, though, the corporation's "best people" aren't always the right people for the start-up job. Sometimes senior-level corporate managers or officers with responsibility for ventures at this stage may turn over day-to-day responsibilities to more junior people, which means the venture never receives the senior leadership a high-risk endeavor demands.

Financing. The trouble a corporate venture faces from its parents is the general skepticism or lack of interest in the venture. The consequence of such indifference can be inadequate funding during the first months, as well as a lack of commitment to future funding. Without some level of reasonable support, the venture simply will not be able to survive.

The Venture Vision: Key Lessons

- *Define the platform and the product/service.* If you can't explain it succinctly, you can't sell it. The venture team needs to focus on what is distinct, what customers need, and how the venture will reach out to them.

- *Draft a plan, not an operating manual.* The first draft for a venture should describe a business, a product, or a process, and explain the benefits that would come from it.

- *Make timetables short, and expect change.* Too many ventures lose steam because they miss self-imposed deadlines. All deadlines are unrealistic in corporate ventures because the territory is new. Applying the Schedule Fantasy Factor can help.

- *Market to the individual, not the world.* At this early stage, segment-of-one marketing, which studies the habits, reactions, and desires of a handful of individuals, yields far greater insight about how people might actually use a service or product. Corporate ventures should steer clear of broad-scale, data-driven market research plans at this stage.

- *Hire a venture team that understands ventures.* The venture team leadership should include a mix of outsiders and insiders who are fully committed to creating an internal platform for venturing. They should have some start-up experience, some outside experience, and an understanding of the parent company.

CASE STUDY

the venture vision

To understand the Venture Vision Stage better, let's look at a company that is pursuing a strategy of corporate ventures. We show how the company moves through the Vision Stage, as measured by the Bell-Mason VDF. In subsequent chapters, we'll show how the framework can pinpoint flaws in other stages in the development of a venture.

Context

Big Global Services Inc. is one of the most respected names on Wall Street and around the world. A hundred-year-old publicly traded firm, its financial services business operates throughout the United States, Asia, Europe, and Latin America. In 1998, the company saw that its base business of mutual funds, brokerage service, and 401(k) plans was eroding. The Street knew it, too, and stock performance was turning lackluster. Financial services have been undergoing enormous change, fueled in part by technology. Global Services knew it needed to figure out a way to catch up.

After a series of brainstorming sessions, a Corporate Task Force generated an idea that could allow Big Global to leap ahead of its competitors and capture a large and growing market—a Web-based business providing preretirement information, planning, and delivery of services to forty-five- to sixty-five-year-olds. Initial research indicated untapped demand, with the target community wanting not only financial planning but also information about health care, insurance, travel, relocation, and continuing education. Global Services believed this business, "Big Global Retirement Online," could become the high-quality "site of choice" for preretirees. They started to use the Bell-Mason VDF to track progress.

As a corporate venture, Big Global Online had some major advantages:

- An existing base of products, services, customers, and partners to leverage
- The parent's brand
- The parent's existing technology capabilities
- A wealth of experienced in-house talent
- A wide circle of proven supplier relationships

The executives sought to move quickly, with the goal of showing something to the executive committee in six months. To speed development of a platform, they decided to use off-the-shelf technology. They engaged outside Web developers to develop a site that could, at a later stage, mesh with the Big Global Services IT systems and databases.

The first key hire was the venture CEO—a director from one of the parent's retail product lines with no previous start-up experience but considerable experience and accomplishment in the parent company. The venture CEO recruited internal people for the rest of the core team:

- A project developer from the IT group (limited Web development experience; no start-up experience)
- A quarter-time person from the corporate strategy group to drive development of the business plan
- A product marketing person who worked previously with VGM in retail products (limited Web experience, no previous start-up experience)

In an indication of the venture's priority, the venture CEO got high-level permission to recruit talent from other internal sources (including IT, human resources, and legal) on an "as-needed" basis.

At this stage, the CEO also hired a host of outside consultants to: develop the Web platform and a demo disk (which is critical for fundraising), and to handle advertising and branding. The CEO decided to use Big Global Services's favorite ad firm, based on familiarity with the parent's business and full range of services available.

The venture team pursued progress on several fronts:

- The team did an initial competitive analysis, looking at existing sites for retirees and assembling a prospect list of potential partners.
- The advertising firm tabulated a total available market (TAM) analysis for use in the business plan.
- Two weeks after commencing, the ad firm presented a first draft of a branding plan, and conducted three to five focus groups for customer profiling and reaction to Big Global Retirement Online. It supplemented the focus groups by conducting telesurveys and sending response cards to prospects, asking them to rate product features and functions. Each focus group surfaced requests for more features on the site ("wouldn't it be great if . . .?"). The venture office was encouraged that potential users were able to identify a wide range of needs that the site could address.
- The CEO, assisted by the quarter-time person from corporate strategy, completed the first business plan. By the time the venture received preliminary approval from an "angel" group vice president and submitted the plan to the executive committee for approval and funding, the report had grown to seventy PowerPoint pages with appendices.

The target market was viewed as a rich and underserved vein of gold, and the venture a potential high-value, alternative channel for the parent corporation's present and future products and services. Top-down market sizing indicated that with less than 10 percent penetration, the venture would achieve its goals. Revenue projections reached $600 million (based on partner advertising, referral fees, finders fees for partner products sold, customer subscriptions and, in year 2, the beginning of sales of the venture's own private label/branded products and services.) But a profit picture wasn't yet established because the revenue model had many different constituent parts and the team needed to proceed with partners in order to extrapolate the numbers. The estimated ramp on revenue for year 1 was a "conservative" $40 million.

While the executive committee found it difficult to have certainty about five-year revenue projections for new ventures, they agreed unanimously that the venture must bring in at least $500 million in that time frame to be worth the corporation's attention. After six weeks of work, Big Global Retirement Online received the green light to build a prototype for $15 million. They had money to burn as they headed into the second stage, Alpha Offering.

In other words, by the end of the Vision Stage, things seemed to be on track. But shortly after its commercial launch, the venture was shut down. Where did it start to go off track? What were the early warning signs?

The Bell-Mason VDF, using data generated by nearly 100 questions at this stage, posed to the venture's senior managers, reveals that the early warning signs were apparent even at this early stage.

Bell-Mason Graph and Analysis

If you look at the twelve dimensions in figure 5-2, you can see that Big Global Retirement Online fell short in every dimension except cash during this stage. The parent company was prepared to spend money—but did they know what they were spending it on? Early

FIGURE 5 - 2

Diagnostic of Big Global Services

warnings were there to be detected, and like snowballs rolling down a hill they grew into major barriers to success.

Once a venture falls apart, people tend to look for one fatal bullet. Or they look at several flaws, and see them as coincidental to each other. In fact, a failed venture is rarely the result of only one weakness. And the flaws are rarely isolated from each other. Rather, they build on each other. Let's take a look at how Big Global Retirement Online fell short on each of the twelve dimensions, to get an idea of underlying problems.

CEO

The CEO had experience as a project leader but no experience or expertise with ventures. Thus he was unable to understand what incremental goals were required, how to assign priorities, and how to manage others in key tasks. With no ability to lead the integration of functional areas, the CEO was ill prepared to prevent individual units from devolving into a series of managerial silos. His inexperience in venturing, along with that of the director of marketing, showed itself in the expensive branding effort they invested in. The ad firm, rather than customer insight, drove venture development.

Team

A lack of venture experience and a mix of fractional team members and outside contractors and consultants scattered over multiple locations exacerbated a lack of integration. The use of an experienced management consultancy made some sense, but given their own lack of experience, the CEO and development leader didn't know how to guide and manage them properly. When things started to slip, the team's response was to blame the vendors for inadequate implementation, rather than to identify and address the underlying causes (which included an inadequate core team).

Board

Management inexperience was compounded by the absence of a board of directors or advisors to provide mentoring and counsel. No venture-defined or venture-driven governance process was in place to guide growth and decision making with the parent, and to insulate the venture from traditional corporate culture and practices.

Cash, Financing, Control/Operations

While funding was generous, it was neither performance-based nor pegged to incremental milestones. An initial budgetary decision by an executive vice president indicates only the lack of governance, not a long-term commitment. Moreover, the team had no real understanding of "straw man" platform development, in which planning is based on reasonable assumptions that change as the business develops. Thus they had no real sense of the development schedule that the Web/software contractor was assembling, and they were unlikely to keep control of the schedule going forward. Because this venture's platform, first-product/service feature set, and partnering strategy kept expanding in an ad hoc way (to satisfy every suggestion the focus groups generated), the venture team had no way to get a handle on cost structures and product mix pricing.

Business Plan

The length of the business plan should have been a tip-off. Large chunks of it were a tutorial intended to explain the Internet landscape to the parent company. At the same time, it provided only a superficial overview of the competitive landscape embellished with top-down market statistics and market sizing based on percentage penetration. Perhaps its central weakness was the lack of segment-of-one analysis, relying instead on focus groups, which are unable to provide a comparable logic of customer approach and prioritization

Platform

Development could not keep up with a constantly moving target of platform specifications, which were in flux owing to changing features, partners, products, and pricing strategies. While the vendors had Web and start-up experience, those from the venture who were defining and managing the development process did not. The result? Mixed agendas and conflicting priorities. Such problems magnify as the schedule clock ticks.

Product/Service

The offering was already moving toward "feature glut" without either appropriate prioritization or an understanding of whether the features could actually be built.

Delivery

Regardless of whether the Web contractor providing platform development was up to the task, the CEO and team lacked the experience and expertise to make that determination or manage the process. The absence of a fundamental integration with strategic business and marketing efforts spelled the beginning of the end.

Marketing

The venture team relied too much on the corporate approach of big-budget branding, focus group testing, and mass-market testing prior to figuring out specifically who the customer was. This decision stemmed from the politically motivated decision to use the parent's ad firm.

Business Development/Sales

The venture team took stabs in the dark on aggregate forecasts (multiple types of pricing structures for different products, services via different partners—a little of everything) without understanding context and cost of each at a micro level.

Epilogue

Now let's lift our eyes from the individual dimensions and take a good look at what they tell us about the whole. What we see is the danger inherent in separating vision, strategy, and implementation at the earliest stage in the venture's development. The risk is especially pronounced when the venture lacks the core team, governance, and outside board to remedy the situation. The risks were not apparent in the Vision Stage. But they became more and more obvious through the second, Alpha Offering, stage (when schedules slipped by months and costs mounted) and third, Beta Offering, stage (when tests showed that customers' verdict was generally "great idea, lousy implementation.") In fact, what Big Global suffered from was a failure of vision rather than implementation. The team never consistently translated its vision, or embodied it in the operational prototype, or even understood it at a granular level, because they never really fully understood the customer and segmented the market. Failure is at this fundamental level: the inability to translate and adapt a high-level venture vision into an integrated view of what the customer wants and the venture can provide.

6
stage 2

the alpha offering:
building while planning

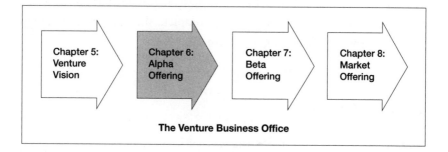

| Chapter 5: Venture Vision | Chapter 6: Alpha Offering | Chapter 7: Beta Offering | Chapter 8: Market Offering |

The Venture Business Office

If you want to make an apple pie from scratch,
you must first create the universe.

CARL SAGAN

In this chapter we describe how a corporate venture moves from the Venture Vision Stage to the creation of an alpha version of the platform and first product or service. In effect, the venture uses this stage to create an alpha version of the whole business. This alpha version should typify how the venture will deliver the customer solution from end to end. Throughout this stage, the venture's marketing team has one overriding purpose: to better understand the market and the customers who will pay for this product or service. Indeed, understanding the customer drives the refinement of the venture's specification for the platform and product. Understanding the customer also helps refine the selection of partners and alliances critical to product delivery. As implementation moves forward in this "build" phase, the team constructs the first real business plan and refines it incrementally, as they learn more. Table 6-1 summarizes the challenges of the Alpha Offering Stage.

If in the Vision Stage the venture team learned whether the targeted customers actually needed something, in this second stage they learn how customers will want to use that something. The second stage of building a venture requires detailed research on potential customers and segments, establishing performance standards that the product or service will try to meet, and selecting the features that distinguish it. In addition, the venture team must now move to complete the partnering strategy and aggressively begin filling in the core team.

TABLE 6 - 1

Stage Two Challenges

Challenges	Circumstances and Context
Convergence of planning and building	A need emerges to start building the platform, refining the strategy, and completing the first full business plan all at the same time. This increases the pressure on all efforts, and requires a unique team and quality start-up process to pull it off.
First "real" implementation of platform and product/service	This involves an intense development implementation effort in a short period of time with partnering and contingency planning. This demands lockstep integration with marketing to refine specs.
First customer set validation and prioritization of next segments for expansion	These decisions are driven by marketing prowess in qualitative analysis and targeting and correctly interpreting customers' needs. In turn, this drives development of sales, service, support, business development, and partnering.
Schedule and funding pressure	This requires managing expectations of corporate funders and directors, especially in the face of schedule and performance slips.
"Corporate Antibodies"	In this stage, start-up development is nose-to-nose with corporate s.o.p. The venture needs focused attention and protection of the VEO and VBO if it is to stay on track.

At the end of the stage, which may last nine months, the venture will have produced an alpha version of its platform and first product or service—not yet ready for prime time, but with all its components built or represented in an integrated fashion, working as a system with measurable performance. With the alpha version in hand, the venture team sets out to raise significant funds and obtain more specific feedback from prospective partners and customers alike.

The Gap between Corporations and Their Ventures

The Alpha Stage is the most difficult stage for any new venture because it requires the venture team both to flesh out its plan and to start building the first version of the product at the same time. In a traditional business, this convergence of planning and building would seem impossible. But the growth of Internet-based businesses has made us rethink our venture-planning process. We have realized that, unlike building a new type of automobile or drilling a new well, the most typical Web-enabled venture businesses require less infrastructure development. Changing and rebuilding a Web site for an Internet-based business "on the fly" is far easier than, say, retooling plans for an assembly line.

Without being fully operational, the alpha version ought to give an observer a full sense of the final service or product. At the end of the Vision Stage, the team can describe the product or service, but at the end of the Alpha Stage they can touch or examine the product or fully identify the technology or people needed to provide the service. If it is an Internet-based service, a mock site—perhaps created on an extranet—should be fully functional. So armed, the venture will be ready to begin building a formal beta version of its product or service for testing in the real world.

Finally, the Alpha Stage is where most of the difficult issues with the parent arise and must be resolved. Cultural conflicts are especially pronounced, with the growing independence and differentiation of the venture culture rising in contrast to the parent's status-quo approach. Also, issues of the future of the venture begin to take center stage. In particular, discussions and debates arise on such matters as outside funding, the creation of equity and the percentage of parental ownership, degree of autonomy, governance issues, and the efficiency of functional links to various departments and business units in the parent company. Keeping corporate expectations on track while managing ongoing changes in schedule, platform and first product/service specifications, and market planning is a continuing challenge for the fledgling venture.

Things are made more challenging at this stage because of a natural tendency for corporate leaders and a less experienced venture team to keep moving ahead, even if they haven't properly analyzed, absorbed, and accounted for changes indicated by slips in schedule or misses in performance. Worse yet, we have seen some corporate ventures head to market too fast: feeling pressure from corporate oversight, schedule slips, and increased "burn rate," they short-circuit the next Beta Offering Stage altogether. This acceleration is a recipe for disaster. Most later-stage venture failures can be traced back to mistakes made during this stage.

In a sense, the Alpha Stage is the "swing factor." It is now that roots are put in the ground. Everything else grows from here. Decisions made during this brief time will echo through the rest of the process and directly determine whether the corporate venture will be a success or a failure. In the Alpha Stage, stakes are put in the ground. The subsequent two stages are all about refining the implementation of the venture around these stakes, so making sure they are appropriately developed here becomes paramount.

Stage 2: The Alpha Offering Stage

The objectives of this stage are reasonably straightforward:

- Build the alpha version of the platform and product/service

- See how it works

- Factor in changes and refinements to the basic specifications

- Understand and resolve implications for the venture's positioning, business model, value propositions, as well as the effects on functional strategies and plans of the rest of the venture's departments

The process by which the venture team achieves these goals is complex, however. They need to demonstrate five key capabilities at this stage:

1. The marketing team's ability to gather and correctly interpret the nuances of customer behavior for strategic market planning

2. The development team's ability to build out the first alpha and establish a process for testing and incrementally refining its specifications

3. The ability to integrate the marketing team's increasing understanding of target customers and segments with the development team's platform and product specification process and build-out

4. The ability to quickly understand the implications of the specific alpha platform/product performance to the venture's business plan and path forward; the ability to use this output as the basis for strategic refinements and contingency planning as needed across the venture

5. The ability to manage funders' and board members' expectations while setting the performance bar for the next round of funding

The Business Plan

Ideally, the venture completed Stage 1 of the process with a concise, ten-page business plan that captured the thinking of the entire management team and set in place assumptions that the team takes up during this second stage of venture development. Now the team assembles its first real venture business plan (expanding it to about twenty pages, minus appendixes). The newest version of the business plan is based on the more detailed information and refined set of assumptions, fleshed-out and integrated departmental plans and implementation specifics, and a refined timetable and funding strategy for market entry. As during Stage 1, a written business plan forces the venture leaders to carefully consider their objectives, the market they want to serve, and the character and features of their product or service. In our view, business plans force managers to probe their own assumptions and define their purpose in the clearest possible terms. Questions the venture team should ask themselves during the Alpha Stage include the following:

- Have we created the equivalent of a "private placement memo" that we can put in front of investors?

- Have we created a schedule with major milestones linked to dates—including key aspects that are tied to external and internal events?

What makes for a good venture business plan? We look for certain things, as do many venture capitalists:

- a robust executive summary (two to four pages—this almost always gets read);

- a *logical* value proposition and business model based on exposure to target customers;

- a thoughtful view of the competitive landscape (a venture always has competitors, even if it's the status quo);

- a description of market sizing, qualified by the logic of the venture's approach, prospective customer profiling and supported by extrapolations of industry statistics (rather than the other way around);

- and an overview of the partnering strategy.

When it comes to financials, we have noted that assumptions driving the numbers are much more important than the numbers themselves. It's also important to lay out the logic and rough schedule for development, market entry, mean time to revenue and profitability, and steady state operation. Funders pay a great deal of attention to the team section: Who is on the team? Are the founders visionaries? What are the team members' experience and expertise relative to what the venture is trying to do? What roles aren't yet filled (and how critical are they to the venture's progress)? It's a good idea to enhance this section with a good roster of advisors and directors—if they are known to be good, funders infer that the venture is likely to be good, as well.

This first full business plan can be seen almost as a private placement memorandum, differing little in content from the traditional private placement flipbooks. Within the venture, the business-planning process also forces a degree of discipline on the team. The ongoing, dynamic planning process encourages the team to look further outward, beyond the initial product/service to subsequent products and venture sustainability, financing strategy, budget outlays, inventory, delivery, exit strategy, and so on.

The team's elevator pitch and power presentation, first developed during Stage 1, should be updated and refined, because they remain vital tools for "selling" the venture to its various constituencies.

Finally, the venture needs to create a new type of schedule for itself, balancing and integrating all the venture's functions, and linking them to the incremental, key milestones of its plan (the date of the first beta testing, for example). Even during the first weeks of the previous Vision Stage, the venture will have already measured the pace of progress and made adjustments to create a more realistic timetable. These measurements should continue to gain momentum, and, as they do, the team should report them on this major milestone schedule. The purpose is not to create a date-certain calendar but rather an event-driven calendar. Because the exact length of time for every element of the plan is ultimately unknowable in advance, it is more important to achieve key incremental milestones and report the time it takes to reach them—and then apply that experience and knowledge to future steps.

More often than not, what throws a schedule off are external or internal events over which the venture has no control. The parent postpones a funding decision by two weeks. A key supplier of software necessary for the alpha cannot deliver as promised. The venture leaders must consider every internal and external relationship on which the venture depends and calculate the factors that might delay the schedule. They will always face surprises, but they can anticipate some surprises better than others. This is the reality of new venture contingency planning.

The Platform

During Stage 1, the platform was largely a concept—a model for how new businesses could be created, who would use them, and how they would be delivered. Now, in Stage 2, the development of the platform becomes much more focused on the practical aspects of the product or service. Refining the platform is a constant activity during this stage. Questions the venture leaders must ask themselves now include the following:

- Have we created a checklist of key platform "ingredients" that are critical in developing a sustainable platform that continually enables new products and services?

- Have we defined what levels of performance will meet a minimum "acceptance test" for the product or service at both the alpha and beta levels?

- Have we embedded a continuous development architecture in the platform?
- Does our development schedule map together scope, time, and budget and let us measure our progress as we build the alpha?
- Have we courted, recruited, and committed partners who are critical to the launch of the venture?

Throughout the Alpha Stage, the work of the venture can be frenetic. There are so many things to do and keep track of. What cannot be overlooked, however, is whether the concept of the platform, fleshed out and "hypothesized" in the first stage, still makes sense when a set of tougher, more detailed criteria are demanded and a first working version of the platform and product is complete. We suggest that at the beginning of the Alpha Stage, the venture team create a platform checklist that covers the specific items listed in the accompanying box.

VENTURE PLATFORM CHECKLIST

- AN ITEMIZATION OF UNIQUE, PROPRIETARY, AND/OR DEFENSIBLE COMPONENTS: attributes that customers value and that distinguish the product/service from competitors and other players in the market. What makes an initiative unique can range from specific technologies or processes, to the particular aggregation of existing capabilities with a new kind of integration.

- ARCHITECTURE: a structural framework and specification that allow the venture to continue to consistently and efficiently construct specific products or services from a base of primary "enablers" and fundamentals. This architecture is inherent in the first product or service that has been developed and launched; awareness and adherence to architecture ensure product family compatibility and interoperability in subsequent releases.

- STANDARDS: corporate, market, and/or technical standards established in the development of the platform and first product/service

- FORMAL DESIGN AND QUALITY PROCESSES: the documented process (the venture's development bible) for systematic and quality-assured development

- A FIRST PLATFORM, PRODUCT/SERVICE DEVELOPMENT PLAN: a complete development plan and schedule that sets metrics and incremental milestones, and estimates when resources will be required

- PLATFORM, PRODUCT/SERVICE SPECIFICATIONS: the definition of the platform and product/service, specifying all the components and how they integrate and analyzing what parts to make, what to buy, and what to partner for or license

- DELIVERY OVERVIEW AND SPECIFICATION: a front-to-back outline of the contractors and partners who are necessary to deliver a service or product. This is especially important with Web delivery businesses and other specialized manufacturing or value-delivery processes, where multiple vendors may be involved.

- CORE TEAM: a team with the appropriate depth and breadth of industry and organizational experience and expertise: the CEO, the development leader and architect, strategic marketing and business development heads, a manufacturing/delivery leader, customer care and sales leaders, finance head

- RESOURCES: what level of resources is available, what is needed but not currently on hand, and an indication of a clear path by which to acquire it

- VALUE NETWORK: the network of value-added suppliers and other alliances that are the "infrastructure" for the development and delivery of the product/service

- GLOBALIZATION STRATEGY: when and how the venture will extend its reach globally; in what way its value propositions are extensible; what the implications are for operations and partnering

- VENTURE PLATFORM "FUTURES": a list of sustainable competitive advantages that could have potential value over time, and ideas about next products and services

- OPERATIONAL MANAGEMENT: the core team's ability to maintain venture management excellence and control, with cross-functional integration, efficient team problem identification and resolution capability, management by objective, forecasting competencies, and so forth

Acceptance Test. With this checklist in hand, discussion about platform and technology should move to the question of an "acceptance test."
In an acceptance test, the venture leaders agree on what levels of performance they are trying to achieve with their service or product and,
indirectly, what standards they will need to meet if they want to move
forward with the product or service. Defining these "tolerance" levels
requires thinking through all the basic aspects of the platform and how
it relates to target customer needs and perceptions of value. The integration of the marketing and development teams' worldviews should be
clearly evident. If the venture will be offering a Web-based service, what
are the acceptable response times? What are the expected delivery times?
How long will customers wait before they receive an electronic confirmation of an order? These considerations may seem technical, but they
are part of defining the character of the venture and the benchmarks of
quality for its first products.

The development of an acceptance test is closely linked to the creation of a "continuous development architecture"—a system of gathering operating information and measuring progress that the venture will
use over and over again. At the Alpha Stage, venture leaders need to establish a process that allows them to constantly monitor every aspect of their
business, gather the relevant data, analyze it, and then respond to it. In
effect, the venture leaders must ask themselves how they will know if their
product or service is on the right track, and what to do when data present clues about how to make it better. In many cases now, especially with
Web-based ventures, these information-gathering and analysis processes
have evolved into powerful software packages and services that the venture can or should specify as part of its platform design. For example,
some systems can be integrated into the overall design and specification
to monitor and report on Web site traffic and customer behavior, and
others can extend customer care capabilities to track customer trends
and test new product concepts. While the venture won't really exercise
this continuous improvement system until the Beta Stage, it must be
readied now as the platform is built. The system will prove indispensable for venture leaders making decisions about glitch fixes, inadequacies
in system performance, feature pruning, next product services—the
host of trade-offs and "calls" that the team must make daily, some of
which have significant long-term implications.

Time/Scope/Budget. Throughout the Alpha Stage, the venture needs to develop another system of measurement, one that is able to map whether the amount of money being spent matches the initially predicted "burn rate." Slips are not unusual at this stage, given that this is the first time the platform and product/service have been assembled, but the team must discuss and resolve financial ramifications and strategic implications (short-term versus long-term). The team must make another measurement with the Schedule Fantasy Factor (actual time divided by predicted time, first mentioned in chapter 5) in the Alpha Stage and make adjustments accordingly. A readjusted time, scope, and budget map should be part of that process. It should allow the venture team to focus on what they still need to accomplish, and at what expense and over what period of time, to create an appropriate beta test version of the product or service.

As you can see, much of the thinking and development of the platform components during the Alpha Stage require measuring and creating data-gathering tools so that, prior to beta test and launch, the venture will be equipped to determine how well it is doing and whether it will meet its projected targets. But at this stage the venture also has the task of identifying and courting partners—for example, technology vendors or potential financial investors, as well as specific channel partners. Some of these partners will play no role during the development of the alpha. But strategic partnership efforts need to begin now if partners and alliances critical to beta and launch are to be in place. Typically enough momentum builds during the development of the alpha to support the venture's partnering efforts. We use a simple template, the Strategic Partner Profile, to systematize development of this information. (See Appendix G at the back of the book.)

The Market

During the Alpha Stage, the venture does not deal with large numbers of customers directly. But its leaders ought to be thinking and strategizing about customers constantly. During this period, the marketing team needs a complete strategy to define the customers and determine how to reach them. Here are some questions the venture team must ask about marketing during the Alpha Stage:

- Have we created customer/application profiles of those most likely to benefit from the product or service?

- Have we created product/service positioning, value proposition and descriptions of the competitive environment?

- Have we completed the initial prioritization of target customers/segments? Have representatives signed up for the beta test?

- Have we created a preliminary sales plan?

Customer/Applications Profiles. During the Alpha Stage, the venture has to continue to interview and refine its views of its future customers, a process started in Stage 1. Who are they? Where are they? Is there really pent-up demand for a new service or product? How are potential customers getting by without it now? How would the venture be able to persuade such customers to embrace a new product or service? What customers have what kind of resistance to the venture's message and products? Who does the venture target first, second, and third in order to make the forecasts of sales?

These are not idle queries. They are core questions that face every venture. Any new service or product, regardless of how appealing, will face barriers from customers who are instinctually cautious about trying something new. Most big corporations launch new products after lengthy focus group and pilot testing. A venture does not have that luxury. But it can pursue, at relatively little cost, something that few large corporations do: a careful examination of the needs and habits of potential customers.

We recommend that venture teams use what we call a customer/application profile (which we first referenced in chapter 5 and included as Appendix E). Along with segment-of-one interviewing, it is a fundamental marketing tool for assembling and standardizing basic information gleaned about target customers and applications.

Filling out the profile requires more than simply identifying who is the most likely to buy your product or service. If you are creating a corporate travel service, you must determine how corporate travel decisions are made. Who inside a company makes those contracting decisions? Do they typically have long-standing contracts? What material do they read, or who do they listen to that might influence their decision? Are there professional societies for corporate travel planners, and are they an effective channel for new product introduction?

The next set of questions is linked to the way a customer might use the product or service. The answers create a "topography" of the user's application. The venture marketing team must understand in what kind of specific site or settings the product or service would be used. How many people might use it? And what kind of technology or software would customers need to make your product or service useful to them?

One of the great impediments that new ventures face is that many would-be customers are loath to change their current arrangement, even if offered a superior service or product. That is why the venture must, at this stage, understand what it will take to close a sale. To answer that question, venture leaders ought to examine the current solution providers and understand their business models intimately. These are the companies with whom the venture will be competing before long, and they are unlikely to stand still while a newcomer tries to displace them. What the venture is trying to learn is how, specifically, adoption of the venture's products will meet the customer's stated needs and prove measurably better than the competitors' products. Then the venture must explain whether the quality of the product or service is compelling enough to motivate the customer to action or change.

Learning this level of detail about potential customers is not easy. Part of it comes from a deep understanding of the industry. Venture leaders need to be immersed in it, even if they believe that their product or service is sufficiently distinct from the existing players. The goal is to understand the mind-set of the most likely customers and the spheres of influence that shape their perspective. Careful study of the industry as a whole is an obvious requirement. But in many cases, this kind of profile involves first-hand observation of and discussion with potential customers.

If, for example, the goal were to market to suppliers of auto manufacturers, it would be very rewarding to spend time at the site of one of those customers. There you could see how decisions are made day to day, at what level decisions are made, and what tools are used now to deal with the problem the venture claims to solve. If the goal were to create an online supply-chain network for auto suppliers, it would certainly be critical to see how some auto suppliers currently use the Internet. One of the many problems faced by Covinsint, the Web-based B2B network established by the three Detroit auto-making companies, is that many auto suppliers were still communicating by fax.

How can a relatively unknown venture gain access to the inside world of a company that is not yet a customer? This is where corporate ventures have enormous advantages over a freestanding start-up. During the Alpha Stage the venture can leverage the existing customer base of the parent company, as well as identify internal SBUs and other companies that can be readily approached as possible venues for customer/application profile research. Some companies might be willing to do it as a form of free consulting. Others could be drawn into the planning by offering access in exchange for equity or the promise of free service for a finite period. If the right people are sent inside a company, they should be able to determine how the venture's product or service could be used there, and by analogy, break into the market, or how it must be changed to compete.

This approach of "watching the customer" borrows from the techniques of the most sophisticated mass marketers. Procter & Gamble has been known to place video cameras in customer homes to see how customers use an everyday product. Other firms collect such tapes and resell them to market researchers. They understand that the ability to see how the customer actually behaves is far more useful than reams of survey data.

As the venture team is stepping up this and other marketing research in this stage, it is using the results immediately to refine the venture's positioning and customer segmentation and prioritization.

Positioning. The venture leaders now must look again at their description of their positioning—their statement of how the venture is unique and what benefits it will deliver—which they initially conceived in Stage 1. They need to test it against reality and update it on an ongoing basis throughout the Alpha Stage. Positioning is critical because it is customer-oriented and benefit-driven, and because it presents an opportunity for establishing a leadership position in a new space. This process is time-consuming and difficult. And most team members come to it with a "knee-jerk" desire not to "limit" the venture's reach by defining it too narrowly. That can be a danger. What a venture needs is a clear definition of its position—what business it is in, where its inspiration lies, what solutions it will provide and for what type of customers with what kinds of needs. The venture that claims to be all things to all people and cannot define the real-world problems it solves will never be attractive in a competitive market. Conversely, the rewards for good positioning of a venture are huge: Positioning unifies and focuses the venture team around a single set of statements and shared strategy, which every aspect of the venture then reflects. The level of complexity and iterative refinement in developing solid positioning is apparent in figure 6-1.

Customer Segmentation and Prioritization. Other than positioning, this is the primary area for marketing development in the Alpha Stage. New ventures with innovative products and services try to build markets and constituencies from the bottom up, through evangelism and persuasion, testimonials and reference selling. Decisions about where to start—which customers to target, in which order, and why—begin to coalesce in the venture's customer first segmentation plan, which we call the Market Segment Development Schedule. The Market Segment Development Schedule evolves in the following fashion:

- First, the team completes profiles of like customers and tests receptivity to the product or service value proposition.

- Second, the team builds a logical view of the size of the segment of potential customers, using those profiled to hypothetically represent the segment as a whole and filters quantitative segment data and analysis accordingly. Also factored in are any additional product/ service development requirements deemed necessary to deliver on the product or service value proposition for this segment of customers.

- Third, the team develops an overview and a strategy of how of to reach that desired segment and close sales, which involves understanding the resources realistically required to be successful, in time, money, people, and capabilities.

- Finally, by completing these overviews for each segment being targeted, the team has the fodder and framework for determining their optimal rank ordering. This rank ordering is reflected in the venture's overall schedule for market segment development.

FIGURE 6 - 1

Positioning Strategy Process Model

An iterative process, involves successive approximations

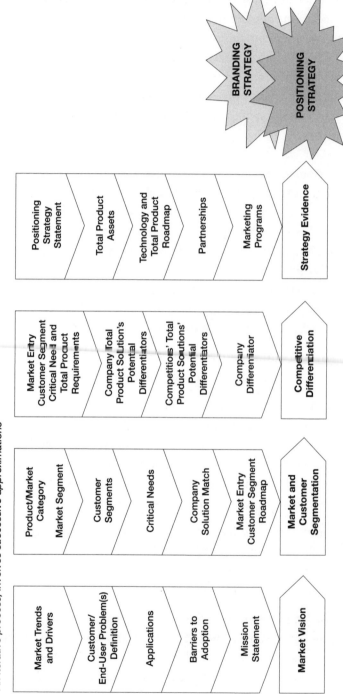

Source: © Rosemary Remacle, Venture Partner, Sevin Rosen Funds.

Understanding the differences among customers is important because ventures commonly make the mistake of assuming that their first customers are illustrative of the whole market. That is rarely the case. It is more important to take some aspects of the behavior of one segment of customers and see if a marketing plan can apply them to other segments. Of course, the marketing team must be aware that there will be significant differences. Ventures that learn how to close sales with particular segments of customers quickly learn how to ramp up growth. Equally important is the process of customer/segment prioritization—knowing which customers to pursue first. Figure 6-2 illustrates the process.

Sales Plan. During the Alpha Stage, the venture has no finished product or service, no customers, and no customer revenue. But a sales plan is well underway.

As we have discussed, the marketing team's task is to figure out which segments of customers offer the greatest potential for success and in what order they should be pursued. The job of the sales team is to close on these targets, building unit sales to volume. The job of the marketing team is to fashion messages and evidence that generally reduce

FIGURE 6 - 2

Market Segment Leadership Road Map

How many customer segments can the company support?
For how many customer segments can the company supply (total product) strategy evidence?

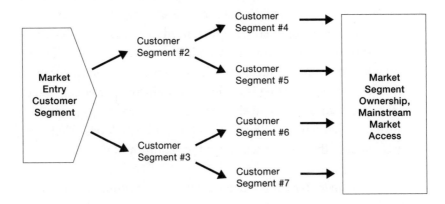

Source: © Rosemary Remacle, Venture Partner, Sevin Rosen Funds.

the barriers to sale and educate and precondition customers, making it easier to convert them into sales. The process for planning this crucial element of the venture business begins in earnest now.

The head of sales should be on board; ideally it is someone with extensive experience working in a start-up, building sales from the ground up. The sales leader needs to be intimately involved in every aspect of early marketing planning. It is particularly important that the sales team fully understand the alpha and be kept abreast of every change in design and focus. And it is very useful for the head of sales to be a member of the venture team when the first round of possible beta test customers are selected. At this point, the sales personnel should be able to contribute to understanding which market segment the venture is trying to penetrate.

Many ventures will discover that, at first, their pool of potential customers is rather large. It is the task of the sales leaders, with help from the marketing team, to design a system, to identify attributes of likely early adopters in each customer category and segment. The team must also determine how barriers to sale will be overcome, and develop a model of what the lead time to individual sale is likely to be per category and segment. This activity amounts to a type of forecast—one that will be continually revised—about who will be the best early adopters of the venture's first product or service. Targeting that first group, as we have discussed, begins in earnest during the Alpha Stage.

The sales team should base its strategy on a deep understanding of the venture's competitive position. A preliminary sales plan should consider all the various channels, geographies, organization, sales cycles, and "model" costs that the sales team has verified against similar products or services in the market. They then need to match that sales strategy against the marketing strategy to see if the two actually complement one another. In many ventures, the lack of consistency and integration between sales and marketing is a common problem. The goal is to get the sales leader to understand the venture at its earliest stages and be sensitive to "what works" at both the alpha and beta levels. That way, every element of the team understands the venture as it develops.

Beta Customer Targeting. The corollary of customer/application profiles and a sales strategy is the ability to select customers who will eventually be beta testers. Beta testers are not simply potential customers. They are early-stage customers who will provide feedback on the product or service. Selection of beta testers should not be random. Prime candidates include people sampled in the segment-of-one interviewing process, prospective customers, and infrastructure players identified in the customer/application profiles and in the Market Segment Development Schedule. Determining your target market is difficult and critical. It requires considering every aspect of the business, including delivery, customer care, and technology. The sales team must select target customers on the basis of whether the venture can reach them, not just because the team thinks they would benefit from your service or product. In many cases, selling and signing up early customers who want to test the product will require different sales strategies and marketing approaches. Corporate parents' partners and VBOs can be invaluable in this process.

The Team

During the Vision Stage, the team probably comprised a few founding visionaries, talent on loan from the corporation, and some temporary consultants. Building an alpha requires a larger team with a longer-term commitment. The goal is for most of the senior people to be on board by the end of this stage. Thus building the team and making sure it is well balanced is a central activity of the venture now. The venture should ask the following questions about its personnel at this point:

- Is the CEO a leader and team builder across departments? Can he or she lead and manage the team?

- Is the venture team evolving so that it is integrated, with a clear strategy and purpose in recruiting?

- Is the team orientation a balance of "manage" and "do"?

- Is the board formed, active, and diverse?

It goes without saying that the venture's CEO needs to be a dynamic leader: part manager, part salesman, part networker, part crisis coordinator, part fundraiser, part decision maker. What is distinct about a CEO inside a corporate venture is that he or she can have a close and trusted

relationship with the parent company while still conveying a fully independent spirit and entrepreneurial culture inside the venture. Much has
been written about the skills a corporate CEO needs. Inside a fast-paced
corporate venture the CEO is culture leader, recruiter, spokesman, and the
insistent voice that every aspect of the venture be measured and assessed.

Despite all these roles, the CEO must also be a delegator if he or she
is to be an effective leader. No corporate venture can be micromanaged.
Instead, the responsible CEO will spend much time making sure that
both insiders and outsiders are brought into the venture as advisors,
partners, staff, and consultants. By insiders, we mean members of the
corporate parent who invariably want to be associated with a new venture. The CEO must court them assiduously but still constantly ensure
the venture's independence. At the same time, the CEO will be looking
for people far outside the company, people who can breathe dynamism
and new talents into the venture.

The Venture Team. At the Alpha Stage, the venture team should be
rapidly taking shape. The CEO will be in constant recruitment mode
and, with others, be designing a systematic method for recruitment. This
method will become indisponsable after the beta test, when there will be
an extraordinary rush of hiring. The purpose now is to think about how
to hire quickly, what incentives to offer, and what the compensation system will be. Often these decisions require delicate negotiations with the
parent company, which looks askance at hiring people on an entirely
different pay scale.

In addition to the development and marketing staff already on board,
the most important new people to hire are a chief financial officer and a
chief business development officer, because financial planning and partnering strategies are coming to the fore. But other critical positions must
be filled at this stage as well, as the venture moves from planning to
intensive implementation. Marketing is expanding to include the product manager; the sales team is moving from high-level business development to operations. The development team in particular must fill out
the technology and product teams with appropriate implementation
specialists and technologists, either by direct hires or by adding consultants or outsourcing altogether. In Web-based businesses, for example, or
with custom integration efforts of existing packages, this filling out of

the team is especially obvious. The venture team needs to be tightly integrated, constantly updating one another, and sharing feedback. Part of the CEO's responsibility is to make sure that the venture team works creatively together, united by a single purpose and vision.

Team Leaders. The members of the venture team will also be distinct from what is normally found in large corporations in that they must be both managers and practitioners. At most large corporations, the head of sales is a superior manager who is many years removed from actual sales work. The same is true of most division heads. But in a venture, everyone from the CEO on down must be able to take on any part of the business. The CEO should be able to do spreadsheets as well as the financial staff can. The head of marketing should be as comfortable in a high-level development meeting as on a sales call. Everyone should be able to give the elevator pitch, Power Presentation, and run the demo. While this balance of skills clearly builds venture morale, that is not the primary reason that team leaders must be jacks of all trades. In far too many corporate ventures, the top leaders have been selected primarily because they have thrived at management in previous posts.

The venture team can take a few other steps to foster cohesion. One is to make sure that the existing team leaders interview every senior hire. New recruits will have to work with every member of the team, so it is important to take a team approach to recruiting. Similarly, there should be regular teamwide discussion about the implications and fit of the new hire within the venture, and how the venture is evolving, from every department. This cooperation will prove even more important as volatility increases during the Alpha Stage. What may be a small change from a marketing perspective could have huge ramifications for the technology side. Or imagine that, for sound technical reasons, delivery times change from three days to four. This kind of adjustment could change the appeal of the service or product for the potential customers the sales force is now wooing.

The Board and Advisors. During Stage 1, the corporate venture is so embryonic it is typically too early in the game to attract the caliber of board members it will need to guide and govern it. But at the Alpha Stage, when the real planning of a company that can be fully described is taking place, a board of Directors must be assembled. (This entity should *not* be confused with the venture business office's board of advisors. While some members of one board may be on the other, the functions and purpose of the two boards differ. A VBO board guides the Venture Business Office's operation and portfolio development, whereas a single venture within VBO portfolio has its own board of directors and advisors at work on a more micro level, dedicated to its development.) The corporate venture board of Directors should be small—five people should be enough, one or two of them from the parent company. At least two others should be outsiders, who can provide sound advice that may at times be at odds with the prevailing view at the parent company. At least one member of the board should have direct, start-up experience. If the venture is involved in e-commerce, then at least one director should have that kind of background.

What does a board of directors do for a still fledgling company? Providing seasoned advice and counsel, assisting in recruiting, helping with strategic partnering, and making high-level introductions are all reasonable and important contributions. During the Alpha Stage, the board will also be instrumental in making the case for, and helping to raise, additional financing (both inside and outside the corporation, depending on the particular venture's strategy).

The Board, of course, should be able to operate in a fashion that is sensitive to, but independent of, the parent's positions. Ideally, it should be a separate legal entity. Many companies balk at that and simply create a board of advisors instead. That can be a fair substitute. But sometimes the venture's immediate interests will diverge from—or even be in conflict with—the parent's, and on those occasions it is exceptionally prudent to have established operational "arm's length." First and foremost, the venture needs to be able to define and pursue the best course to ensure that it will not only survive but thrive, with the parent company's understanding and agreement that the venture's independent success will return value to the parent. For example, when a venture wants to create a value network that might include corporate competitors of the parent, the venture and its board should be able to endorse that step without fear of reprisal from "upstairs." Or if the venture seeks to enter a market segment the parent company has rejected for its own business, the parent, similarly, should not be able to co-opt the decision process.

Still, it is natural and understandable that parent corporations tend to limit board membership to "corporate insiders" such as executive officers and directors. It would be a surprise if the parent, without prodding, were to include outsiders—with concerns of confidentiality breaches and Wall Street whispers, excluding outsiders only makes sense. But a new venture must avoid this kind of caution if it is to get the type of advice and counsel it needs to succeed. Alignment of the corporation's and the venture's strategic goals and agendas, specifically addressed at the time of the venture's formation, should continue to be monitored on an ongoing basis as the venture develops.

If all of a venture's board members are insiders, the board tends to function less as a true board of directors and more as a less financially powerful version of the parent's board of directors, complete with the corporate culture, hierarchy, and priorities. Such an internally focused board will almost certainly place the parent's needs, not the venture's needs, first, and no corporate venture can afford that kind of a handicap.

The issue of whether board members are "insiders" or "outsiders" typically appears as decision-intensive matters arise during the Alpha and Beta stages. For instance, the board must choose whether to seek outside venture capital, whether to acquire or associate with partners, and what kinds of compensation and control these new entities will hold within (and over) the venture's evolution. A heterogeneous board—a mix of insiders and outsiders—will be more likely to offer a balanced approach to these types of critical decisions.

We urge the parent corporation and venture leadership to consider the following guidelines when building the board:

- Keep membership to no more than six people. With more members, the atmosphere begins to be less collegial and more like a committee—with all the attendant discord and politics that go with committees.

- Balance senior managers from the corporation with outsiders, whose experience with venturing and the product or service itself clearly fills the needs of the project.

- Choose "outsiders" committed to championing the needs of the venture before other needs; that is, avoid naming members who are merely "buddies" of the parent leaders but who have no compelling interest in seeing the venture succeed.

- Consider bringing on "outsiders" with well-known expertise, in order to build credibility for the parent and the venture alike.

- Consider the members' motives and career arcs, because board memberships carry nontrivial legal and fiduciary responsibility.

- Do not underestimate the role of equity compensation in motivating the directors. Having "skin in the game" motivates members to pay close attention to the venture, and to more carefully consider the quality of the advice and counsel that they offer.

- Lastly, don't think of the board of directors as a static entity. It is important to keep in mind, even as the venture leaders are recruiting and closing these first directors, that the needs of the venture will change as it evolves. Board membership should be equally dynamic; the composition of the board should change along the way to better serve the venture's evolving needs.

It is worth briefly considering the role of the more informal board of advisors. Advisory boards are particularly important in bringing an early infusion of outside expertise, venture experience, and access to outside networks. They also bring "reflected glory" and credibility to the venture. And they can be as large or small as desired, typically with one-year commitments as a start. As we have discussed in reference to the formation of the VBO board of advisors, they are easier to form than boards of directors, because members incur no legal, fiduciary, or operational responsibility. And individual advisors provide senior expertise and experience to augment or complement the core venture team's capabilities and experience. Ideally, the venture team leaders can contact an advisor frequently and informally for counsel and other forms of assistance. Compensation for these individuals is not burdensome—usually it's a small amount of equity or honoraria.

The Financing

During a venture's Alpha Stage, the level of investment required is still relatively small and not the primary concern. But it soon will be.

That is why much of the financing questions during this stage involve thinking about how the venture can be perfectly positioned to raise funds at a rapid rate once the beta test is launched during the next stage of development. Questions to be asked about financing during the Alpha Stage should include the following:

- Do we have cash on hand for the next six months?

- Do we know our cash needs for the next twelve months? Are we developing sources for that cash?

- Is our team performing and meeting milestones in a way that builds confidence for future financing?

Some financial issues cannot be ignored. During the Alpha Stage, the venture needs at least several months of cash on hand. The amounts needed remain relatively limited. In many cases, the venture will require less than $500,000 a month, or enough to build the alpha and maintain a payroll of most of the team leaders and their small but growing staff. At the Alpha Stage, these funds may still be coming exclusively from the parent company. Outside venture teams can testify as to how distracting fundraising at this stage can be, when the venture team needs to devote so much attention to the basic design and operational details of the venture. It is invariably easier to raise money, on the outside or inside, when more of the first product or service has been developed and can be tangibly demonstrated, in support of the venture's business model.

Nonetheless, the team does need to think about what future cash needs will be. Some of this information will emerge as the team puts together its time, scope, and budget plan. Understanding how much money the venture will need and when the demand for resources will be greatest is a necessary planning tool. It is the only way a venture can avoid the eleventh-hour scrambles for an infusion of cash. It is also a way of projecting cash requirements for the parent corporation in such a way that it would not be blindsided by a sudden demand for more capital.

It is sound policy during the Alpha Stage to create a strategy for where to raise future funds. This strategy should be a chief focus of the board and the CEO, who should be consciously making alliances with possible fundraisers or partners who would be interested in an equity stake.

The most urgent money issue during this stage, though, is tracking whether the venture is staying within the expected budget, performing according to objectives, and meeting expectations. It probably is not. Everything that happens during the Alpha Stage almost dictates that some amount of change occurs. Some vendors may turn out to be more costly than projected. Search time for partners and team leaders may have increased. An initial test of some Web-based features of an e-commerce offering may have required a second, third, or fourth iteration. Obviously, every correction eats up more cash, and each of these steps needs to force adjustments in the overall financial plan.

The deeper question, however, is whether the venture is taking all the steps in advance to make future fundraising possible. Even in a fast-paced universe of corporate venture building, the tactical steps needed to raise money require time to assemble. One company we worked for knew early on that the key to raising significant amounts of money after completion of its beta test was customer testimonials. The market was relatively narrow in scope, and the venture leaders knew that if a few key players were to advocate their new online purchasing service, investors would be more eager to put more money behind the venture.

Unfortunately, customer testimonials cannot be created suddenly. They require, to begin with, customers who are using a product or service, not just customers who have familiarity with the venture and support the idea. After all, investors will call anyone who gives a testimonial to find out the true depth of support. In short, thinking about fundraising at the Alpha Stage requires thinking through all the steps that will make fundraising possible. Done correctly, many activities that seem far removed from fundraising—sales, identifying vendors, selecting beta customers, and so on—become consciously linked to the goal of raising more money down the road.

The VBO's Role in the Alpha Stage

The VBO's role becomes more active and pronounced at this stage with virtually all its constituencies: the venture, the corporation, and the outside venture community. This is the turning point in development, marking the first real implementation of product and venture build-out—something you can "see and touch" and assess as an independent entity. This is also the turning point on stepping up the investment and

SUMMARY OF "MUST-HAVES" AND "RED FLAGS"

ALPHA STAGE "MUST-HAVES": ESSENTIAL ELEMENTS TO HAVE IN PLACE

- Detailed platform, product/service specifications and development schedule: continuously refined
- Early customer/market research and validation
- Reduction and prioritization of targets/segments
- Refined positioning and launch strategy
- Core team in place
- Partners identified or, if playing key development role for launch, in place
- First full business plan (twenty-five pages excluding financial data and appendixes)
- Demonstration that displays basic operability of product or service
- Venture executive officer in place, ensuring linkages to parent
- Parent-venture governance structure agreed (including decisions regarding how a future venture will be spun out, and the level of sweat equity for venture employees)
- Funding (inside, outside, or both) according to parent ownership decision
- Alpha for marketing and development: first testing, with partners and small number of customers, of product/service efficacy (does it work?), of vision as first executed (great idea and great execution)
- Continuous development architecture for partners, processes, etc., in place across all departments
- Platform partners (vital to extranet alpha test) on and operating as projected; others being closed for beta
- Platform/first product or service: refined and updated based on alpha results and now beta- and pilot-ready
- Beta plan refined and formalized by all departments. Refinement based on alpha results from the development, marketing, business development, support, and delivery/operations teams. Beta plan should include selection of beta testers, agreement on a process for frequency of contact and support, tracking and information gathering, information distribution and teamwide analysis.

ALPHA STAGE "RED FLAGS": FACTORS THAT DEMAND IMMEDIATE ACTION

- Parental "business as usual" governance structure
- No VEO
- No action regarding venture status (e.g., wholly owned by the parent corporation and retained on the inside, inclusion of outside investors and significant degree of operational independence)
- Team incomplete, or made up of internal people who are part-time and geographically dispersed
- No outsiders (on team, as partners, as advisors, on board)
- No spec or architecture, just a "general direction"
- Venture business plan no different from a divisional project plan
- Marketing research quantitatively driven and tactical only
- No formalized, rigorous alpha test plan and execution
- No incremental validation of marketing plans and customer behavior
- First segment and infrastructure customers not participating in alpha
- Infrequent sampling of alpha testers; ad hoc and incomplete collection of information from testers
- Response from alpha testers: great idea, lousy execution—site doesn't deliver promise of high-level concept
- Partners not on board; parent vetoes venture's choices
- Development people only on team: very incomplete
- No VEO, no corporate cooperation on launch, marketing and sales, channels
- No governance structure for determining performance and setting expectations
- Inadequate funding; inadequate "carrots" to attract talent

---

the path-forward risk. With the oversight and assistance of the VBO, the venture's ability to navigate through the hurdles of the Alpha Stage and perform against these major venture milestones largely determines its success or failure in later stages. The VBO's role and responsibilities at the Alpha Stage include the following:

- *Venture management.* The VBO should be active in the oversight and management of the venture and its progress. A VBO executive may serve as an observer or director on the board or even as venture advisor. The VBO may also be called on to help identify and recruit additional advisors and directors—which in turn tests the quality of the VBO's venture-development practices and management capability.

- *Beta targeting.* The VBO is responsible for sifting, selecting, and "seeding" appropriate SBU contacts as next-stage beta test sites and for follow-on pilots. The VBO is typically highly active in arranging initial introductions and aiding in identifying the value that stems from independent venture-SBU business relationships. A VBO executive should also attend all venture-SBU meetings. This corporate relationship is also important as a demonstration of the VBO's position and value to all its present and prospective portfolio companies. It also serves as a signal to the venture capital community and others outside the company that the VBO is a critical player.

- *Corporate antibody protection.* The VBO must act as a funnel between the venture and other corporate resources. At the same time, it must protect the venture from unreasonable corporate interference and delays.

- *Funding.* The VBO should establish an investment step-up analysis and decision-making process. New responsibilities emerge depending on the outcome of each investment decision. For example, if the VBO decides to let a venture "go forward," the VBO goes into high gear on fundraising on the venture's behalf both inside and outside the corporation. If the decision is to "hold," the VBO helps reset performance goals/milestones and closely supervises the venture as it works to meet them. If the VBO decides to "kill" a project, the VBO looks for ways to harvest venture accomplishments to date for corporate use. The timing and types of these kinds of investment decisions test the quality of the VBO's operation and its fundraising savvy, both within the parent organization and within the venture community at large.

- *Other relationship development.* The VBO must leverage its corporate clout to line up venture access/introductions to other potential customers, other industry players, vendors, and so forth.

Corporate Assets Available to the VBO

Platform. The corporation will likely have core capabilities and assets that will be an advantage to the venture as it creates its platform during the Alpha Stage. This can result in arrangements like joint development (e.g., linkages into specific development groups for aid with platform and product integration), access or reduced fees or clout with outside vendors, password access to key customer information databases, and manufacturing or other delivery asset advantages.

Also, because the corporate parent will often have SBUs that are potential early users and reference sites, the venture can use these relationships to profile the sales process to similar organizations outside the company. Ideally, the corporate parent's SBUs can also become early, marquee customers, hastening the venture's market development ramp.

Market. Here again either some or all of the corporation's marketing assets help the corporate venture. The company's existing research base, for example, can be an invaluable resource for learning about the history of customer behavior, market segmentation, specific customers, and other industry players. The corporate brand can also act as a "halo" for a start-up venture. In some areas—financial services or consumer goods, for example—the storehouse of information on marketing and sales is enormous. The venture can use this information to make a more sensible and detailed business plan for the Alpha Stage.

A corporate parent can also provide the key introductions to potential customers or companies willing to serve as targets for customer/application profiles. Ideally, the corporation helps bring in key partners to the venture who will stay with it through the launch of the business. And in general, the corporation can act as a cheerleader, fundraiser, and promoter of the venture, building excitement even during the Alpha Stage.

Team. Corporate parents can be very helpful in building and supporting a venture team during the alpha process. They bring a high degree of domain and industry expertise in their area, and the venture would be foolish not to seek it out and leverage it for its own purposes. Many top people in the parent company will join the work of the venture either on a full-time or a part-time basis. If a venture can incorporate top talent from the parent company to provide vertical area expertise, and use that connection to maintain a strong information flow between the venture and the parent, it has a likely formula for a successful relationship.

Financing. Once again, the advantage that a corporate venture has over a freestanding start-up company is that it can rely on its corporate parent for both hard and soft dollars. During the Alpha Stage, this will include not just the supply of cash, but more office space, equipment, accounting, and consulting services, which might otherwise have come out of the venture's bottom line.

Common Mistakes: VBO Beware

Business Plan. The venture "disconnect" that comes with corporate planning techniques is the tendency to think in strict time blocks or over-long five-year plans. The venture plan does not operate on a traditional calendar. Since corporations operate within established guidelines and with fixed priorities, time-based planning makes sense for them. But because corporate ventures are dynamic, they are always in the process of creating and refining their plans. Therefore, corporations examining their ventures must be provided with an appropriate context and set of metrics—standard venture-development milestones—for evaluating progress. Otherwise, the likelihood is great that the corporation won't receive the venture plan well or won't understand it well, which will result in "analysis paralysis," lack of interest, or general delays on decision making of all kinds associated with the venture.

Platform. One error corporations make during the Alpha Stage of the venture is to see the platform as a point product only—as merely a single, one-off project, rather than an ongoing business that could produce many services or products that have applications in many different business. By thinking in terms of a project, the corporation is apt to view missed deadlines, or changes in the alpha, as signs of failure rather than appropriate adjustments. Another common problem is the imposition of the corporation's legacy architectures and mandated standards on the venture's platform specification. While the desire to build on existing architectures is logical from the corporation's point of view, it often is an unnecessary if not toxic burden to the new venture. Further, it may render the venture's resulting platform noncompetitive. At the very least, it complicates and often derails the venture's development process, undermining the coherence of its architecture and the quality of its output, as well as its ability to control costs and manage schedules.

The Team. The downside of the corporate relationship when it comes to building a senior team is the parent's reluctance to see the venture as an independent new entity that needs to play by different rules to succeed. As a result, some of the parent's recruiting, hiring, and compensation bureaucracy spills into the venture. This is particularly true when it comes to defining compensation and incentive levels that may be very different from the standards that the corporate human resources department uses. Another related shortfall is the tendency to load up on corporate managers in senior leadership roles in the venture, weighting the venture in the direction of corporate culture and control. Even if outside specialists are hired to fill out the team or brought on as consultants, they still report to managers who very often have no base understanding of the tasks and the relationships they're responsible for managing—which is always a recipe for trouble. Resistance to outsiders being brought in at the "inner-sanctum level" may cause the corporation to shy away from recruiting outside directors, or even forming a board of advisors that includes highly qualified outsiders to help the corporate venture through its development challenges.

Financing. Again, without appropriate context, corporations often over- or underfund ventures. Overfunding the venture may encourage premature spending and commitment to a path before its time. Overfunding also removes one of the motivators of team progress in outside ventures: investment that's triggered by performance rather than budget allocations. The flip side is that too little money for recruiting, testing, and marketing will force the venture to move "hand to mouth" and underfund these critical efforts. Loss of quality is predictable. Underfunding can also cause the team to postpone solving problems revealed at the

Alpha Stage. Often the team's best hope is to address these problems later when more serious money comes in. And yet fixing something downstream is almost certain to cost more and be more painful than fixing it up front. The corporate parent should be funding the venture at an appropriate level that allows for "misses" and readjustments, and investment decisions should be triggered according to preset governance guidelines, not as an ad hoc corporate budget review.

And finally, the issue of whether to solicit outside involvement and funds (especially with venture capital firms) seems always to raise conflicts with the parent corporation—and to bring out the antibodies *en masse*. These conflicts ultimately boil down to the corporate parent's desire to retain control. It can be seen in everything from the corporation's resistance to outside and conflicting points of view, or the misperception that outsiders bring no discernible value. In other circumstances, the corporation will persist with the desire to maintain majority interest and not face dilution, which can often retard, if not undermine, the venture's ramp to growth.

The Alpha Offering: Key Lessons

- *Refine the positioning, fill out the written plan, update the pitch.* The only way to ensure that the team sings in unison is to make sure they're using the same songbook. Agree on a common investor pitch for the venture that everyone on the team can recite; develop a more detailed business plan with a spelled-out launch strategy. Get a first version of the offering built. The tendency is to overanalyze before building. Often, design requirements can't be defined until a "working" product is available. Don't worry, it'll change often anyway.

- *Set standards, and measure against them.* The devil is in the details. The character of a venture depends on benchmarks and constant measurement. The venture must define minimum levels of product/service performance that it must meet in order to move forward.

- *Create and refine "customer profiles."* The venture needs to know who they are, how to reach them, and how they'll use the product—and must devise a rank-ordered segmentation strategy: which segments, in which order, and why. Large companies take years to launch a product; start-ups don't have that luxury.

- *Fill out the team.* A critical issue for the venture at this point is filling out the team, especially hiring the CFO and chief business development officer.

- *Because you're soon going to have to raise money, start planning how much and from whom.* Up until now, funding has come from the parent company. To avoid blindsiding the parent, it's important at this stage to identify future cash needs, and when they will arise.

CASE STUDY

alpha stage

This case illustrates an extremely common dilemma for corporate ventures, or any venture for that matter: how much evidence—or, on the other side of the coin, effort—is necessary before a company decides to scuttle a venture? Let's look at the joint corporate venture spawned by Fortune 500 companies Cataco and Dataco.

Context

This example illustrates a corporate venture that was disbanded early in Stage 2. On the surface, the venture failed because of its inability to deliver key business partners and sponsors within the time frame set by the parent corporation. The actual, root causes of the venture's inability to deliver tell a more complex story about inappropriate expectations and artificial deadlines, and confusion about ends and means. Was this the wrong decision made for some right reasons, or the right decision arrived at arbitrarily and incorrectly? Should there have been a different ending, and should the parent have netted greater value? Let's take a closer look.

Like every other industry, the Internet had turned the catalog business upside down. More frightening, the catalog business in particular had either one of the greatest opportunities or one of the greatest threats from new technologies. This was partly because the

Internet behaves much like an interactive catalog. Many things were quite familiar—database marketing, remote merchandising—and many things were wholly unfamiliar—interactivity, price, and product transparency.

Many industries had formed "purchasing alliances" to aggregate buying power against suppliers. Several had built exchanges to facilitate spot purchases. Few had organized the sales and marketing side driven by competitive and regulatory fears.

The catalog industry businesses within Cataco (a printer company) and Dataco (a consumer database company) had been mutually successful business partners for years. An annual strategic planning process yielded an initiative to extend offerings to this key industry. A midlevel executive responsible for the existing catalog business developed the initial concept and built support for a more detailed planning exercise.

The concept was radical: to create an online department store for catalogers, which would be promoted from each of their catalogs. The venture and catalogers would also collaborate by sharing purchasing data with each other to facilitate direct-marketing efforts—after all, knowing about all purchases is better than knowing about only your own. To this point, the department store concept, online or offline, was heresy to the catalog industry—they simply didn't allow their products to be displayed alongside a competitor's.

This idea had the potential to cannibalize the print business, the database business, and even the catalog businesses. But it also had the potential to grow into an Internet-based multichannel retail powerhouse leveraging the skills of each. It would have a network effect unlike anything anyone had ever seen. And the catalogers inherently knew the power of the network in their business. The bigger the customer database (names plus purchase recency, frequency, and value), the better. The key question always centered around what the cost of collaboration would be (i.e., margin loss, market share loss, initial investment).

The catalogers would keep their own proprietary sites and did not need to offer all their merchandise to the new venture. The idea was that any revenue or profit cannibalization would be more than offset by revenue created, or retained, by this new superbrand of direct retailing. They would create another Amazon, or maybe this was the Nile—except that the service would be created by the leaders in direct marketing, which the Internet represented.

The venture considered two different market-entry strategies: to start with the smaller catalogers and work up (the CatalogCity.com approach) or to start with the biggest catalogers and work down. They chose the latter because it appeared to be the quickest way to lock in the biggest networks.

The key issue for the catalogers was cannibalization of revenues (price comparison) and brand (direct merchandising). They often spoke out of both sides of their mouth on this issue. Our catalog is the mall, why let other merchants in? But then, most customers comparison-shop across catalogs anyway, so why make it easier? The biggest pushback came from retailers who sold exclusively branded merchandise, such as Lands' End. Multichannel retailers that already offered others brands, such as Nordstrom, offered less resistance.

Ultimately, the parent sponsors pulled the plug on the venture owing to the inability to sign up enough partners in the predetermined time frame. The looming question still looms—was this decision prescient or merely shortsighted?

Bell-Mason Graph and Analysis

Figure 6-3 shows what was going well and what wasn't. Let's look at what exactly was happening:

Platform

The platform for innovation looked strong. It was a solid business-to-business platform—with potential products such as direct marketing data, direct marketing services, and procurement. It was also a solid business-to-consumer platform—with products such as individually customized Web sites, paper catalogs, and even merchandise. There was virtually no limit to the types of goods or services that could be sold through the business. The strength lay in the unlimited possibilities the platform enabled. The weakness lay in the realities of building the first product at a reasonable cost.

FIGURE 6 - 3

Diagnostic of Joint Corporate Venture of Cataco and Dataco

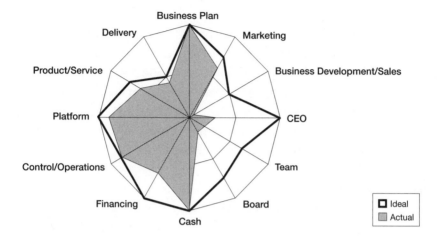

Product/Service

The offering looked strong. It leveraged the catalogers' assets (merchandise selection, quality, delivery, and price) as well as the investors' assets (database marketing, Web development for retailers, and customized printing services). The alpha had been tested with individuals and focus groups and subsequently enhanced from their feedback. The venture team retained a professional branding firm to create an "endorsement" brand that appealed to catalogers and consumers alike. They also hired a professional design firm to create a look and feel that was comfortable to novice and advanced Internet users alike.

Delivery

A clear strength. It leveraged the catalogers' core capabilities—fulfillment and customer service. Market research showed that potential customers were very positive about the venture's delivery plans because the current "pure-play" Internet retailers were having tremendous difficulty making timely deliveries. The alpha test revealed one weakness with the delivery system, which related to the necessary integration from the Web site back into cataloger legacy systems. While the issue was known, the detailed solutions were not known, and in fact, would likely need to be customized for each cataloger.

Business Plan

The business plan was high quality. A team deeply skilled in marketing, technology, and finance had developed the plan, and it had been "stress tested" by several independent catalog experts and potential investors. The drawback may have simply been length—which indicated a "throw-everything-at-the-problem" mentality, rather than focus on a couple of key issues.

Marketing

Without doubt, the plan's primary strength lay in its analysis and segmentation of consumer and cataloger needs. The market analysis included prominent secondary research around "direct" shoppers and catalogers. Primary research included a statistically valid and comprehensive survey on buying attitudes, preferences, and behaviors. In addition, the marketing team held a significant number of focus groups and did a great deal of one-on-one interviewing and observation. On top of all this, they conducted well over two dozen interviews with people working for catalog companies, to test the concept and understand adoption barriers.

Business Development/Sales

The distance between market research and sales proved to be substantial. Everyone loved the concept, but everyone also thought that the realities of implementation were nearly impossible to overcome. The first customers, as always, proved to be the most elusive. Nobody wanted to be first. And the bigger the target, the more difficult it was to get action—or for that matter to find someone who could take action; it always seemed to be a committee decision that required the CEO's approval.

CEO

In this case, the venture's leader was a manager with substantial energy, intelligence, and industry knowledge, but he had never run a start-up before. In fact, he was a midlevel career executive at one of the corporate investors. He couldn't get the resources of either parent to work for him when he needed it. And he often felt compelled to take charge himself and not ask for help when help was needed (another earmark of inexperience). The most obvious situation occurred when meeting with the CEOs of the catalogers who were needed as partners for the venture to fly. CEOs like to meet with peers, not midlevel executives pitching disruptive ideas. At this point, a certain level of trust was required, trust that would be available only through the personal relationships of the parent investors' executives. Yet the venture manager didn't ask for this help.

Team

The venture did not have any permanent employees—all were consultants. While the consultants' skill sets were critical to venture progress, the fact that no permanent employees were aboard signaled to everyone, both inside and outside, that the endeavor was still a project, and not a venture.

Board

Essentially, the venture had no board. The board, such as it was, consisted of one senior executive from each of the corporate investors, none of whom had time to devote to helping the venture. No advisory board had been established, and no outside advisors were used. Neither corporate partner/investor had a formal venture business office, although both had several different ventures underway in separate areas of their organizations. So the antibodies were abundant in all interactions with the corporate investors. The venture executive officers (corporate sponsors) at each company were members of top management. Accordingly, neither had much time to spend on helping the venture, other than to receive basic status reports every couple of weeks. One executive in particular spent less than an hour a month with the team.

Cash

The parent companies were basically funding the venture month to month based on its progress. So at one level, the venture leaders had deep pockets. At another level, they didn't have *any* pockets. But at the time of our review, they had spent a couple of million dollars and had authorized several million more.

Financing

A key milestone was getting top catalogers to sign letters of intent to join the network. The venture's potential for closing future financing rested on achieving that milestone. The viability of building the service or getting consumers to use it would be secondary. In fact, if the catalogers signed the letter of intent, they were agreeing to endorse and market the service to their customers.

Control/Operations

Primarily because all the employees were consultants, they were governed by very strict contractual requirements related to cost, deliverables, and time frames. The larger issue, of course, is that there was ultimately no permanent and qualified team to whom to transfer this operation.

Epilogue

The Bell-Mason analysis recommended immediate action in three areas. First, the venture executive officers at each parent needed to spend significantly more time; in particular, they needed to take accountability for signing up the first catalogers. Second, they needed to begin the search for a new and more seasoned venture leader—preferably one who already knew the major players in the catalog business. Third, they needed to begin to recruit a permanent team—which included establishing a board of advisors with venturing experts and other outsiders who could provide independent and objective counsel to the management team.

A year after the venture was scuttled, the closest comparable service, CatalogCity.com, continues to gain significant traction, as evidenced by the fact they have signed up many catalogers on the venture's original list. Although their financial status is not public, CatalogCity.com has successfully entered into agreements with some of the biggest names in the catalog business and attracted early funding from sources such as Bill Gates and Yahoo!.

7

stage 3

the beta offering:
testing the waters

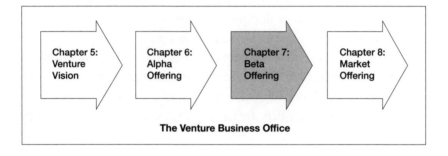

| Chapter 5: Venture Vision | Chapter 6: Alpha Offering | Chapter 7: Beta Offering | Chapter 8: Market Offering |

The Venture Business Office

I have not failed. I've just found
10,000 ways that won't work.

THOMAS EDISON

In this chapter, we examine the stage of development in which we see ventures rapidly mature and, quite suddenly, take on many of the aspects of more established businesses, such as the management of sales and customer service. If the first two stages have been devoted largely to fleshing out an idea and sketching out the business offering, the next two stages shift to developing the initial product and expanding its market.

The venture CEO comes into this stage with an updated plan for building the business, money, and key people to execute that plan, an alpha version of the actual product, and connections to those elusive, and critical, first customers. The next key milestones are transitioning from an "alpha" offering to the "beta" offering. The alpha product is the first fully operational version of the first offering to the market. It operates in a very controlled environment, usually internally, with limited customer exposure. The beta version of the product or service is also tightly controlled, but it must now operate in the real-world environments of actual customers (beta testers). This Beta Offering Stage ends when all refinements to the platform and first product or service are made, and the venture is poised for public launch. Table 7-1 gives an overview of the Beta Offering Stage. This stage is particularly difficult, for three reasons that we will explore in more detail later in the chapter.

The Beta Stage can last as short a time as a month or extend to many months (or even years in industries such as biotech). During this time, the venture team is engaged in building and operating a product or service to meet the needs of a limited number of real world customers, partners, investors, and suppliers. By its very nature, it is far more complex

TABLE 7 - 1

Stage Three Challenges

Challenges	Circumstances and Context
Containing the offering development schedule	At this point it is critical to balance the desire of marketing to add more features and functions with the desire of product development and finance to get a working product done on time and on budget. This challenge is compounded by the phenomenon that customer feedback *does* get much better the closer the offering is to launch.
Getting testimonials from customers to use for marketing purposes	The dilemma at this point is to get a company to endorse publicly a product that isn't working completely right yet. This issue is compounded by the phenomenon that big customers have huge legal protection systems in place that deter endorsements of products or services offered by others, especially new companies.
Raising money for the next stage before this stage is complete	The money needed in the next stage to launch a product in market is substantial, relative to the prior stages. It is particularly difficult to raise these funds before market evidence of a successful beta test is clear. Unfortunately, funding in the prior round typically can't cover product development and the market launch costs, so this funding round and its issues can't be avoided.

and real an undertaking than articulating the initial business concept. It is also more than simply a product or service performance test. An optimally conceived Beta program tests virtually every aspect of the venture. Through this testing, venture teams are likely to discover weaknesses in their plan or mistakes in their assumptions and will need to revise and fine-tune to prepare for the full market launch. This is a natural and productive part of the venture development process. Some, however, may find themselves so far off the mark when Beta Stage results are in that the VBO and other investors decide to completely retool or even pull the plug before going to market. This "natural selection" process in venture development, guided by a clear system of stage metrics and reality checks, not only permits but also encourages such decisions.

The Beta Stage is also a period in which major, unpredictable changes may occur, which can throw initial schedules into disarray. Suppliers that were selected in the Alpha Stage don't meet expectations, prompting the venture to scramble for a new supplier. When the venture finds a supplier that meets its specifications, that supplier might offer a slightly different set of features for the product or service. This kind of change has a ripple effect through the sales, marketing, and delivery plans that have developed until this point. For instance, during the frenzy to build industry exchanges in the late 1990s, two transaction engine suppliers, Ariba and Commerce One, dominated the market. They exploited their dominance to extract high prices from potential customers who had few other choices. A second-tier supplier, RightWorks, offered much lower prices but also less functionality. One client who initially selected Commerce One and tailored parts of its product development to the vendor's specifications switched to RightWorks in the Beta Stage, which caused specifications to change yet again. This, in turn, caused development's schedules to slip and increased its costs.

The Gap between Corporations and Their Ventures

Changes need to be coordinated more closely than ever in this stage. And it is in this coordination where we see a marked difference between the behavior of a corporation and the behavior of the ventures it sponsors. The strict silo divisions of a traditional company are an anathema to a venture. Because throughout the Beta Stage, venture leaders are testing, getting feedback, and making changes to their plans, the right hand of the venture must always know what the left hand (and both feet!) is doing. More precisely, the marketing, sales, delivery, and customer service arms of the venture need to be constantly kept abreast of every change that developers are making—and vice versa. The classic example is that developers cut features and functions from the first offering to make schedules and budgets with plans to slip them into a later version, and in so doing they cut some of the key features and functions that customers desired and expected (and that the venture marketing team has promoted).

And vice versa. All too often, the sales or service teams make promises to customers that don't get fed back to development. Or when development does hear about them, the development team deems them to be lower priority—and the customers' interests and expectations are not adequately addressed. That is a mistake, for in the venture process, the sales and service teams must become a mechanism for product and service refinement. What better place to look for new offering ideas than in the customer service (i.e., complaints) department? An entire industry sector, customer relationship management, sprang up around the need to capture and analyze sales and service information to enhance product design—and virtually every other function in the venture. Inside a venture, this communication between front-line employees who touch the customer and the venture developers is an essential part of preparing to launch a new product or service.

For the corporate venture, the Beta Stage needs to be a tightly controlled process within the chaotic real-world setting of a customer. Say you're involved in the Beta Stage of a corporate venture. You're at the front end of being "out in the market" with your new product or service. You are soliciting feedback. You are baby-sitting your product at the customer site to ensure smooth and appropriate use, closely observing customer-product interaction. You have established an easy way in which customers, industry analysts, partners, and suppliers can react and comment on what you are selling. If they like what you have to offer, even if there are refinements and changes to come, positive customer feedback validates the venture's approach, and the marketing at this stage helps build the reputation of your soon-to-be-launched venture. Word of mouth, the grease of missionary marketing, is as important to build in the Beta Stage as it is in the next stage, Market Calibration and Expansion.

In this sense, the ambitious and, frankly, self-promoting character of the aggressive corporate venture will be very different from the low-key approach favored by most large and conservative corporate initiatives during the development stage. The corporate venture craves recognition, even as it is still involved in a work-in-progress. Many non-technology companies, burdened as they are by cautious management teams and nervous investors, are more risk-averse than their technology counterparts. Fearful of alerting their competition, they hesitate to show their hand before a new product or service emerges. They discourage any public exposure to marketing and testing—even when it is limited— until they are ready to release something that is "bulletproof" to the rest of the world. Yet this is standard operating procedure in the technology industry, and in particular in the software sector. And it is a fundamental means of getting early validation that the venture is on the right track. Having a full beta test actually reduces the risks associated with launching a new company with innovative new products/services. As the Bell-Mason VDF makes clear throughout this chapter, the corporate venture cannot survive on secrecy. Strength comes from the ability to solicit feedback, to absorb it, and to respond as necessary. During this stage, the preparation done earlier to ensure that the right beta customers were selected will prove critical. Now is the time in the venture's life cycle when the venture needs the full cooperation and input from those beta users. If one of the beta users also happens to be the venture's corporate parent, this stage can be harder or easier, depending on how engaged the corporation is. What is critical is that the users at the parent be as open about how they use a product or service as any other beta tester.

Many of the questions in the VDF that help undergird our tour through the Beta Stage of the corporate venture may seem either overly general or even repetitious. That is both intentional and deceiving. It is necessary at the Beta Stage to revisit the questions venture leaders have already asked at earlier stages: Do we have a continuous development plan? Are we meeting the milestones of our original plan? Are we incorporating the feedback from advisors, partners, and potential customers? At the Beta Stage, the venture will have more people involved, more feedback arriving every day, and, of course, more at stake. Without doubt, once the business is launched, correcting fundamental problems becomes harder and more expensive. That is why we insist on probing some areas several times.

But if these questions seem at all simplistic, it is because the venture leaders are not taking time to consider what a complete answer might be. Most venture team members will assume, for example, that their product or service is ready to scale by the Beta Stage. But what does scalability require? How quickly can it scale? Has every potential obstacle to scaling been addressed? It is this level of granularity that corporate venturers must be prepared to explore if the Beta Stage is to succeed.

Stage 3: The Beta Offering Stage

The objectives of this phase are easily stated—to test and refine the product/service and, by implication, the rest of the venture's programs, gain early market acceptance and customer testimonials from a beta product, and to use Beta Stage results to secure funding to do a full market launch—and not easily accomplished. The key skills that the venture will need to demonstrate are the following:

- Ability to test the business model thoroughly and quickly to identify refinements

- Ability to prioritize changes in product/service and programs in order to balance the perfect world against the real world

- Ability to synchronize the changes across sales, development, and finance divisions to maximize implementation efficiency and consistency

The Business Plan

While keeping the plan updated may feel like an exercise in corporate administration, it is quite the opposite. Often the business plan goes unattended during this stage because the team is extraordinarily busy building and marketing that first product and new information seems to change the basic plan almost daily. Yet few things are more dangerous to a new venture than an outdated plan. An up-to-date plan is the basis for executive alignment and communication and validation with the outside world. The venture team must ask certain questions about the business plan at this stage:

- Have we updated the business plan to reflect what we have learned from the beta test?
- Does the entire management team agree with the newest version of the plan, including the launch schedule?
- Have outsiders validated the assumptions in the updated plan?

The business plan, we recall, is a living document. The venture team must continually update it to reflect whatever they learn from both the alpha test and the beta test. One of our clients learned in the Beta Stage that customers really didn't want to pay a fee for every transaction, but instead preferred paying an up-front subscription because it capped the cost of high usage and was easier to audit. Implementing that change in fee structure involves a fundamental change in the business model. At this point, the venture managers must decide whether to ignore the input (probably not smart), or rethink the product design and partners that were part of the original plan (frustrating). But this decision cannot be made in isolation. Everyone on the senior team must participate in the analysis and decisions related to changing the business plan. If the input is accepted, the business plan should be updated to reflect new priorities.

Rewriting and updating a plan is the formal way to force agreement among venture team leaders. It is dangerous to assume that the management team of a venture shares a common understanding of the venture business plan and strategy. In the frenetic pace of building a corporate venture, it is easy for individual team members to lose sight of the initial purpose and lose track of the changes that have occurred along the way. That it is why it is so important to schedule regular—at least weekly—meetings of the senior team. These meetings should not be merely a series of status reports (indeed, if members simply report on the activities of their divisions, that should be taken as a sign of trouble.) Instead, these meetings should be an assessment of the data gathered by every component part of the venture with discussion among the members, where challenges are voiced and next steps to resolution agreed upon.

Such meetings not only build group cohesion, they also provide each part of the venture an opportunity to plan strategically. For example, if the marketing leader understands the schedule and milestones for raising cash, he or she is better positioned to link marketing investments to business realities.

The constant reality check for every new venture ought to be the judgment and feedback it receives from the outside world and the corporate parent. That is why it is so important during the Beta Offering Stage that the venture consciously seek out formal and informal validations of its business progress from the board, investors, advisors, industry experts, and so on.

The Platform

Because the platform is the basis for the venture to produce subsequent products and services out of the foundation created for the first offering, it is critical to assure that the platform is being well-built. Questions the venture team must ask themselves about the platform at this stage include the following:

- Is development governed by both schedule and problem identification?

- Is the first product or service meeting performance expectations?

- Are the fulfillment or delivery elements of the venture ready to scale after the Beta Offering Stage?

The Beta Stage is a controlled yet public test of the venture platform. Until this point, potential customers have had the chance to consider

BRITISH TELECOM'S BRIGHTSTAR:
PUTTING THE D INTO R&D

In 1998, Harry Berry, a British Telecom executive, was recruited to form a new type of corporate incubator. Named Brightstar, it was chartered to commercially develop promising new technologies from the R&D division of British Telecom, BTexact Technologies. Brightstar offers BT employees the opportunity to develop their unique technology ideas into commercial venture propositions, and create additional shareholder value for BT, as well. Brightstar nurtures these fledgling ventures through their early stages, working hand in hand with venture capitalists and other partners to bridge the gap between BT and the outside world.

Although it is too early in the game to measure return, three things seem to set Brightstar apart:

- FIRST, FOCUS. Brightstar has, as a key element of its platform, BTexact's rich pool of related technologies and services, including 14,000 patents, on which to set its new venturing sights. Brightstar has implemented a highly structured process for finding and developing ideas into businesses, using explicit criteria and screening at each stage. Berry describes his role as a farmer of ideas from within the organization, rather than a hunter of ideas outside the organization.

- SECOND, VENTURE INFRASTRUCTURE. Brightstar has built a network of experts and partners outside of BT to help guide and develop these fledgling businesses—support that includes bringing in outside capital at an early stage. And they have tightly integrated the use of these experts and partners into the developmental process. For instance, the second iteration of the business plan goes before a ten-member Advisory Board comprised of various subject matter experts—five from BT and five from outside sources. The next iteration of the business plan goes before a five-member investment committee made up of the most senior management from Brightstar. The Brightstar-sponsored business proposal must pass this hurdle to gain additional funding needed in order to develop a rigorous investment offering memorandum, which is then used to gain outside financing.

- THIRD, TEAM. Brightstar focuses intensely on the founding team from inside BT and also freely uses its assets to assist the team and accelerate venture development. Harry's thirty years of experience implementing major change programs at BT taught him one unbending lesson: people make all the difference. Great ideas, great technology, and great plans all break down if the people supplying or demanding the ideas don't enthusiastically buy in. So the first thing Harry wants to see is the passion, commitment, and inspiration in the founders of the venture. This passion is then matched by the recruiting efforts of outside VCs and partners to complete the founding team.

While the folks at Brightstar are currently focusing on only one aspect of corporate venturing—early venture building from within—they appear to have built a platform—an incubation "engine"—for doing this innovatively and effectively. With nine ventures already created, the months ahead will tell.

the venture in theory, or in a scaled-down operational prototype or alpha. Now they are "tasting the food," so to speak. The purpose of this stage is to assess the venture's ability to deliver according to specification and to capture and respond to feedback.

During the Beta Stage, venture managers are torn between meeting the schedule expectations of their parent company and their partners, and pausing to correct what they believe are potential flaws. These decisions arise all the time. Imagine, for example, that during the Beta Stage a potential customer testing your Web site access tells you she needs real-time inventory levels, not last night's inventory levels. Meeting her request will require significant reworking of the product architecture, and changes will need to be made in all the marketing and sales material. So the larger question to be quickly pondered is: Are her requests individual and exceptional, or indicative of a larger pool of customer/segment requirements? Are the delays in schedule and costs of additional development in making these changes worth the possible gains in downstream customer acquisition?

Ultimately, the venture CEO must make this "call." But he or she needs to make it in the context of weighing the interests of every part of the company. The tendency to ignore small flaws in the name of keeping to a schedule must be resisted. The whole purpose of the stage-by-stage approach to venturing is to take enough time to identify and correct possible flaws before the launch.

In the same vein, the Beta Stage is when the venture managers ask themselves at what cost they can meet their performance benchmarks. In the rush to prepare for the launch of a venture, they often overlook or rationalize details that aren't quite up to original specification. A Web site that promised response time within a second may in fact not respond in two seconds. Is that a problem? Perhaps not. But a series of small performance failures can quickly snowball into a large problem: a product or service that no longer meets customers' initial expectations—and the implications of this can be quite serious.

Performance questions also arise because the conditions for developing the venture change as a company moves from alpha to beta to launch. A component of the system that behaved a certain way and achieved a certain speed during testing in the controlled environment of the Alpha Stage needs to behave similarly and maintain that speed once it is mass-produced: Does the venture have the capacity to measure and maintain that performance? It is inevitable that performance declines in all sorts of ways as the venture moves from creating a prototype to something that is marketed to, and tested by, a larger audience. That is why the Beta Stage of the venture needs a process to monitor performance issues constantly.

Ultimately, the platform and first product or service offering need to be ready to be scaled by the completion of the Beta Stage. Here *scale* means not just size and scope, but the full network of partners, staff, inventory control, sales, and delivery that help distinguish a mere product from a business. In many ventures, the leaders are so excited about their product or service that they overlook details in the support network that are required to sell, distribute, and service their creation. When Encyclopedia Britannica launched its online version of its famous reference work, it marketed and advertised it brilliantly—so well, in fact, that what they forgot to do was create a powerful enough Web site to handle the flood of traffic Britannica.com attracted. For more than a week after it launched, the major story about the encyclopedia's Web site was that readers couldn't access it.

Here again we see the need to synchronize all the elements of the venture carefully. A product that is developed well ahead of schedule is useless until the venture has the sales and customer service staff to support it. Such problems speak to the need to begin developing every component of the venture plan well before it is necessary. The Beta Stage becomes much more manageable if many of the disconnects between one part of the venture and another have already emerged at an early stage.

The Market

The marketing and sales plan goes through significant refinement in the Beta Stage because real data are being collected from the initial customers around pricing, use, adoption barriers, buying behavior, and the value proposition. The venture team should ask the following questions at this stage:

- Have we updated the marketing plan to reflect experience from beta?

- Is the marketing communications master plan complete and executing?

- Is the sales plan and process in place and operating?

- Are the strategic partners and other alliances critical to market entry now on board?

- Is the customer service program specified and operating to support the beta test?

For the marketing operation, the Beta Stage represents the critical opportunity to observe and interact with customers using the venture's product or service in their own environments, in a way that most closely emulates how the product will be used and received on a broader scale when it is launched. The opportunity is to use the beta to essentially test out the principal elements of marketing's positioning and programs, and sales and service programs. The team is able to do this "end to end," from first customer contact through delivery and post sales customer support, in a way that allows the team to extrapolate implications to the launch and tweak its approaches—one last time, in a protected and private way, before going out to the public. This is also an opportunity to align partner's roles and activities, as well.

Accordingly, the marketing, sales, delivery, and service teams must have a system in place to methodically capture all aspects of beta test response and related field information. Invariably, it is during this process that the venture can begin to calibrate the reality of the challenges it will face in generating, closing, and supporting sales. Most ventures unintentionally underestimate the effort and lead time required for closing sales. The goal here is to use information gleaned in the beta process to refine the profile of the sale, from lead time to resources required. A more accurate, representative sales profile is literally worth its weight in gold as the team constructs and refines its aggregated sales forecasts and revenue projections—all crucial in setting expectations for the venture's early performance in the marketplace.

By the end of the Beta Stage, the marketing and sales teams should be equipped with a process and system for tracking leads, prospects, and conversions to sales. At the Beta Stage, the venture needs to think of all the aspects of marketing that are required during a launch of a product or service and prepare to move into the implementation phase of its plan: For instance, public relations, collateral Web sites, direct-mail campaigns, and appearances at trade shows and industry events. The marketing communications master plan strategically integrates and syncopates the development and implementation of these programs and activities, in a fashion designed to cost-effectively build word of mouth and "buzz"—shown time and time again in the venture world to be one of the most compelling tools for missionary market development and early sales interest. The strategic PR program planning and materials preparation typically begins some three to six months prior to launch and starts to execute during the Beta Stage. Its goals are to build support among industry analysts and influencers, and utilize customer and partner testimonials to support the venture's public introduction.

The Beta Stage tests the current sales resources of the corporate venture in various ways: Were they able to win cooperation from the right beta customers and partners? Have they been able to pique curiosity among other potential customers and partners? Have they been systematic in their approach to sales and business development, coordinating their efforts with the rest of the venture team? Are the primary systems and backbone of an infrastructure in place to support rapid growth of the sales organization? Building that infrastructure gives rise to a new set of questions that help define a sales operation: Has the Beta Stage permitted the creation of a complete sales process? Are there adequate sales materials? Is there a formal mechanism to retrieve comments from the field and apply them to the beta-test version? Is a customer relationship management database in place? Putting systems and processes in place now helps streamline operations in the next stage, when the organization expands and swings into high gear for marketing and sales.

Along with sales, customer service program fundamentals are something that should be in place *before* the venture goes to market. Beta customers need a mechanism or process through which they can report problems or ask questions. Will it be an e-mail service, a chat room, or a call center? Are queries going to be answered within minutes, hours, or days? How will these queries be routed within the venture for efficient resolution—and to dispatch additional customer assistance if it is required?

Beyond this immediate application, customer care is fast becoming a high-level strategic function in the venture, one that is key to customer satisfaction and a vital source of information about the target market. It should be established by the Beta Stage, used to support beta users in a way that can be extrapolated to test the appropriateness of its plan and cost of delivery, as well as its readiness for launch. In many corporations, customer care is still seen in a relatively narrow vein as a technical matter, peopled with mid-level operators (e.g., How many service reps can field how many calls per hour?). In the bosom of the corporate venture, however, customer care becomes a far more critical and strategic function, acting as a magnet for customer satisfaction, a source point for and referendum on new features and product ideas, and a unique collection point for market data and insight. As such, it is very important to have a leg up on this vital program, with a plan for its full-scale operation in place and fundamentals operable to support the beta, in order to test and refine it prior to launch.

The Team

At this stage, recruiting is in full force to fill out the venture team to run the business. The venture's size will double, triple, or more in fairly short order, in order to meet its goals. Obviously this growth brings several challenges: Key people must spend more time recruiting, and also more time managing and controlling a larger organization, and the burn rate will suddenly accelerate, which makes mistakes more costly. Example questions include the following:

- Is the entire management team in place, and do they demonstrate the ability to work together?

- Is the board in place and actively helping in all areas?

- Are the partners critical for market entry on board?

When should the corporate venture have its full senior team in place? Some will argue that until the venture has been launched and the market has expanded, the need for a full complement of senior team leaders is unnecessary. We disagree. When the venture launches, every element of its plan will be in operation. It is now that the venture needs high quality, venture-experienced people leading the charge in the various functional areas of the business. As Regis McKenna, Silicon Valley marketing guru, has always maintained, "You don't get a second chance to make a first impression." Having the best people on board invariably helps boost the quality of the venture's first foray into the public marketplace, which is critical to its missionary marketing and sales efforts. The point is not to simply bulk up with headcount, but to hire judiciously and with laser-like focus, to match the best people with the specific roles at the right time. And this is a huge challenge. Several things help. For instance, having "debugged" and formalized the venture's end to end structure and process for recruiting and hiring in the previous stage better prepares the venture and boosts efficiency in this one. Also, having a back up strategy is important; e.g., pre-identifying and retaining senior level people to come in on an advisory or consulting basis to "fill in" while the venture continues to focus on finding the permanent hires.

It is also extremely important for the venture to have an integrated team, where members work together well and identify and solve problems in an efficient, collaborative way. The Beta Stage, because it requires so much coordination and checking of the various components for the organization, mitigates against a silo mentality, in which each executive operates an independent fiefdom. As we have pointed out, ventures cannot survive without internal cooperation far in excess of that found in most larger companies. Also, having the full team on board and working well together in the beta testing period provides an all-important preview of how they will operate when complexity increases yet again, exponentially, when the venture is launched. Team members should clearly agree on the plan for the next six months, and they should be saying the same thing whenever they discuss the venture with anyone outside.

From a purely practical standpoint, it is important that, relatively early in the venture, knotty human resource issues are resolved with the parent company. Compensation, vesting, benefits, bonuses, and so on must be resolved if the venture is going to succeed in bringing on relatively senior people. If the team is fully on board by the Beta Stage, the venture should be able to introduce a whole series of venturewide management processes that will create a greater degree of discipline. It will still feel like a start-up, but it should feel like a well-run one.

One indispensable figure on the management team at this point will be the chief financial officer. At this stage, the CFO's role should be one of chief educator of the team on all financial issues, as well as a source point for financial strategy expertise and keeper of the financing plan for the venture. He or she should make clear that everyone understands profit and loss statements and can read the balance sheet, and that the core team leaders are clear on the funding strategy. The purpose is to imbue the team with a sense of fiscal responsibility, whether they are in human resources, marketing, or sales.

By the Beta Stage, the small board the venture has assembled should be meeting at least once a month. And more than just meeting, they should be acting as an extension of management, consulting on new problems, enforcing the discipline of measurement, and acting as advocates within the parent company. The board should also act as a reviewer and critic of the product or service. It should question the assumptions of the marketers and sales force and compare the existing experience with previous start-up experiences.

The board must also be working diligently to recruit supporters, key personnel, more strategic partners, and customers. Like the sales staff, the board can largely act as evangelists for the venture, helping conduct marketing with missionary zeal.

In most cases, the venture will have identified partners and forged agreements with them long before the Beta Stage. But now the venture leaders must determine whether these partners are really on board and how they will make good on their commitments. Each relationship should be framed by a Strategic Partner Plan, which the venture team initially outlined in the previous stage: it is now fully fleshed out with specific commitments, delineating each party's responsibilities and deliverables according to a timetable and budget. Considerations are down to the tactical, operating level. Let's posit, for example, that one of the partners is a national association—such as the AAA—whose membership list is critical to your customer base. The AAA and the venture must have determined exactly who does what. Is the AAA distributing venture marketing materials? Are they participating in the beta test and/or helping to identify beta customers? What if their members call them about the venture's service? Are they prepared to answer questions or make referrals to the customer care division? Will they be prepared to sell the venture's products or offer special access or rates to the venture's service? These details must be established and the delivery process refined before the venture launches and expands in Stage 4. So during the Beta Stage, the venture's marketing team must pay as much attention to partners as it does to potential customers.

These practical concerns are the nuts and bolts of a the partnership—and where, many times, the relationship breaks down. At the Beta Stage the venture leadership must "check the temperature" of the partners, to make sure they are motivated and fully engaged in the project—and delivering according to expectation. If they are not, the venture must determine why not. Perhaps the partner's commitment wasn't as complete as the venture leadership perceived it to be, or a significant "influencer" on the partner's executive staff has now gone cold on the deal. Perhaps the partner's internal operations and mechanisms for distributing the venture's materials don't really do the job as planned. Perhaps the venture's offering conflicts with a product now favored by another division in the Partner organization. Staying on top of partnering and alliance details, from high level strategies to daily operations and coordination, is a full time effort. It is also why the business development and relationship management position in the venture is so vital.

The Financing

The venture needs to raise money for launch before a beta test is complete. Current funding which gets the venture through the test period will erode quickly now that product development, marketing, sales, and customer care are gaining momentum. Questions about financing at this stage include the following:

- Do we have cash on hand for the remainder of the beta test? Do we have financing lined up for the market launch period?

- Do we have the critical elements necessary for fundraising, including performance efficacy, testimonials, letters of intent, possible revenue?

- Are we hitting key venture development and financial milestones?

During the Beta Stage, fundraising becomes a priority. It should not become all-consuming, however. The key is to have enough money to execute the plan and have a significant contingency—after all, the worst time to raise money is when you don't have any. A venture should always assume that its own plan is "aggressive" and figure that it will need to live off the previous round of funding for 30 percent longer than anticipated. Whereas the earlier stages required relatively limited funds, the money needed here is more significant. The venture will be completing engineering on the product, filling senior and many midlevel positions, and engaging in extensive marketing and sales activities.

Knowing that this cash is available is very important to the venture's morale and focus. If the venture already feels the financial pinch at this stage, then it must start aggressive cost containment at the same time that it is spending more than ever. Cost containment is a good general principle for all businesses, of course, but underfinancing the venture at this stage is penny-wise and pound-foolish, particularly as the venture verges on showing tangible results and business model validation which will increase its value going forward.

Fundraising requires more than asking for money from potential investors. There is simply too much competition for investment when capital markets are tight. Most discriminating investors will demand to see a few signs of early success in the Beta Stage venture, such as a list of beta customers, testimonials from those customers, letters of intent from committed customers, and perhaps even the earliest signs of revenue.

At this point, many ventures find themselves engaging in a delicate balancing act. They have customers who are eager about the concept and pleased with the beta. What they now reasonably wonder is whether the venture can continue to produce its product or service once it goes into full-scale market expansion. In some cases, pursuing a pilot program before moving on to a full-scale launch requires less immediate funding and is an incremental way to reduce risk around full-scale introduction. The down side is that, at the end of the day, doing a pilot adds additional expense to the total funding required by the venture and requires more time in the schedule, but it makes sense as long as the pilot's net results continue to help push the venture toward a full launch.

In most instances, though, the skilled investor will still want to know how a venture can prove that it can move beyond the Beta Stage. That is why a venture will need "evidence" that it is ready to move into market expansion. To secure future sales, the venture management must often make special deals with the first customers. Most investors understand that. But during the Beta Stage, the venture must start exploring with its test customers what it takes to make preliminary purchase agreements or secure letter of intent. Such agreements are extremely helpful in the fund raising process.

As with every stage of the venture, it is imperative to take steps to measure success at hitting key milestones. From a finance perspective, those milestones might be staying within expense tolerances in the budget, achieving validation of valuation equivalent to comparable endeavors, and recognizing first orders. From an operational perspective, they might be the team hitting its schedules and delivering betas on time and on target, setting up management processes and systems, people hired, customers in the pipeline, customer care program developed, etc. During this stage, the venture must also flesh out the full set of financial metrics and performance targets it will use when it launches: gross margins, inventory level, and so on. As always, the venture leaders need to measure these metrics against the various stages of product development to determine whether the venture is on course.

CARGILL eVENTURES AND DEMANDTEC: DELIVERING ON THE PROMISE OF CORPORATE VENTURING

DemandTec is a nearly three-year-old start-up on the fast track to success. The venture produces software that enables large retailers and manufacturers to optimize every merchandising decision, to make the most of opportunities for growth for profit. The company's software platform evolved from the founders' earlier work with applied mathematics in pricing optimization. Now, DemandTec's operational software platform links corporate business systems with "every item on every shelf," enabling customers to make very dynamic product pricing and merchandising decisions and trade-offs, across all types of products and tailored to different locales. Current customers number three of the top five drug chain retailers, including Longs Drugs, and two major grocery chains.

By November 2000, DemandTec had beta results, and its CEO and founder, Mike Neal, was ready to raise a second round of financing. Crosspoint Venture Partners, a well-known Silicon Valley–based VC firm, was one of those Neal approached. Cargill eVentures, via an introduction facilitated by Crosspoint, was another. "I was interested in exploring the possibilities of including a corporate investor, one who could bring industry savvy and connections, and whose parent company could be an early customer, as well," Neal said. "Cargill was a great potential fit."

Jim Sayre, CEO of Cargill eVentures, agreed. DemandTec was perfectly aligned with his firm's mission of transforming global supply chains, by investing in and incubating new technology ventures to spur innovation and lower costs of doing business for Cargill, its partners, and customers across the globe. Neal was somewhat cautious about Cargill eVenture's ability to act decisively, with a speed and efficiency common in the venture capital world but often lacking when the investors and partners are corporate. He need not have been concerned. Within the space of the several weeks, Cargill's corporate venture group had completed a focused due diligence and had offered oral commitment; within eight weeks, the full second round, including Crosspoint and Cargill eVentures, was signed, sealed, and delivered.

Cargill eVentures assumed an observer role on the board, and got busy delivering the kind of value Neal had hoped for. They scoped out appropriate application areas within Cargill, along with high-level strategic business unit contacts. Cargill eVentures managed all the introductions—and continued to "run point" as the relationships and projects matured into independent business deals. "Jim Sayre was at every meeting with us," noted DemandTec's CEO.

As DemandTec continues on the way of explosive business growth, Cargill eVentures's value as a corporate resource grows along with it. For example, the venture is beginning to explore the potential of expanding its business to Europe: Cargill eVentures helped Neal create an appropriate agenda and used its corporate contacts to set up all the meetings for him.

"Having venture investors who not only understand your venture but also have the know-how and contacts to pave the way for you in the corporate world is an incredible advantage," Neal said. "We have benefited immensely from having Cargill eVentures as an investor and partner in building our business."

The VBO's Role in the Beta Stage

In this stage, the VBO should concentrate on bringing value to the venture from corporate, and vice versa, in three key areas.

- The VBO must assist in making all corporate partnerships work. Since solid execution by these partnerships will be critical for a successful first offering, and navigating large companies can often be frustrating if not downright impossible for entrepreneurs, the VBO provides invaluable assistance in navigating the corporate backwaters. This type of high-level business development and relationship management is a crucial element of the VBO's value to portfolio companies, the venture community, and other partners and customers.

- The VBO must use its influence to help make the first customer trials work. If a large corporate customer knows that another known and respected large corporation is behind a new venture, it is much more likely to exercise patience or flexibility with the initial offering.

- The VBO must continually assess the venture's performance against all key metrics for this stage of development. Subsequent feedback must be focused on problem solving, not simply criticism for missing deadlines. These metrics include everything from product development schedules to product performance relative to its value proposition to analysis of financial needs.

Notable Differences between Corporate and Independent Ventures

Remembering our definition of a corporate venture—a venture with corporate interests represented on the board or one owned more than 20 percent by a corporation—it is important to understand how it differs from a venture without corporate ties. At this stage of development, the corporate venture often deals with issues that are different from its independent venture cousin. For example:

- *Platform.* The corporate venture must be mindful of how its platform and first products fit—both strategically and politically—with the platform and products of its corporate investor. The philosophical difference is that the venture should complement, rather than compete, with its corporate sponsor.

- *Market.* The corporate venture may be forced to expand or tailor its market focus to be interesting to the parent. Independent ventures have laser-like focus on market segments as they get started. The corporate venture sometimes gets pushed to address a broader set of customers by the parent, which requires a more sophisticated first product and usually takes longer to develop and costs more. The corporate venture might also get pushed towards a market that is less ideal, for its own purposes, as a first target, but is the clear preference of the corporate parent.

- *Team.* The corporate venture, especially one being built inside a corporation, typically has a greater percentage of team members who come from the parent organization. The downsides: while they are certain to have corporate understanding and domain expertise, they may be "fractionalized" or on temporary assignment until permanent employees can be hired, and/or they have little or no useful startup experience. This combination inevitably slows the venture development down.

Notable Differences between Venture Investing and Building

At this stage of development, the VBO plays very different roles relative to ventures it invests in and ventures it actively incubates:

- *Platform.* From a venture-build perspective: the venture platform leverages and extends the corporate platform's capabilities. And the venture may in fact use many other services from the parent rather than build or buy them independently. This convenience sourcing may actually be a competitive disadvantage to the venture as it limits the degrees of freedom around assessment of alternative sources. From a venture-invest perspective the relationship of VBO to the venture is clearer. The venture seeking the corporate partner is often looking for one of two very specific things (in addition to funds): It wants them to supply a key product or service to the venture, or it wants them to be an initial public customer.

- *Market.* From a build perspective, the venture often gains access faster to better customers than an independent entity would, because a relationship with a built venture can be more visceral than that from a venture investment. From an investment perspective, accessing new customers and segments brings many times the value, but serving the same ones differently does not. So rather than bringing customers to the venture (build), customers are brought to the corporation (invest).

- *Funding.* From a build perspective, we've seen two extremes on funding: from raising all Beta Stage funds from other corporate investors to raising all Beta Stage funds internally. The first approach is intended to validate the merits of the business, as evidenced by external investors. The second approach is intended to maximize ownership and value for the parent corporation when Beta Stage risks are deemed low. From an investment perspective, the key challenge is to put a value on strategic assets that are committed to the venture. The wild card is the value of strategic assets, such as the commitment to be the first customer, the ability to use the parent's brand name in marketing material, having access to sales and marketing resources, or having access to manufacturing and distribution capability. Retaining an investment banker to value these assets isn't a bad idea.

Corporate Assets Available to the VBO

Business Plan. Corporations can be extremely supportive in helping their ventures plan for the actual launch. The sheer size of the parent will usually suggest that they have a corporate communications group that is skilled in how to roll out new products or services to big markets. These are resources that few corporate ventures have. Many independent ventures have spent millions of dollars hiring public relations and advertising firms to assist them with market launches. The corporate venture, by contrast, can save a great deal of time by working with the corporate parent team. The caveat, however, is that the venture must have an understanding of the unique role and types of techniques used by new venture PR specialists—perhaps even retain someone of this caliber or have a senior communications strategist on the core team—if it is to appropriately direct and manage the corporate communications effort. The plan for communications should come from the venture and not the parent's corporate PR group. This coordination should be fully engaged at the Beta Stage.

Platform. At the Beta Stage, the corporate parent must provide as much help as possible to keep the venture's partners involved and close to the ventures. Many of these partners will be units within the parent corporation, so it's crucial for the parent to send subtle messages about the need to remain supportive of the venture. Many of the partners, especially in the technology and development side, are vital to the completion of the Beta Stage, especially when more changes have to be made to respond to feedback. Keeping those partners close, informed, and happy is one of the parent's key tasks.

Market. Corporations can provide their ventures with the most invaluable of resources: brand name first customers. Indeed, working closely with the parent company, a venture can find customers most interested in participating in a beta test of a product or service. Without this connection, finding agreeable customers—who may well turn out to be real, paying customers—can be like blindly drilling for oil.

Team. As the final senior team comes together, the parent corporation may be the source for missing talent. We have earlier cautioned about the dangers of relying exclusively on internal talent to lead a venture, particularly if they have no start-up experience. But the parent company can offer other in-house talent that understands the industry, as well as access to a network of people outside the company who could bring substantial knowledge to a venture.

Financing. Clearly a corporate venture benefits from the fact that the parent provides the initial funding. This direct availability of funds increases the venture's stability and certainty during its first year. But it also requires the venture to maintain a full-time relationship with the parent, constantly keeping it abreast of its progress, its setbacks, and its changes. This parent/investor relationship often poses a greater internal management burden for the venture, in that it must deal more regularly with cultural antagonisms and lack of venture understanding.

Common Mistakes: VBO Beware

Business Plan. Not all relationships with the parent corporation will be idyllic during the Beta Stage. Corporate supporters will remain nervous when they see the number of business plan changes that occur during this period. They will assume, erroneously, that a significant change in a product feature or service-delivery timetable suggests an initial failure.

SUMMARY OF "MUST-HAVES" AND "RED FLAGS"

BETA STAGE "MUST-HAVES": ESSENTIAL ELEMENTS TO HAVE IN PLACE

- Product/service efficacy proved by beta test; effective front-to-back integration
- Key partners on and operating as projected
- "Tweaks," as opposed to major overhauls, completed on platform; first product/service based on beta/pilot feedback
- First customers/segments targeted and represented in beta/pilot; marketing and sales' assumptions and programs tested
- Service and support programs modeled and refined, based on beta/pilot feedback
- "Continuous development architecture" (i.e., systems and processes across all departments) in place and working for beta/pilot tests
- Venture leader (CEO) and complete team in place; advisories and board in place
- VEO (corporate senior executive on venture board) in place and facilitating venture/parent relationship
- Launch program for venture and first product/service underway
- Significant sweat equity in place to keep core team
- Next product/service in development, with targeted entry for three months after venture launch
- Governance operational and working according to plan
- Funding secured for market entry and venture scalability in next stage

BETA STAGE "RED FLAGS": FACTORS THAT DEMAND IMMEDIATE ATTENTION

- No formalized, rigorous beta (and, if required, pilot) test plan and execution in place
- Marketing's plans and assumptions about customer behavior disproved by real beta feedback
- Failure of attempts to "scale" with pilot (e.g., don't meet market/product/service/delivery requirements and/or quality standards with increased numbers of users)

- First segment and infrastructure customers not participating in beta/pilot
- Infrequent sampling of beta/pilot testers; ad hoc and incomplete collection of information from testers
- First features and functions (e.g., beta/pilot customer requirements) off the mark
- Crucial partners not on and/or operating with difficulties
- Parent vetoes or holds up decision process for venture's choice of partners
- Team comprised of development people only: very incomplete
- Team comprised of inexperienced corporate insiders; short on outside expertise and leadership; lack of outsiders as advisors and board members
- No corporate senior executive serving as "evangelist" board member to ensure relationship; the parent doesn't cooperate in the launch, marketing and sales, or channels
- No formal governance structure in place for determining performance and setting expectations
- Inadequate funding; equity inadequate to attract talent

Corporate parents will be more likely to urge rapid completion of the venture rather than the more deliberate refinement and adjustments recommended here. In truth, corporate parents are usually lousy at real beta testing. Often we see them rush from an alpha test to an actual launch as time frames and budgets get tighter. This may be the most common and serious mistake we see at this stage. The VBO must not let an alpha product go to market; it will waste good money on an extremely low-probability effort.

Platform. Corporate relationships with existing suppliers are often the source for venture partners. That connection may serve the interests of the corporation, but it does not necessarily help identify the ideal. In the Beta Stage, the venture discovers whether the partner truly adds value. Come the market expansion stage, the venture will depend entirely on partners for execution and product delivery. The Beta Stage is the time to test them hard, and to question the corporate parent's assumptions in recommending them if there is any reason to doubt their performance so far. The venture should actually simulate scaling efforts with partners at this stage.

Marketing. In marketing, corporate parents can suddenly become competitive with their own ventures. Indeed, some corporations make the mistake of becoming very territorial about their customer databases, refusing to share key information. Alternatively, they may make referrals to customers but insist that they rigidly control the introduction and interaction process. If the parent company meets once every two months with a customer, the venture will be allowed to approach the customer only on that schedule. At that point, the process of seeking allies and customers who could provide feedback become bureaucratic, extended, and somewhat worthless.

The Team. The mistake, which derives from convenience and speed, is that the venture becomes too reliant on in-house talent. This is particularly true with members of the board of directors and board of advisors, but it certainly is true with the senior management team as well. Here, more than anywhere, it is critical to have advisors and board members who come from well outside the company. In some cases, the best advisor will be someone with no connection at all to the parent company. The venture needs people who can give unbiased advice and be relatively unconcerned about the parent's internal politics. Finding such people is a challenge for most ventures.

Financing. Corporations go astray when they try to play the role of all-or-nothing investors. We have observed corporate parents who insist on funding 100 percent of the VBO's operation and ventures, in order to keep control and ownership, and/or maintain the wall between itself and the outside community. We also have clients eager to embrace the Venture Business Office but then insist that all funding come entirely from someone else. In these cases, the corporations treat their willingness to help build the venture as their ownership stake, but then they prefer to use someone else's money to advance it. This creates a predictable scenario when the venture is successful. Recognizing that the venture within its own walls has produced, say, a technology that would have a major impact on the industry, the parent company suddenly wants to own it all, blocking out investment from potential competitors. But because such financial enthusiasm comes late in the process, the parent's role becomes uncertain, and the relationship between the parent and the venture becomes uneasy at a time when the venture needs the parent's support most.

The Beta Offering: Key Lessons

- *Get a second opinion—and a third, and a fourth.* By the end of the Beta Stage, a promising venture team will have to make it a priority to obtain an essential resource: objectivity. It should consciously seek out formal and informal validation of its progress and concept, from customers, suppliers, partners, the board, investors, and advisors.

- *Customer feedback is crucial—get it.* At the Beta Stage customers have an opportunity to provide concrete feedback. It's easy to ignore problems in order to meet the schedule. But the purpose of this stage is to address problems, not postpone them.

- *Get ready to start selling.* At this stage sales contracts will be slow in coming. Valuable sales processes and metrics track the entire sales pipeline—referrals, first meetings, length of time to close, win/loss analyses—and build reliable forecasts based on ongoing results.

- *Put the whole team on the field.* Now is the time to avoid culture clashes in the future. The way to do that is to have the full senior management complement filled out by the beta-testing stage. It's at this point that senior managers are required to think about the purpose and direction of the venture; with a full team now, the venture won't have to rehash the same issues later.

- *Partners are about to become crucial—make sure yours are ready.* Now is the time to determine whether the venture's partners are fully committed and energized. The marketing team must be paying as much attention to partners as they are to customers: Do they have confidence in the venture? Do they have conflicts? Do they have the information they need?

beta stage

Fabco Corporation builds a new venture intended to revolutionize its supply chain. It does all the right things in the Vision and Alpha stages. They only get it half right in the Beta Stage, which elongates the stage, delays the launch, delays revenue, and ultimately permanently delays additional funding. Unfortunately, the piece that went well was the product build, which was expensive. The piece that didn't go well was locking down the beta customers. So the company spends tens of millions of dollars building a scalable product, only to scrap it when the beta customers don't materialize fast enough.

Context

Fabco is a multibillion-dollar global supplier of metal fabrication services to the heavy manufacturing industry. In early 1999, Fabco was the second leading supplier of these products in the world and after losing a battle to acquire a global competitor, it slipped to fourth place in size. This setback appeared to be permanent, as no other viable acquisition candidates were visible. Determined to grow, the senior management team at Fabco decided in a senior management retreat to undertake several initiatives to grow the business "organically." One of these initiatives involved finding ways to leverage the burgeoning Internet. One group brainstormed the name of a URL for their largest relationship within their largest customer segment: www.metalfabricators.com.

The biggest issues facing Fabco in this endeavor were senior management experience and capacity—not one member of the management team had substantive experience with start-ups or the Internet, nor did any of them have time to dedicate to building a plan. The effort would be led by Bob Smith, a top advisor to the CEO responsible for new service business development. Smith assembled a cross-functional team of senior managers from technology, e-business, finance, marketing, and strategy. None was full-time, however, and their roles after the planning stage remained unclear. The team also retained a consulting firm to help drive the planning effort.

The most immediate tactical action was getting together a viable business plan around this amorphous idea: to find the right set of products and services for the right customer segment charging a price commensurate with the value proposition. The largest source of conflict in this effort would ultimately come from the very mission given to this team, which was to develop a significant business proposition that leverages but isn't constrained by the company's core competencies. The bolder the idea, the farther from core competencies the venture strayed. And in fact, the boldest ideas competed against or cannibalized Fabco—ideas such as selling competitors' products, increasing price transparency, selling direct rather than through the sales force, and trading production and delivery capacity with competitors.

On the other side of the coin, the more logical the idea—such as selling product into the consumer market, entering new international markets, and selling domain knowledge—the less value it created, given the core business. The implications were profound: This would be the highest risk-return profile the company had ever undertaken, especially outside the core business and at this scale. The typical capital investments for the company had a 90 percent probability of returning 1 percent more than the cost of capital. This would be different. As the CFO told the board, "Within the next twelve months this investment will yield somewhere between a total write-off and a billion dollars in market capitalization and I honestly can't tell you where in between it'll land with any confidence."

The first stage took approximately six weeks to complete; the output was a top-level analysis of the market potential and the cost of building the business. The team did initial market validation using a firm that specializes in understanding the behaviors of early adopters in emerging markets. The resulting concept business plan was presented to senior management to gain funding approval (to hire business consultants) to build an investment-offering memorandum, a.k.a., a Stage 2 business plan.

The initial high-level concept centered around selling personal and professional products and services to the 2 million metal workers in the United States—everything from steel to welding equipment to NASCAR event tickets. Based on this idea, Fabco agreed to spend $350,000 to retain consultants to put the concept plan together. To little surprise, the team quickly concluded that the target audience neither spent enough nor spent enough online nor influenced enough spending to build a business. In addition, well-funded competitors with significant advantages amply supplied most of the B2C offerings.

So the concept would undergo its first iteration. The team decided to drop the B2C components and extend the B2B components. Basically, they would build a full set of business functions around the metal fabricators' business—joining, cutting, bending, and stamping metal. Fabricators essentially take raw steel from a mill and transform it into a variety of interim and end products used in manufacturing industries such as transportation (planes, trains, boats, and automobiles), industrial machinery (earth-moving machinery and factory machinery) and construction (structural steel). Taken together, this amounts to over $400 billion in spending represented by captive and independent businesses in the United States alone, with tens and possibly hundreds of thousands of businesses, most being under $10 million in revenue.

The Stage 2 took approximately four months and produced an interactive Web-based demo of how the service would look and operate. Also, a detailed business plan sought $20 million in funding to get through the Beta Stage. The prototype and plan were presented to the parent's board, which approved the investment, subject to interim milestone verification.

Bell-Mason Graph and Analysis

The Beta Stage was scheduled to take eight months to complete and be ready for a full market launch. An analysis using the Bell-Mason VDF halfway through the stage indicated serious problems, as figure 7-1 shows. However, the management team believed that the issues were generally known and that they were working on fixing them. Nevertheless, the issues weren't recorded anywhere, and accountability for resolution fell to various groups, not individuals.

FIGURE 7 - 1

Diagnostic of Fabco Corporate Venture.

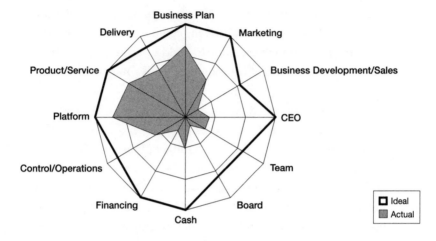

Platform

The platform was essentially the ability to serve any business need for any type of fabricator, whether buying steel, finding labor, or finding new business. And of course, this model could be extended to dozens of other industries. So the strategic options that the platform enabled felt limitless. A key to the platform was integrating the best of breed products in various categories so that uniqueness and sustainability would be created through the customer relationship, not the product features. This relationship would result from having the most suppliers, an objective, comprehensive product offering packaged in a simple interface while capturing the most important information to manage the business. This information spanned from fabricator ratings of suppliers to customer ratings of fabricators to welding process expertise to detailed product descriptions to pricing information.

Product/Service

The features of the service represented one of the biggest risks for this venture. Features, even functions, are not homogenous in a

$400 billion industry. The key was getting enough out in the market initially to attract a large segment, such as farm machinery, but not so much as to weigh down the development and delay the launch. Also, these features needed to be significant enough to move quickly to adjacent fabrication segments such as auto manufacturing. Triaging features and functions proved to be extremely hard for the management team as they defaulted to adding, rather than trading, new capabilities.

Delivery

Delivery presented an interesting dilemma for a software and service company in a physical goods industry. Clearly the venture was offering an Internet-based service, but the target segments were probably the biggest technology laggards in all of industry. And those who were using technology had significant investments in enterprise resource planning systems to do buying, customer relationship management systems to do selling, and human resource systems to do hiring. So systems integration would be a major issue in the delivery.

Business Plan

Generally speaking, the plan was a good one. It had thorough high-level market analysis and detailed product development costs; and the understanding of the infrastructure into which it was selling was superior. The only insufficiency proved to be testing assumptions with the "segment-of-one" customer interviews.

Marketing

The operative words were *targeting* and *segmentation*, since a $400 billion dollar U.S. market couldn't be entered uniformly. The intersecting selection criteria revolved around "need" and "access." Market entry would need to focus on those with greatest need and then be filtered by ability to access the company (or in other words, the venture would have to leverage Fabco relationships). Another challenge dealt with the low-technology adoption rates in the industry, which was a barrier to entry. Segmentation was difficult because of the severe fragmentation of the industry according to any number of criteria, such as size, sector, and technology use. But in the end, the market analysis was more like classic corporate top-down plans rather than bottom-up new venture plans. The lack of extensive segment-of-one customer interviews to validate assumptions indicated this shortfall as well.

Business Development/Sales

Given that no one had ever sold anything like this to these customers before, sales was a real wild card. A direct sales force would be needed to get the venture off the ground, and the sales team hoped that some critical mass would enable some more cost-effective approaches for building out the market. Sales could be the hidden Achilles' heel of the whole effort, since this level of "thinking" would result in changes to features and potentially the value proposition.

CEO

The venture faced serious challenges. The CFO-turned-CEO underwent a huge change in job description—from the CFO of a Fortune 250 industrial company to the CEO of a dot-com technology company, a role for which he had no prior experience. The team faced significant hurdles attracting marketing, business development, and technology people from outside the company fast enough. Many slots were filled with Fabco people on a full-time, but interim, basis.

Board

No formal board had been established for the venture. The informal board consisted of the venture CEO and the parent company CEO; there were no outsiders. They met once a quarter for an hour or so.

Team

The only non-Fabco member of the management team was the CIO. He had no experience either with start-ups or with the metal fabrication industry. A significant portion of the remainder of the team consisted of consultants. On alternating months, they were nearly furloughed for cost reasons.

Cash

The venture started the Beta Stage with $20 million in cash intended to fund the team for eight months or until the customer testimonials from the beta service could be used to raise more money.

Financing

The venture capital markets were evaporating just as quickly as the public equity markets had gone south. Funding was available only to ventures that demonstrated substantive progress toward having positive cash flow. From a financing perspective, it would be critical to demonstrate market acceptance. In addition, corporate investors, such as steel companies and gas companies, should gain significant strategic advantages from this new channel in the form of lower costs and broader market access.

Unfortunately, the team had never raised money in the market before. They had unrealistic expectations about the time and effort required. The head of marketing at one point said that he thought they'd have money in the bank in sixty days, even though he hadn't had the very first conversation with a potential investor. They still hadn't raised money six months later, and in reality, they had had few serious funding conversations with qualified investors.

Control/Operations

This venture had more control than any start-up ever deserves. It was blessed to receive the procurement policies, the recruiting policies, and the management decision criteria and cycles of its parent. Legacy cultural habits from Fabco permeated the new venture. As the first step in the product development stage, the new venture's management team hired a top strategy firm to "pressure-test" and "refine" the concept they had just decided to fund for $20 million. Few, if any, start-ups would undertake such an effort. The results cost several hundred thousand dollars, took away a month of time from the entire team, and didn't lead to any changes.

Epilogue

Pulling the plug was the right decision. In fact, the plug could have been pulled earlier since the problems were evident a couple of months into the Beta Stage. A formal advisory board or board of directors would not have let the venture proceed as it did, unsupervised. Of the six or so ventures pursuing similar goals at the time, only two remain, and their long-term success isn't assured. The highly fragmented nature of the industry, high supplier switching costs, and the lack of overall information technology usage make for a hostile venture environment. But for these guys, all we can say is, solid idea, bad execution.

8

stage 4

the market offering:
calibrating and expanding

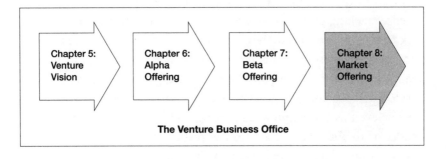

| Chapter 5: Venture Vision | Chapter 6: Alpha Offering | Chapter 7: Beta Offering | Chapter 8: Market Offering |

The Venture Business Office

*We didn't lose the game;
we just ran out of time.*

VINCE LOMBARDI

Once the beta test stabilizes and the venture has applied its lessons to its product or service, the venture is ready to launch formally as a genuine business. At this point, it should not feel like a great leap. The venture has identified its markets. Customers are being lined up. Partners are on board and ready to play specific roles. Advisors and board members are active. There is a steady word-of-mouth buzz about the new business.

Now it must carefully calibrate demand and prepare to expand the market for its offering. Information derived from the prior stage has been analyzed and the venture's "dials" adjusted accordingly, to prepare for formal launch. The strategic communications plan is in place, ready for implementation, along with testimonial and analyst support to begin the public introduction of the venture and its first products/services.

As its name implies, the Market Calibration and Expansion Stage is two different substages crammed into one very tense period. First, it is the "calibration-of-demand" period: the first three to six months of the venture's life in the commercial marketplace. This is that uneasy time when the first real customers start appearing and you find out whether your plan for business was based on correct assumptions. Everyone involved in the venture is on pins and needles over those initial sales. Intense tracking of customer feedback, and a hyperfocus on sales—or lack of them—is a daily activity across the venture. And while the venture team is focused on this process of market calibration, it must be ready to "pull the trigger" on plans for its expansion—next products/ services, next customer segments, new geographies. It has to be ready to do this even as it continues calibrating and tweaking its fundamental model of the business, based on the reality of the market's response. Every venture-development stage has its challenges, but, assuming the venture gets this far, this stage often produces the most difficult ones. At the conclusion of the prior stage, the ante—and the burn rate—goes way up. The gun is fired, and the race is on to "make the numbers" and build the business to steady state. Table 8-1 delineates the challenges of this fourth stage of venture development.

The Gap between Corporations and Their Ventures

While the venture is rapidly taking on many of the characteristics of larger, more mature organizations, it is still a new venture. It still lives by the rules of new ventures. While the team can feel good about getting this far, the venture still has a long way to go to be viable. One of the biggest differences between corporations and their ventures will be seen in the market launch itself. Mature companies are accustomed to launching new products into existing sales and distribution channels, often with a big splash and significant global advertising and fanfare.

TABLE 8 - 1

Stage Four Challenges

Challenges	Circumstances and Context
Changing key elements of the venture while in the market in response to what has been learned from the market experience	The inclination is to not change anything, but to push forward. Feels like failure if the business strategy has to be adjusted. (It isn't. It's natural.)
Getting the sales and marketing engine firing on all cylinders	New companies with new products have an uphill selling battle. They are unknown and they are being compared to the known. Complicating this is a new sales force that is trying to gain access to new customers, get them to switch providers, and overcome implementation barriers. Many types of marketing investments require serious scale (e.g., television advertising)—sponsorships that start-ups don't have. Yet marketing is the front end of the sales process and is therefore crucial.
Coordinating everything after the sale—delivery, service, support, billing, receivables	Two words: exceptions and bugs. The standard processes should cover 80% of your cases. Unfortunately, the remaining 20% will take 80% of your time. Additionally, bugs will naturally surface in your processes and systems and will require immediate attention.
Getting customer service structure and info flow right	Customer service in a start-up is a senior-level function, not a midlevel technical fix or simple 800 number support. It's a primary source of customer understanding; a venue where all the other strategic functions can live and learn (product efficacy, feature/function/benefit weeding and feeding, other marketing research, next product sampling, sales, quality of delivery, etc.).
Not running out of cash	Costs are ramping up quickly with the expectation that revenue will start to flow according to the assumptions in the business model. Too often, revenues and margins are lower than the model. The question is always "for how long?"

For new ventures with new and innovative products, this style of intro wouldn't make a lot of sense—even if the venture were to have enough money (which it rarely does!).

Remember, new and innovative ventures sell their first products/ services most efficiently by building a solid base of customer referrals and other third-party endorsements, persuading customers to buy and building constituencies of support by creating word-of-mouth "buzz."

The elements of marketing that especially enhance this effort are things like strategic public relations tailored to the needs of new ventures that stress editorial "proof points" and industry and product leadership editorial coverage—and tend to be much more cost-efficient than other programs. Even customers whose needs and requirements perfectly match the new venture's first product and services still need to be convinced: After all, they are taking the risk of buying something that hasn't existed before, from a start-up that is new to the scene. Building constituencies and finding early adopters takes lots of intense work and relationship development. Ironically, a new venture can't "buy" its way into the market. It has to prove its value first—which is a good thing, because the venture typically doesn't have a lot of excess cash at this stage. The cash it does have will cover new hires and many other elements, including postlaunch revisions. We suggest to ventures that they think through some key strategic contingencies in these regards, so they aren't caught flat-footed in the face of new information or unpredicted market change. For example, during the calibration phase, significant product modifications may be required, or the business model or partnerships may need to be reworked. The venture will ideally have enough cash in reserve to support itself while it works through these changes.

Getting to this stage does not happen quickly, as we have tried to convey. It is a result of months—or even years, in some industries—of careful strategy development and deliberate research, measurement, testing, and process improvement. The venture's objective at the outset is to build and launch a profitable, growing business as soon as possible. We consider this fourth stage to be the ultimate beginning of the scorecard for this fledgling business. Everything else to this point has been simply preparation for being in market. Now all activities are aimed at creating a profitable and growing revenue stream. The venture team must quickly incorporate critical changes that improve the performance of the product or service, strengthen relationships with critical partners, maintain enthusiastic support from the parent company, or bolster the venture's ability to sell and support its product or service.

One of the greatest changes in this stage is that the venture team must augment missionary marketing programs, such as strategic public relations, with other marketing programs, such as advertising, promotions, and co-branding efforts. At the same time, the team must use these programs judiciously, because of the step up in expense for the business value returned. By the beginning of this stage, the venture should have a "marketing master plan," which lays out the marketing communication ("marcom") and channel support strategy over the next year, and gives concentrated detail for the venture's first six months in the market. This master plan integrates all the primary marketing elements along with required resources and schedules. It ties the projected performance of each marketing element to the venture's immediate business goals in this stage.

Another significant element of the venture at this stage, customer care, differs markedly from customer care functions in large established corporations. In new ventures, customer care begins as a crucial strategic function, not a midlevel technical support capability. It is a key source for customer access and, as such, an opportunity to better understand a number of things: product efficacy and acceptance issues; venture positioning; feature/function/benefit mix; two-way market research for next products; sales leads; and program feedback. In fact, just about every element of the venture has something to learn from customer care.

In this chapter, the questions that we have selected from the Bell-Mason VDF point specifically to becoming a self-sustaining business. In each area, the focus is now more narrowly on measuring success, gathering feedback data, and then recalibrating and refining aspects of the enterprise without losing its essential character. The goal is that, by the end of this stage, the venture will have "stabilized" its business model and plan—and revenues will be generated much more predictably, as forecast in the updated plan.

Most surprisingly, the venture may discover customers and uses for its products/platform that it had not envisioned earlier. This is the kind of unplanned event that may make or break so many new businesses. One of the most famous examples of this phenomenon occurred during the clinical trials for a new heart medicine in the early 1990s. During the clinical trial studies of sildenafil as a heart medicine, the team discovered that the drug also increased blood flow to the penis, allowing men to reverse erectile dysfunctions. Viagra was born and today generates over a billion dollars in revenue for Pfizer.

Stage 4: The Market Offering

The objectives of this phase are, again, easily stated—find customers, become profitable, and get the next version of the offering to market— and not easily accomplished. The venture will need to demonstrate certain key skills:

- An ability to sell the new offering to new customers at the right price and cost

- An ability to deliver an end-to-end offering without incident under a variety of situations

- An ability to provide postsales support and service to keep new customers happy, and to collect important feedback from customers

- An ability to manage financials prudently and begin the move toward having positive cash flow and hitting the numbers in the business's economic model

The Business Plan

Is a business plan still necessary as a venture gets ready to launch its product or service into the market? We think so. The venture can head in new directions as a result of beta-testing data analysis and subsequent refinements. The business plan sketched out in the first stage probably did not anticipate those new directions—and so now the venture team needs to update the plan to reflect these changes. Now, every aspect of the business and its plan is "live." As the venture prepares to deal with real customers in true market conditions, revising the plan—and making sure that it includes a way of measuring the success of the launch period—remains the glue that can hold the team together during what often is a frenetic and volatile period. The business plan remains the central control document for the venture, as well as a sales tool for prospective partners, funders, and high-level recruits. Questions the team should ask about the plan include the following:

- Does the plan explicitly outline the key milestones toward being cash flow positive?

- Does the plan have the next two product releases scheduled and linked to key milestones such as revenues, funding, and hiring?

- Does the plan explicitly articulate the interim milestones and metrics that signal whether calibration and growth are proceeding according to plan?

Until this point, the venture has been measuring a series of activities that show accumulating knowledge about the market, customers, and partners. Now, operating in a real marketplace, the milestones become more traditional, more unequivocal. At this stage, the team needs to measure objective and hard data against the business assumptions. For example: How long is the sales cycle? How much do we spend on sales and marketing to sign up a customer? Does pricing work? How much does it cost to deliver? What is our customer care cost per sale? How close are we on our original assumptions and projections, and have we factored in the variances to update the overall plan and business model?

These questions should keep an eye on moving toward positive cash flow. At the outset of any venture, all sorts of financial compromises need to be made to sign up customers and spread the word. In some cases the venture will reduce prices. In other cases it will maintain prices but throw in additional service for a finite period. These steps may be essential, but investing too much in marketing and sales can be trouble if steps to increase revenue or cut costs do not quickly supersede them. One major mistake dot-coms made was to assume that they could "buy" their way into market share, by spending enormous amounts on advertising and marketing to build brand recognition and capture "eyeballs." They thought that the Web created a complete new business environment—and a complete set of new rules to go with it, which obviated past venturing practices and common-sense customer sales and market development as measures of success. They had things entirely out of sequence, spending enormous amounts for brand recognition without knowing whether customers were likely to buy their product or not. In addition, they spent great sums on branding before perfecting positioning—while they ignored the fact that brand had to be earned over time. Many fledgling companies spent millions of dollars on Super Bowl commercials in 1999 and 2000. Worse yet, these ad purchases consumed 90 percent or more of marketing and sales budgets for this single event! Many planned multiple expensive broadcast advertising spots as part of a standard ad campaign, and raised funds with that end in mind. It was a grand experiment, an extraordinary roll of the dice, a departure from venture best practice of the past. And we now know how this "irrational exuberance" ended.

Suffice it to say that new ventures cannot afford such a high-risk strategy. Corporate ventures in particular should be far more prudent in their marketing budget to avoid incurring the distrust of the corporate parent. That is why we insist on creating a set of sound business and financial milestones that guide the company at this stage.

What a venture is striving for at this point are signs that it is on the right track to profitability. If the product is selling, the venture team should know why (is it just a function of early promotional marketing?) and who is buying it (are these the customers the plan anticipated?). That is why the leaders need to pay close attention to metrics such as the conversion rate of contacts to sales, or the delay between first inquiry and sale. These measures will be the building blocks of future financial projections because, after a few months, they allow a venture to see the length and duration of its sales pipeline.

As the product or service enters the market, there is a tendency to think that it is like the Tasmanian devil: once loose, impossible to control. This is wrong. What makes a corporate venture different from its parent is that it has been designed to accept changes even at this late stage. The parent's tendency is to see *any* failure to meet expectations immediately as a symptom of *complete* systemic failure. Rather than tweak a product or change a strategy, the corporate parent may simply throw in the towel at the first sign that things are not working out as projected.

But the fact is that every venture must adjust to the realities of the market, regardless of the preparation that has been made. Large numbers of new and real customers involve too many unpredictable factors. Many of the necessary changes are small. The question is whether the venture leaders know how to identify them and then act quickly.

Price and pricing strategy are always potent topics for analysis during market calibration. If the lead time to sales extends, and leads don't convert at the rates the business plan projected, there's almost always a knee-jerk reaction to lower the price to see if that will stimulate demand and break the "logjam."

But is the price really too high? Before moving to discount pricing during the calibration stage, the venture leaders need to ask serious questions about why the product or service is not selling. Perhaps the customers believe that it is not delivering the value they expected or perhaps they don't how to measure the value. Maybe the learning curve is too steep or the changes to current systems too great for new customers, especially when they didn't have the undivided attention of the venture team that accompanied the Beta Offering Stage. Indeed, it is helpful to examine the differences between the customer experience in the Beta Offering and the Market Calibration and Expansion Stages. There you may find the reason for customer resistance.

But there are other reasons, too. Some can be swiftly fixed: Your sales team, for example, may not have the right skills or tools, which means they either need to be trained or augmented. Or your competitors may have introduced a rival product since the beta test. Again, the venture leaders need to respond to the competition—but they need not immediately surrender. A new venture can make its early sales at full price only rarely. In most cases, pricing is not the real issue anyway. It is more likely that the venture has not communicated, or convincingly supported, the value of the venture's product or service to the target customer. Short of establishing that value and overcoming barriers to the sales, no price change in the world will make much of a difference. Sometimes, big customers know they have leverage over small suppliers and are simply trying to get the best deal. Instead, what the venture leaders need to do during this stage is to tweak and make small changes in the product/service offering, marketing mix, sales approach, and customer service, with an eye to increasing the venture's appeal to early customers and building positive exposure, "buzz," and sales momentum.

The Platform

As the venture prepares to launch its first product or service, the platform remains the basis by which it is delivered. The venture team has to resist the temptation of focusing exclusively on its first product, even as it responds to customer response and other information. Indeed, even as the team is introducing and stabilizing its first product or service, they must be developing the second one. They must also be sifting through market response to catch hints of additional product or business opportunities that the platform might enable. Questions the venture team should ask themselves about the platform now include the following:

- Are product development and marketing meeting weekly to review schedules, changes, and market feedback?

- Is the product achieving expected performance goals?

- Is business scaling/growing according to the plan?

The close, coordinated relationship among the senior team—which should have already been established during the earlier stages of the venture—must continue once the venture goes to market. In weekly meetings, the venture leadership must now examine lots of new data. There will be a continual and heavy flow of market feedback from customers, partners, vendors, investors, and analysts. The question is how to efficiently gather, analyze, and act on it. And even then, every department within the venture has a specific perspective and agenda related to it. For example, marketing will explain that more resources need to be devoted to broadening the reach of the product. Finance will insist on cost controls. Product development will want to add new features or services quickly.

None of these arguments will be easy to ignore. But the venture leaders should establish certain priorities. The business process and information systems established for this type of critical decision making are vital for getting the venture "engine" running smoothly and efficiently. What results from this superstructure is the process and connectivity to enable the venture team to get, share, and make high-level venture decisions based on market feedback. They must screen, categorize, and prioritize bugs, key product features, thoughts for next products or services, tips for marketing and sales improvements, bottlenecks in installation or delivery processes, whole product "completers" for customers and partners or things that fall into the category of custom development for a particular segment or marketplace, and so on—as well as information that is interesting but nonactionable in the venture's current stage (and that may be more appropriate to a partner or other referral source).

Then how does the venture team decide what merits more attention over some other item? This is one of the important aspects of the venture CEO's job: ultimately driving, arbitrating, and managing the creative conflict and decision process across different departments in the venture.

The question every venture wants to know at this stage is whether its new product or service is delivering on its value proposition. Is it reducing a customer's costs? Is it introducing new efficiencies in the market? Is it delivering on the value proposition as forecast? The venture cannot be a passive observer in answering these questions. It must continually return to customers and measure performance as deeply as possible. Ideally, the Beta Offering Stage allowed the venture to work closely with companies to see how they actually used or did not use the product/ service. Now that it is available in an open and competitive market, the venture should go back to those customers and others to see their usage patterns and measure their satisfaction. In fact, where possible, this data-collection capability should be built into the product or service so that the customer's effort is minimal. For example, a Web-enabled venture that designs coupon programs to connect merchandiser to retail site to customer should have a built-in tracking mechanisms to automatically record descriptive information about the coupon use: when, where, how many, by whom, for what purpose, aligned with what other programs, and so on. This type of information becomes vital for analysis and supportive proof points on the venture's value propositions to its customers and partners.

The approach differs considerably from merely sending out customer satisfaction surveys. Understanding performance should take on the same level of meticulous probing that was used in the segment-of-one marketing we described earlier. Customers who report themselves as "very happy" with a service may not be using the service in the intended way. That could be good or bad news, but the venture team must observe it closely to understand it. Indeed, many companies we have worked with find that the greatest source of inspiration for innovation is when customers "misuse" the venture's service.

That is why understanding customer habits becomes a preoccupation of the venture leadership at this stage. There are the real behaviors of the first targeted customer segment to track, along with all its variations, as well as the next and subsequent segments. Is the prioritization of customer segments still correct? One clue: Customers in different segments often respond differently to the same attribute or feature of a product, because of the different profiles of their use. (Remember those customer/application profiles and the Market Segment Development Schedule? Here's one of the reasons they are so useful.)

We worked recently with a financial services company that was launching an online sales portal. The company spent a great deal of time driving down response time on a key customer question from ninety minutes to forty-five. During the Beta Offering Stage, half the respondents said they were satisfied with the improved response time, and half thought it was still too slow. What explains such differences? It turns out that the consumers for this particular service were two very different types of people, correlating with two different customer segments the venture had previously profiled, and each used the service for entirely different reasons.

In the next stage, even more segmentation is likely, and it is important to understand how each customer segment responds. Again, the venture team needs to approach customer research as intensely as it did when they were trying to identify the appropriate target segment. If at this point the team can better understand customers' motivations and habits, the venture stands a better chance of developing future products/services from its platform.

A crucial performance element for any venture will be delivery. If you make it easy for a customer to find what they want and order it, you had better make sure they get it. Thus a close alliance with delivery partners is crucial—whether they are software providers and Web-enabled vendors whose packages are integrated with yours or completely stand-alone, outsourced capabilities such as hosting or other partner relationships. Once market expansion begins, the venture should be ready with a complete, front-to-back process flow, points of responsibility, and tuned information systems to make sure the venture has real-time access and control on where orders are in the pipeline and how they're being handled. The importance of delivery to any sales venture suggests that, even when a strong relationship with a delivery partner has been established, it is wise to have a backup plan.

Once the venture team has appropriately calibrated the venture in the market, they're ready to expand it. But what does expansion mean? Instead of issuing revenue reports at the end of each month, helter-skelter, it is important for the venture to institute a formalized process to account for revenue during its first year. One key metric is revenue per salesperson per month. Using such a measure will allow the venture leaders to chart the sales team's progress, isolate nonperforming salespeople, and establish targets. If the venture fails to make its revenue numbers one month, the leaders need to develop a thorough explanation. If target numbers are missed, something is awry in the system—either in the plan or execution of the plan. Is the sales gestation period taking too long? If so, why? Where are sales breaking down? Is the contract so cumbersome and complex that it is discouraging sales? Or is growth being prompted by an unexpected customer? If so, are there more like them?

The purpose of these questions is to treat every point in the launch that is not working according to plan as a clue to a breakdown in the system or possibly an unanticipated opening in the market that promises further expansion. The box below highlights key elements of the corporate venture operations of Motorola.

CREATING STRATEGIC VALUE FOR MOTOROLA

Motorola Ventures (MV) is the strategic venture capital arm of the global communications and embedded electronics company. MV actively invests in early-stage companies with high growth potential in areas of strategic interest to Motorola's current and future businesses. Wireless LAN, broadband, smart cards, telematics, and next-generation silicon applications are a few of the technologies within MV's investment scope. Typical investment size varies from $1 million to $10 million per investment. The company maintains operations in Boston, Chicago, and Palo Alto.

This foray into corporate venturing, which began in 1998, wasn't the first for Motorola. In fact, the previous attempt was an arguable failure, mainly because the relevance of the investments strayed too far from the core business. Jim O'Connor, a managing director at MV, explains that today, strategic value is the key—both value to Motorola and value from Motorola. Without the ability for value to be added in both directions, an investment doesn't make sense.

Take, for example, Motorola's investment in Graviton, a provider of wireless sensory information networks. Graviton appeared to be an extremely attractive financial investment given bluechip venture investors such as Kleiner Perkins in prior rounds. However, it was the potential strategic value from a codevelopment arrangement that drove the investment decision. The complementary nature and potential from combining Graviton's offering with Motorola technology made the decision clear.

O'Connor stresses the importance of the noncash contributions that corporate venture groups make to new ventures. He also acknowledges that the private venture capital community, perhaps deservedly so, often knocks their corporate cousins in this same area.

But MV takes a unique approach with its investments *after* it funds them. The venture group is divided by function in three ways: business developers (deal sourcing), finance (terms and conditions), and venture managers. This last group is special. They dedicate the majority of their time to helping portfolio companies navigate the corporate hierarchies to ensure that they get the right attention. In fact, MV uses a three-champion approach to managing portfolio companies. One champion is the venture manager, the second champion is a senior business manager from the unit that sponsors the venture, and the third champion is the senior technology manager. In other words, they invest most of their time with a portfolio company after they finance it, not before, helping them with the operational issues of growing a new business and helping them navigate the complexities of large corporate partner.

To ensure that strategic value is being captured, the MV team measures it at very granular levels of detail. In keeping with the company's Six Sigma approach, MV methodically tracks incremental as well as long-term strategic measures, calibrating direct and indirect impacts on revenue creation and cost reductions—in addition to the market value of the ventures themselves.

The Market Plan

It should be plain by now that *marketing* during this stage of the venture means far more than promotion and advertising. It requires active, engaged systems for collecting customer data and measuring the performance of every marketing activity. In most large corporations, marketing is fractured into strategy, corporate marketing, and product marketing per SBU, with lots of standardization around tactics and campaigns. For the successful new venture, all these aspects of marketing are integrated as one, with business strategy continuing to drive "inspired" implementation, to build awareness of the new venture and its product/service innovations in a way that cost efficiently reduces the barriers to sales and builds a position of leadership. Continuous information collection tells the marketing team if they're succeeding—and establishes the channel that helps the venture leaders know whether the relationship between product and customer is working. Questions the venture leaders should be asking about the market plan during this stage include the following:

- Are customers validating product and business model performance?

- Is our marketing plan driving the sales plan, and are sales the focal point of discussions?

- Is customer service/satisfaction feeding data to marketing, sales, and development?

It is one thing if your customers are buying your product or service. It is another if they are truly integrating it into their operations and making it central to their business. In many cases, customers will use a product or service only briefly, or use it in isolated or stand-alone way. The goal of the venture, and the aim of the marketing and sales team, must be to get customers to embrace a product enthusiastically. Ideally the customers themselves will become the greatest ammunition for marketing, willing to tell other industry players or even their own customers with similar needs that they use your product. This is the venture equivalent of having computer companies place the "Intel Inside" sticker on computers that use Intel microprocessing chips as part of their hardware. What the venture should be actively looking for is customer validation that the product or service works and meets or exceeds the benefits envisioned. Indeed, the marketing system should also be geared to use beachhead customers to spread the news and subsequently use the product across their companies and/or communities of interest, expanding the kinds of use and possibilities for additional innovations and benefits.

It is sales' job to understand the specific dynamics of the customer buying process including all those people who impact the final sale. The sales team should also diagnose when and where others in the venture can assist. Driving sales at this stage becomes the priority of everyone in the venture—everyone who can help in a particular call or sales process should do so in a highly consultative way. Here are some examples: Sales calls on development to assist in a customer call, to help the customer size the integration effort required if the venture's product is to be purchased; sales asks the CEO to make a high-level call to an executive vice president who otherwise wouldn't make an appointment; sales asks marketing for additional evidence of specific application performance and customer references, or requests connections to other partners for sources of leads; sales even asks the CFO to reassure a strategic customer of venture's financial health. As we have stated earlier, word-of-mouth reference and missionary marketing and sales are the most effective means of building a "grass-roots" beachhead of early sales. This same technique, constantly refined, should be methodically applied from each segment to the next, building momentum and volume.

As the venture is introduced to the market, the customer care team becomes a hub of activity and market information. As we mentioned earlier, customer care in a new venture operates in a critical strategic role, not just a midlevel technical support capability. Because it is a key source point for customer contact, it provides a unique opportunity to better understand everything from typical user difficulties with the current product or service, to requested new features, to market program validation and research—information critical for refining just about every aspect of the venture's work and guiding just about every major program or initiative.

Customer care in a new venture is, in reality, a sophisticated and complex operation led by a high-level member of the executive team. It comprises different mechanisms and means of customer access, and it is progressively augmented by powerful software packages that provide a "dashboard" of integrated efforts: a toll-free number, e-mail, a Web site, and so on. The structure underlying it is critical in connecting the customer in the right way to the appropriate solution source, and in also gathering research and customer information for internal routing and analysis.

The greatest waste of customer care personnel is for them simply to "put out fires" on a one-off basis. This does nothing to reduce future calls of a similar nature from irate customers and yields little information about how the venture can proactively fix recurring problems. The worst possible solution is to leave customer care as an island. Instead, it should be a gauge of how the company is doing at any give time, providing solid indicators of where trouble lurks and pointers to future possibilities as well. If this department doesn't work effectively when the venture is launched, it can easily bring the rest of the business to its knees by leaving unhappy customers with unsolved problems, whether they be simple or complex. Dips in quality aren't easily tolerated by the venture in any department—but a high-quality customer care operation is something a venture simply cannot do without.

One of the keys is to make sure that customer care has full access to every part of the business and that it formally notifies every department of the venture about chief complaints and suggestions it receives. Customer care's leader should also be in attendance at weekly, high-level venture reviews.

The Team

Ideally, the new venture has completed the hiring of its core team in previous stages. In this stage, their individual capabilities and effectiveness as an integrated leadership team will be tested. The CEO, in particular, takes center stage in pulling everything together now.

At the same time, the corporate venture is expanding its hiring, as the rate of implementation of the business plan steps up during this stage, especially if initial market feedback is positive. Managing and pacing this growth and headcount become a major new responsibility. The venture may also undergo considerable disruption by transitions during this period. Employees "borrowed" from the parent company may be preparing to return to their old jobs. Consultants who helped start the venture may reach the end of their engagement as their full-time replacements are hired. These transitions force the venture to activate a longer-term human capital strategy as it starts to expand. The following are key questions the venture leaders should ask now about the team:

- Is CEO leading the business while delegating to the management team?

- Have we established paths for recruiting appropriate candidates? Are we bringing new hires on board at a rate that supports business growth, but that is in balance with our financial outlook?

- Are the disciplines working together as evidenced by meetings, problem solving, and cohesiveness?

- Is the board still active in recruiting customers, partners, and investors?

The CEO. The role of the CEO of a corporate venture is more demanding now than at probably any other time in the venture's development. The initial CEO/founder often gets switched out during this stage, as more senior candidates with experience growing and operating larger businesses are recruited to the role. On the inside, he or she drives operating performance and review, both at the senior level and throughout the venture, based on management by objectives or a similar system. The CEO must be able to arbitrate and optimally resolve cross-departmental conflicts and be comfortable making quick, significant decisions without conclusive data for support (by the time it's in, it's too late!). As each department is working furiously to build its capabilities and does its daily work in the marketplace, the CEO must also be integrating and refining the high-level view of impact on the venture's strategic plan. The CEO must now also learn how to actively manage the venture's board of directors. On the outside, the CEO continues to make high-level sales calls and strategic alliances. He or she is the venture's chief evangelist and industry spokesperson, building relationships with the financial community and acting as a resource to press, analysts, and researchers alike.

Seasoned, talented venture CEOs are not usually in large supply, given the unique mix of skills, experience, and leadership ability required. Most are highly qualified, senior people—but many are also first-time venture CEOs who are learning on the job. Typical problems that ventures encounter with first-time CEOs is that they get too much daily involvement, or too little. The micromanaging CEO can effectively tie up the senior team by refusing to delegate, so that decision making and venture progress suffer significant setbacks. Yet the completely hands-off CEO is not much of an improvement, letting the team flounder on strategic and cross-functional issues. The net effect of this type of management is a disconnection from the daily rigors of implementation: The CEO makes unilateral strategic decisions without having full understanding of their implications for execution, nor the true wear and tear on the team. The hands-off CEO might reasonably represent the mission of the venture on the outside but provide no central leadership and guidance to the operation on the inside. Corporate ventures need CEOs who deeply understand the business and start-up team integration and can get involved—to the degree required—in virtually any key decision the venture must make. That requires a person who regularly joins sales calls or key customer visits and participates in business development meetings. She or he must also be the chief contact for important partners, there to advise, to cajole, and to tie more closely to the venture.

The CEO must also act as the venture's key spokesperson, both for internal purposes and for external relationships. That requires a dedicated public relations strategy of talking with Wall Street analysts, the press, business forums—anything that promotes the unique features of the venture's platform.

The CEO's constant role is to coordinate the various parts of the venture to make sure they speak and communicate with one another. In most organizations there is a natural resistance to such cooperation, and the CEO must fight that tendency. During this stage, the CEO's weekly meetings need to create the atmosphere in which every division reports bad news and good news. In those meetings, he or she should solicit advice and observations from all representatives of the venture, with the goal of solving problems. If the CEO hears only upbeat status reports in weekly meetings, it's usually a sign that something is being suppressed.

The Venture Team. The venture team itself is expanding now at a rapid rate, in virtually every department, but especially in sales and business development, customer care, operations, and product management. Development continues to fill out in terms of maintenance on the present product/service and starts to gear up for the next release. If this is a corporate venture, governance with the parent must be working to allow the venture to recruit qualified personnel, compensated at market rates for their talents. Throughout, it is crucial that the ever-expanding team continue to work cross-functionally and collaboratively, and in support of sales. It is vitally important that the CEO and team understand when a strategy is not working and when to make a change, by having thoroughly assessed missed, incremental milestones and by evaluating the implications to the strategy's future success.

Investing in headcount in a way that doesn't get out too far ahead of the venture's progress and sales ramp is one of the delicate balancing acts the executive staff has to manage. Overly aggressive growth poses another danger: that the venture's culture, business processes, and systems are not yet well enough established for controlled growth.

The Board and Advisors. The board of directors or advisors for the corporate venture takes on more importance once the venture is launched. Indeed, it should continue to serve as the informal management team, providing advice and counsel to the venture team, working out problems with partners and with the parent company as progress is made. The board also has the advantage of having a critical distance from the venture. At launch time and as the market expands, members of the venture who have been working at full capacity to complete their work will not have an unbiased perspective on progress. The board members bring that perspective, along with seasoned experience, to the interpretation of implementation progress without getting involved in the day-to-day operations.

The CEO is responsible for keeping the board actively involved, using them to their best effect in service to the venture—whether it be guiding them through a difficult partner negotiation, advising them on lead management and conversion to sales indicators, questioning and revising the financial plan and strategy, recruiting senior hires, or referring high-level customers. For the CEO, maintaining this contact with the board will often mean short, focused meetings, impromptu conference calls, and private consultations with individual members. For its part, the board should be querying the CEO and the venture about the impact of every new batch of data. At least one of the board members should have experience in venture sales and marketing so he or she can independently judge the performance on those fronts. The board should, as a result of its close involvement, be in sync with the venture's outlook for the next twelve months, with a detailed view of expectations driving the next several quarters.

Board members' focus and attention to the venture are heightened, not surprisingly, if they also have a financial stake in the new business through some equity interest. Such an arrangement should be made at the outset of the relationship but clarified and reconfirmed as the business goes to launch.

Ultimately, the difference between a good and a bad board can make the difference between the success and failure for the new venture. And what can make a difference between a good and a bad board is its composition: ideally, experienced start-up people will complement board members who are financiers or area specialists. This level of expertise is particularly important when the CEO and some portion of the venture team are inexperienced; that way, the directors or advisors can help guide the venture leadership in appropriate decision making and allocation of resources—in essence, advise them on what to sweat, what not to sweat, and when. Seasoned board members can also be invaluable at this stage of the venture's development, in providing access to their infrastructures and in helping to recruit or vet job candidates.

The Financing

The rate of spending goes up exponentially as every cylinder of the venture is now firing: Every department is in full-bore operation. The venture team measures the overarching financing plan against reality now, and begins to look for indications of the next round of financing. If difficulties are going to arise with the parent, now is the prime time. Thus the VBO needs to be most active in its role on the venture's behalf in this fourth stage.

As it prepares to launch its first product or service, the corporate venture should be closely monitoring its cash, typically with enough of a buffer to cover at least three months of operation (equivalent to the amount of time it takes to efficiently close another round on the outside). At the beginning of this stage, it is not unusual for sales to be slower and for the burn rate to be higher than expected. Even if the venture was funded from the Beta Stage through to the first year of commercial operation (which might have been the case if a corporate budgeting cycle were involved), it still needs to draw down additional capital, based on meeting milestones or successfully recasting funders' expectations. One thing is for sure: Raising money is invariably time-consuming and arduous for most ventures, and especially so now, when it distracts the focus of the CEO and leadership team at a time that's critical for building the business. But if the venture navigates this calibration period successfully and is poised for expansion, it should prepare for raising the next round to finance that expansion. Questions to ask about money during this stage include the following:

- Do our control systems indicate that the business is scaling/growing according to plan?

- Does our management team agree on the "final" funding strategy?

- Are our governance systems with our parent/investors enabling freedom without restriction?

The most basic question a venture must ask at this stage is whether it is collecting revenue. If not, finding out why becomes a priority. The problem may be unrelated to the volume of sales but related rather to a lack of coordination among sales, delivery, billing, and collections. That is why it so crucial to make sure that the various components of the venture work in concert. What ventures need during this stage is a carefully measured pipeline that indicates how many sales contracts should trigger what level of increase in production.

Venture leaders should try to avoid the boom-and-bust cycle so common with large corporate management. Slowdowns result in sudden layoffs and then, when better times come, management has to scramble madly to find employees. The corporate venture must instead look for imbalances in the pipeline early on so that as the company grows, these advance-warning measurements are already embedded. When it works best, growth triggers are tied to and integrated across all functions of the venture—business development, sales, delivery, new product development, marketing, human capital/recruiting and finance—so that the venture grows not in sporadic spurts but in a balanced way, as a whole.

At the beginning of this stage, the venture should have raised sufficient funds to build, promote, sell, and deliver the product or service. More cash needs will arise down the road—and, of course, the successful venture will soon bring in revenue of its own. But soon the venture leadership and the parent company will need to create a strategy for the next level of investment. Will it exist as a stand-alone company and require more private or corporate investment? Will it be sold or acquired? Will it try to make an initial public offering? These questions make up the basic strategic decisions that a corporate parent and the venture must now begin considering.

The VBO's Role in the Market Offering Stage

At this point, the VBO should concentrate on bringing value from the venture to corporate, and vice versa, in five key areas. Remember, the VBO doesn't often do these activities; they must influence and manage the activities of others.

- The VBO must help close sales and continue to manage the "linkage" relationships, particularly if they are with the corporate parent or partners. This includes building the actual sales pitches that resonate with these corporate leaders.

- The VBO must help get all corporate contacts and value providers to the venture to perform according to agreements (usually, this means running interference when bottlenecks occur).

- The VBO must monitor the interim milestone metrics (e.g., sales pipeline, biggest customers, testimonials, and key reference support) that indicate the venture is on plan, and on the right path to future financial success.

- The VBO must keep an eye on cash so that the venture doesn't run out of money before revenues ramp or additional funding is secured, and it must be preparing to team with the venture's CEO and CFO to "sell" the strategy for the next round. (E.g., they must determine how much to raise, why, and from whom, and decide whether to obtain more corporate drawdown, invite other funders to spread risk, and so on.)

- The VBO must monitor the effectiveness of the corporate governance and investment committee process, presenting recommendations at this decision-trigger point regarding next steps and future value delivery for the corporation.

PROCTER & GAMBLE FINDS A TAILOR-MADE VENTURE

Dan Maurer had had a long and rich career in various high-level sales and marketing roles at Procter & Gamble. But by 1998, when he headed into corporate development and became a general manager of P&G's iVentures group, he had a start-up in his future.

The iVentures division was formed to address P&G's desire to experiment with new business models and leverage its existing (and underexploited) know-how. Several criteria guided iVentures's efforts:

- The new venture must provide direct benefit to the parent company. (P&G as a customer is a good filter.)

- Although financial return counts (as a scorecard for any business's success), strategic fit and impact are the first and foremost considerations.

- P&G must be ruthlessly objective in assessing its strengths (core capabilities and assets) and weaknesses (areas where the company is less expert or has no competency) in what it brings to the venture table. (This strongly suggests a partnering approach to venture investment and incubation.)

- The new business ideas need to be "big" ones, in order to get and keep P&G's attention. (It was not part of iVentures's charter to look at simple product extensions.)

These criteria led Maurer to focus on P&G's reservoir of expertise in marketing/brand management, a formidable knowledge base sharpened by continual learning, renewal, and incremental improvement over time. Clearly, P&G had great domain expertise and value to bring around marketing, fundamentals that were clearly extensible and of great value to enterprises across many different industries. On the outside, high-level skills of this type were available, but only in a limited way through customized consulting—a delivery vehicle inherently unscalable across the rest of enterprise and beyond, to its marketing and brand management partners and collaborators on the outside.

For Maurer, the vision of a new venture started to take shape around this challenge: How to scale this expert base of knowledge across companies and industries? Know-how plus enterprise software platform plus Web enablement. P&G clearly had the know-how, but not the infrastructure and software capabilities. Maurer's group immediately started to profile likely candidates and competitors, among them a venture called Magnifi in the market calibration and expansion stage that was in the marketing automation space, its clearest strength evident in the innovativeness of its infrastructure and software environment. "A start up with the right stuff," Maurer noted. And a start-up not already committed to a legacy architecture and point of view.

Magnifi's vision of the business and its potential was very similar to P&G's, and its capabilities were point-for-point complementary. Maurer decided that iVentures should make a significant investment, and soon a new company emerged from the intersection: Emmperative. P&G's "just-in-time" marketing and brand management expertise came over in the form of intellectual property, licensed in perpetuity to the venture. In quick order, Magnifi turned from a technology-driven company into Emmperative, a marketing software company supported by great technology and branded intellectual property . Emmperative delivers software that helps Fortune 1000 companies bring ideas and products to market better, faster, and more efficiently. P&G became a customer, joining Philips, Coca-Cola, and others; it holds its business relationship with the venture independently from its investment, in order to keep both types of relationships pure.

P&G's expectations for the venture? Emmperative will help "reinvent marketing, inside P&G and across the globe." For Dan Maurer? This was a vision and a venture so personally engaging that he "went over" to become Emmperative's CEO.

Notable Differences between Corporate and Independent Ventures

At this stage of development, the corporate venture often looks very different from its independent venture cousin in three key respects, which manifest themselves across all development dimensions:

- *Pulling the plug.* A corporate venture is more likely to be shut down prematurely if early sales don't materialize at the rate forecast. A "miss" in the numbers at this early stage is often enough to undermine the parent's confidence in the venture's ability to make its long-term goals, and it almost certainly invites micromanagement.

- *The safety net.* A corporate venture, especially one with significant corporate ownership or management, may not feel the same do-or-die urgency at this stage that the independent venture feels. And indeed, if the venture fails, the core team may not be out of work. The large corporate investor can often employ the key members of the team in a variety of roles, either in other ventures or within the parent corporation itself. This safety net is evident everywhere—urgency around financing, around marketing, around the plan, around the platform, and around the team. During this stage, this safety net can reduce tensions, and urgency, that might be more understandably present in a stand-alone venture that faces quick extinction should its market launch fail.

- *The propensity to change.* A venture with a strong corporate culture, versus one with a start-up culture, often does not like change, especially at this late stage. Change is interpreted as failure, not as learning and response. Independent ventures will do anything to survive, which means getting revenue at this stage, and that in turn usually means changing something, even something once considered central to the business plan. The corporate venture may be inclined to push harder on the same thing that isn't working (because the problem must exist in the market, not in the venture).

Notable Differences between Venture Investing and Building

Venture investing and venture building have more similarities than differences in the Market Calibration and Expansion Stage. The one exception might be a venture that does not have a substantial number of external advisors, directors, investors, or senior managers on board. Such a deficit is nearly always an early warning sign that the appropriate level of objective performance review hasn't occurred.

The key difference between the two is likely related to ownership percentage—the venture business office is likely to "own" more of a venture they built than one that they invested in with many others. The level of investment definitely correlates with how much influence they have over the venture—either how much they can help or much they can hurt. Corporate assets, and the effort to make those assets valuable to the venture, will usually be more available to a venture where there is a greater rather than lesser ownership stake.

SUMMARY OF "MUST-HAVES" AND "RED FLAGS"

MARKET OFFERING STAGE "MUST-HAVES":
ESSENTIAL ELEMENTS TO HAVE IN PLACE

- Performance of partners and alliances ensured

- Performance and cooperation from parent ensured

- First customers/first sales ramping as predicted (within acceptable ranges)

- Product/service development as continual refinement, "weeding and feeding" based on market experience (venture is now a continual improvement "engine")

- Next release on track for within three to four months of launch

- Calibrations and course corrections to plan based on real customer/market feedback across all departments

- Rapid expansion of team, especially for scaling delivery, service, and support

- Market experience, quality of operations, and relative "stability" of plan driving expansion of business (e.g., to new customer/market segments, new geographies)

- Exit strategy realignment

- Capable CEO, full executive team, full board of directors and advisors (including outsiders) in place

MARKET OFFERING STAGE "RED FLAGS":
FACTORS THAT DEMAND IMMEDIATE ACTION

- Fundamental assumptions about first product/service and customer behaviors prove wrong

- Venture doesn't scale: faulty platform and/or unworkable economics

- First strategic partners don't perform and/or next partners (required for expansion) can't be closed

- Continuous development architecture (systems and processes across all departments) falls apart: no way to keep up with response, or to adequately evolve with customer requirements

- No formal means of marketing/sales analysis from experience; no plan recalibration: control and operations unpredictable, "all over the map"

- Second revision of product/service late; first offering insufficiently unique to hold market
- Other control systems (e.g., finance, personnel) are informal at best, making scaling difficult
- Quality of product or service deteriorating with revisions
- Traffic reduces or remains flat: early adopters provide initial sales, but no sustainable momentum; second and subsequent segments aren't identified, or aren't interested (e.g., venture can't get beyond first sales)
- Parent's sales organization and channel partners at war with those of venture
- Team still incomplete in vital areas (e.g., lacking in marketing or Web capabilities; first-time CEO); no ability to recruit key outsiders
- Parent waffling on commitment to venture (e.g., funding; creation of equity; governance)
- Board inexperienced and internal; doesn't provide venture guidance and support
- Funding insufficient to ramp, allocated according to parent's budgeting process rather than venture capital investment guidelines
- Funding and review haphazard, not driven by venture-development milestones and formal governance

Corporate Assets Available to the VBO

Business Plan. The ability to plan ahead for the next stage of the venture is the key asset that a corporation brings to its venture. Most corporations have a strategy group that could advise the venture whether it should go public or how it can begin looking for a possible acquirer. The corporate venture, via the VBO links to corporate finance, treasury, and investor relations, often has access to high-level financial advice and counsel and a potent network of financial resources and partners.

Platform. When a venture platform and the corporate platform are complementary, the boost for the venture is particularly tremendous, and it makes the VBO's job easier. In vertical integration cases, the corporate investor acts as a natural supplier or customer to the venture. An example would be NBC's investment in Intertainer, an Internet-based provider of filmed content. NBC is both a supplier to and an investor in the venture, the platforms are compatible with one another, and the VBO needs to do little work to get the parent and venture to work together.

Marketing. Clearly the corporate parent can be a major force in marketing a new venture, relying on its partners, its distribution channels, and its sales force. But the parent's sales and marketing divisions should be educated about the venture well before this stage. The venture should be able to depend on them as allies in missionary marketing, even if their methods of marketing are more formal. Assistance can come in many forms, from simple expert advice to "feet-on-the-street" to co-marketing initiatives that piggyback on existing corporate initiatives.

Common Mistakes: VBO Beware

Business Plan. The business plan will most assuredly change now that the venture is "in market." Yet when a large, established company changes its business plan, it is often perceived as an indicator of ineptness. The VBO must be an advocate of these kinds of changes for the venture (up to a point, anyway) and insulate it in such a way that the venture is free to adapt its plan without premature repercussions. The VBO must protect the venture by educating the parent while still holding the parent's interests in hand.

Platform. At this stage, the VBO should ensure that the implemented offering from the venture operates as planned—for example, that it is truly compatible with the parent's internal platforms—or, if it is not intended to be compatible, that the parent still approves it. This is a conversation that the VBO must force between the appropriate product and service developers of both organizations and most likely ratify at the CIO level. Also at this point, the next product or family of products is under active development at the venture—so it is a good time to ensure architectural compatibility or independence.

If products/services are not compatible and were intended to be, it's not always the venture that needs to change—sometimes change is good for the parent. For instance, if a venture requires certain product information (for online searches) that the parent doesn't capture, it may be in the parent's best interest to capture that data, for its own customers' use as well as for the venture's use.

Marketing. Some VBOs make the mistake of not helping the venture get over the initial sales hurdle—and then penalize the venture for not delivering on its plan. Making the VBO understand the sales support the venture needs at this juncture requires considerable relationship building. Leaders of the VBO must actively spend time inside and outside the corporation to nurture business relationships and to help with these initial sales. As the venture coach, the VBO must attempt to stay one step ahead of the venture and perceive when sales are going to be an issue—and intervene ahead of that, aggressively if necessary. One VBO member we know actually sat in the office of the head of sales of the parent corporation to raise—and remedy—the sales organization's failure to support the venture in the ways promised.

The Market Offering: Key Lessons

- *Measure performance.* How a product or service succeeds in front of many "uncontrolled" customers remains an open question. It is imperative to determine whether the venture is maintaining its performance standards now that far more customers are using its product or service.

- *Get customers and mine them for data.* Customer care becomes an active hub of information. Make sure it isn't just putting out fires. Rather, it needs to be collecting information on how customers react to the venture, and then sharing and discussing that information with all venture leaders. The venture must learn how customers are actually using the product or service by observing them, using the same segment-of-one marketing techniques used during the first stage.

- *Synchronize operations with revenue.* Don't build it hoping they will come and don't forget to have it built when they do come. This is a tense balance—not getting too far in front, or too far behind, your skis. In any case, a venture needs plans for both modest and rapid growth.

- *Energize the CEO.* The CEO must be involved in every aspect of the venture, delegating operational issues but deeply involved in sales calls, business development meetings, and partner communications. At this stage, the CEO becomes the chief spokesman and evangelist for the company and the public face of the venture.

- *Think about what's next.* Market expansion is the time to think about what's around the corner. Venture leaders and corporate sponsors should be thinking about the next product the platform will produce as well as a long-term financial strategy.

CASE STUDY

market calibration and expansion stage

It all comes down to sales. When sales materialize, all is good. When sales don't materialize, all feels lost. In this latter situation, an experienced team can turn things around, the inexperienced team will be shutting down the operation.

Context

The Printing Company was one of the most recognized firms in the printing industry. With only two other competitors in a specialized financial printing business, the Printing Company was narrowly focused and very profitable.

For many years, analysts had predicted that its success could not last. Its specialized form of printing for the banking industry, for example, was bound to become obsolete as banking itself underwent changes. Yet none of these dire predictions proved true. Year after year, the printing business thrived.

Still, The Printing Company's executives understood that with their specialized knowledge and their vast, national printing facilities, the company was making a mistake by not trying to integrate technology and e-business to create a new platform for future ventures. Their thinking was crystallized in an e-commerce workshop organized for senior managers in the summer of 1999. In the following three-month period, they developed a "portfolio of options."

In January of 2000, the board of directors gave the green light to a first venture. The goal was to create an online printing service that would deliver customized printing of any sort, available over the Web for retail consumers. Relying on the corporation's sophisticated "mass customization" printing technology, a current corporate strategic partner for product delivery (the first of many partners to cover the intended plethora of products), and a design for a powerful infrastructure for Web ordering and delivery, the company believed that this first venture was in fact a platform for a series of future businesses—a "portfolio-in-one." And it envisioned becoming a central Web destination for all types of customized printing, regardless of product type.

Their goal was to establish a Web site, a business infrastructure, and a partner for billing and delivery within 120 days. That required building a team, and here The Printing Company executives proceeded with caution. They signed up just over a dozen corporate employees to work on the new venture, but with only a fractional time commitment. Initially, they retained an equal number of full-time specialist consultants to get the project off the ground and work side by side with the corporate members of the team. The intention was to move quickly to recruit and hire the permanent executive team, especially the CEO, but months into the intense implementation cycle, they had not yet hired any full-time staff.

That was an obvious problem, but in another respect, The Printing Company executives knew what they were doing. They knew that their own employees and managers didn't have sufficient start-up skills to run the new venture. Effectively, the consultants working full-time served as a shadow team to ensure that corporate team members were learning intensely on the job. But the parent company ran into difficulty recruiting from the inside, given the uncertainties around new ventures and the implications for job security. Indeed, in order to recruit from within, they had to offer their people a "snap-back clause" in their contracts, assuring them that they would have their old jobs back if the venture failed. Also, the parent corporation was not yet ready to create equity in the venture and offer it as additional compensation—which further complicated the status of internal employees recruited for the venture. Finally, the company just decided to pay the venture team members more, which was in turn was very unsettling to most of the internal HR procedures and pay schedules.

Through April, May, and June 2000, the new venture moved ahead with building the platform, recruiting partners, and doing focus groups and usability testing. The period culminated with a beta test of the online printing business. Its initial performance was underwhelming. The Web site itself was slow to load, and even under beta conditions, the venture team found they could not adequately produce the types of custom printing requests they received. But a bigger problem was looming: Those selected to be beta testers were "friends and family" of the venture, so their motivations and reactions to the site were not necessarily reflective of the targeted customer base. Results of the beta were thus likely to be inconclusive and potentially misleading—in short, a vital "miss." Because of the beta testers' likely biased behavior, the venture team could not get a realistic view of what was to come. They would find out only after going "live" in the marketplace.

The venture team felt the urgent need to show results and moved ahead with the public introduction of the venture and its first products and services. The marketing and sales campaigns generated a high level of leads. Indeed, response to initial advertising was four times the typical level, and traffic to the Web site was strong. But converting those leads into sales proved problematic. Many fundamental things now seemed to go wrong. Despite their prowess in 2D printing in the financial services sector, the venture ran into technical difficulties delivering the breadth of personalized products over the Web that had been envisioned. The delivery partnerships the team had forged earlier were not performing as expected—worse, it was not clear that they would be capable of doing so in the future. Having produced a complex development platform within 120 days was an enormous accomplishment in itself. But even the technical integration of front-end Web site and ordering systems to back-end ERP and other partners' packages proved much more taxing to pull off without glitches.

But the biggest surprise for the team was that they seemed to have "missed" with both the range and type of products they offered in the first place. Although they were building the complex infrastructure necessary to deliver on an enormous product mix, it turned out that customers gravitated to a just a few personalized printing products. The platform they created turned out to be far too complex and not nimble enough to adjust to new market data.

By August, the early sales volume was a significant disappointment. The Printing Company installed a new CEO at the venture, who looked at the results to date and concluded that many of the fundamental aspects of the business needed rethinking. In effect, the only choice for continuing operations would have been to take the venture back to the Alpha Offering Stage and thoroughly rework it. After due analysis, the new CEO chose to shut the venture down rather than let it run for a while, get more customer/market information, retool the business, and then "resell" it to management to get additional funds. The new venture officially closed its doors nine months after it began.

The Printing Company didn't look at the experience as a complete loss, however. It saw its nine-month experiment as helping teach the company about what is necessary to launch a venture, a base of education it hoped to use later. Company executives assumed that they could quickly put this new knowledge to use when times are right for the company to try again.

Bell-Mason Graph and Analysis

How did the Printing Company's venture score when measured according to the Bell-Mason VDF? A first glance at figure 8-1 communicates the severity of the problems, now in virtually every dimension of the venture. Let's take a look at them.

CEO

Filling the role of CEO even with a highly qualified consultant is a dicey move in a start-up situation. In the final analysis, he or

FIGURE 8 - 1

Diagnostic of the Printing Company

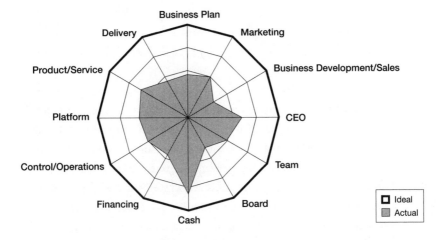

she cannot ultimately be more than part-time and temporary. The longer this situation persists, the harder it is to manage a transition. The CEO has to be the driver, and ultimately the "owner," of the business. Even with a strong recruiting effort underway, the situation wasn't being resolved: The team, the partners, and everyone involved with the venture understood that the full-time CEO was not yet in place.

Team

Nothing was wrong with relying on consultants to help jumpstart the venture. But The Printing Company should have moved more quickly to hire the handful of appropriately qualified, full-time senior management, or else delayed venture development until it was ready to do so. The use of fractional-time employees, and then employees with no equity stake and with a guarantee that their old job was waiting for them, was not appropriate for building the right start-up team.

Board

The board of advisors was comprised largely of Printing Company insiders, the shadow CEO from the consulting firm, a representative of one of the key partner companies, and one outsider. They were diligent and attentive, but they needed significantly more outside start-up experience and expertise to guide them through development and difficult decision making. More outsiders would also have brought more extensive, predictably more appropriate networks to bear, which might have helped as well.

Cash/Financing/Control

The Printing Company financed its venture in distinct stages. It provided $6 million to create a prototype and $5 million to bring it to market. It planned an additional $5 million to operate the venture for six months and then $6 million to scale the business. None of these numbers is unreasonable for a retail start-up. The revenue projected for the first year was $34 million. (Based on its later, brief experience with sales prior to its close, the venture team knew they would never have come close to approaching this figure.)

Business Plan

The venture created a business plan based on a set of starting assumptions but then didn't collect the type of data (through segment-of-one analysis or beta-test construction) that could have revealed that its assumptions were in jeopardy. It subsequently didn't know it was headed for trouble until it was squarely in it.

Platform

The creators of the venture initially believed that it would serve as a platform that would give The Printing Company the capability to personalize printing in many different product categories. The idea was that the venture would become a funnel through which a wide variety of suppliers would direct their products for customization. In practice, however, the first retail consumer target for the venture was more narrowly focused. First things first!

Although the printing company had the right idea about a portfolio of ideas, the senior management team didn't execute on that idea right. Instead of creating a venture business office with lots of new ideas running in parallel, they moved directly into one venture, as a "gate" to subsequent ones.

Product/Service

The venture was propelled so quickly from concept to proto-type to market in its desire to meet the 120-day development schedule that the venture team had little time to reflect about whether they had the right products for the right market.

Delivery

The venture had conceived a very broad spectrum of products and services, available for order online. Being able to deliver them called for a complex platform with highly specialized and inte-grated delivery partners—some of whom were clearly overpromis-ing their capabilities. So not only did the venture end up with a very complex and difficult platform architecture that ultimately didn't match the first customers' preferences, it ended up with one that didn't work reliably.

Marketing

The venture did not engage in enough granular, segment-of-one interviewing of potential customers to validate whether their cus-tomized printing business model would work. The team didn't ask questions that revealed much about specific buyer motivation. The marketing plan didn't call for continuous customer interviewing by the senior members of the team or by the marketing team. Many corporate ventures make this mistake—it's typical and often fatal. Corporate venture teams also tend to focus prematurely on branding (rather than first defining and validating positioning), and this venture was no different. The next issue was testing: Focus groups and telesur-veys were used exhaustively. But the team was testing not the products and services but rather high-level vision and branding elements—again, the wrong move. And when senior-level one-on-one interview-ing was undertaken, it was for usability testing. That is to say, the whole process of venture marketing was unintentionally derailed early in the venture's life and persisted through to the bitter end.

The response to the beta test was a clear warning sign. The initial positive response to advertising was ultimately misleading as well, given that many visitors to the Web site did not want to pur-chase the particular mix of products.

Sales

The inability to convert leads to sales, once the venture was introduced, was confirmation of the "miss" in the customer preferences and product mix. Even then, if sales had ramped slowly, the figures would not have necessarily been disastrous. Nevertheless, misconceptions of customer behavior and buying motivation were far more dire for this venture.

Epilogue

The Bell-Mason VDF helps reveal the many things that The Printing Company failed to do with its venture. In truth, its platform was an enabler looking for a "killer application" to find it. Had the venture team explored target customers' behaviors and motivations more closely and continuously, on a one-to-one basis and at a senior level, or even if they had heeded the later warning signals in the Beta Stage, they might well have been able to forestall the venture's demise. Importantly, though, the venture would have had to rearchitect its current strategies and business model in order to do succeed—and corporate overseers weren't likely to have patience for hearing that, particularly when a venture business office didn't exist to aid in the translation.

Part III

capturing strategic value

9
ensuring the future of corporate venturing

extending the VBO

Not everything that can be counted counts and
not everything that counts can be counted.

ALBERT EINSTEIN

In the telecommunications industry, extraordinary technological advances at the core of the network, such as speed of data transmission, have not made it out to the edge of the network, or our homes. Interestingly, they've made it close, but the "last mile," as it's known, is expensive to implement, with uncertain profitability. Therefore, the telecom companies haven't done much. This gives the impression, at the edge of the network anyway, that not much of value is happening, while in fact it is, it just isn't visible.

Corporate venturing is like the "last mile." All claims for venturing's strategic impact to the corporation are for naught unless they can be efficiently delivered and incrementally measured in the "last mile"— translated back and connected to the corporation's core capabilities and businesses, augmenting and extending the corporation's reach.

For an independent venture capital firm, turning an investment into a greater than "multiple X" financial return over three to five years is success. And, unlike a corporate venturing group, an independent VC's financial-only objective makes this return an unqualified success. The corporate group must operate within a focused strategic investment map, a framework that inextricably links it to an existing base of the parent's core businesses and future expansions. Thus the corporate venturing group must define success differently. Simple financial targets get you only partway to your ultimate goal. The real measure of success lies in the strategic value the investments generate, and indeed, the ability to measure and capture that value.

Unfortunately, this strategic value is often hard to measure and capture, particularly when it doesn't fit nicely into the typical quarter-to-quarter performance expectations associated with mature, public companies. Nonetheless, constructing a framework for measuring incremental strategic impact is crucial if the corporate venturing program is to take its place with other primary vehicles for growth in the corporation. Without this "last mile" appreciation, the corporate venturing program is likely to fail in its mission, and be reduced to the kinds of start-stop action that has so plagued it over the past several decades.

We need a new way to talk about specific VBO performance, about its ongoing progress in furthering the corporate agenda. This chapter will explain how to do three things to get on that path:

1. Identify and measure strategic value against goals

2. Use venturing as a catalyst for corporate transformation

3. Expand the reach of corporate venturing

Identifying and Measuring Strategic Value Against Goals

Measurement of success is key to sustaining the VBO. This is the prime area that invariably sinks corporate venturing programs, or sustains them. The financial value from investing in a new venture is not unimportant, but it is more like immediate "table stakes" in service of the greater measure for most VBOs. Understanding where and how strategic value is created, and then being able to measure it, is essential for the VBO to defend its funding—which it must be prepared to do on a continual basis. Changes in the economy, the venture portfolio scorecard (especially the "misses"), the parent's management team, investor perceptions, and even customer perceptions—all are frequently cited reasons to "rethink" the current value of, and continuing need for, the corporate venturing group.

Some types of value challenge traditional measurement, such as the value that the corporate venturing unit brings to other innovation groups, such as M&A, R&D, and corporate development. As we'll discuss later in this chapter, Cisco Systems uses venturing as a precursor to and filter for M&A. Other organizations use it as a source for high-level, new business development and joint product development. And value is added to the organization in a number of other ways: for example, by overall increases in innovation, learning capabilities, market intelligence capabilities, brand equity, and recruiting attractiveness. Venturing value is often indirect but potent in serving these ends, and we can often see evidence via cases and proof points rather than with traditional statistics.

Direct and Indirect Measures of Strategic Value

Before going any farther, we should qualify what we mean by the terms *strategic value* and *transformation*. Measuring financial value is straightforward—total returns divided by total investment, taking into account the time value of money. Defining strategic value is more complex because it can be measured both directly and indirectly. The direct measures include line items normally found in project justifications such as expected cost savings or expected revenue increases from new products or new markets. We can view the indirect measures as the leading indicators for the direct measures; they might include things such as percent of suppliers using a new service or changes in customer satisfaction from using a new service. Indirect, strategic measures may also include things extremely difficult to calibrate, such as increases in the level of innovativeness at a company or efficient learning about new technologies or markets. Table 9-1 summarizes some of these metrics.

For most corporate venturing programs, indirect strategic value outweighs direct financial value. Because overall financial returns for most

TABLE 9 - 1

Examples of Strategic Metrics

	VBO Metrics	SBU Metrics
Direct	• Cost savings • Revenue enhancements • Investment Rate of Return (IRR) vs. Cost of Capital vs. VCs • Market Value • Real Option Value	• ROI from integrating portfolio company products • ROI from new product/service via portfolio company
Indirect	• Percent of customers/suppliers using portfolio company products • Number and size of new markets entered • Months of market advantage from new products or technologies or partnerships • Number of SBU business proposals filtered and launched • Number of deals "pipelined" for M&A or R&D	• Percent of revenue or cost structure influenced by portfolio company products • Months of business advantage and competitive lead • Number of new leads/qualified prospects • Number of new customers (conversion rate) • Increase in revenue per existing customer

venture capitalists are widely reported to fluctuate in the 20 to 30 percent range, the strategic return would need to meet or beat that hurdle. Consider one example of a supplier who invested $1 million in a plastics industry exchange in 1999. The financial hurdle, after return of principal, would be a $200,000 to $300,000 return. In several instances, this supplier was able to unload nearly obsolete inventories, albeit at a huge discount, that would otherwise have gone unsold and been written off. The "strategic" return, in this case, is yielding several million dollars per year. So without the venturing group, the industrial company would not have had a relationship with this venture, nor a mechanism for moving obsolete inventory.

Measuring strategic value is necessarily less formal, but it is critical that companies ask themselves whether their investment has had a positive impact on their overall strategy. Since it began venturing, Eastman Chemical has invested in twenty-two different ventures. When the company began measuring the strategic value of these projects, it discovered that eighteen of them—82 percent—had created a service or product that their own customers or strategic partners had used or adopted. Clearly, Eastman Ventures had created strategic value.

In practice, parent companies that oversee corporate ventures need to devise a set of measurements, approved by senior management, that can be applied to all business units as well as to the company as a whole. This is the way they can assess whether the corporation itself has been transformed by its ventures. Ford Venture Capital Group (an extension of Ford Motor Company), for example, will not make an investment based purely on the potential of direct financial return. Rather, it evaluates prospective venture investments against four strategic criteria:

- Investments that will benefit the end consumer

- Investments that enhance shareholder value as soon as possible

- Investments of low-asset intensity (the last thing an auto manufacturer needs is more assets on the books)

- Investments that are counter-cyclical to the core business

In the first year and a half after its launch in the early spring of 2000, several B2B exchanges approached Ford's Venture Capital Group with a business case that could reach second-, third-, and fourth-tier suppliers that Ford wasn't reaching directly. But, Ford got out of the business of managing relationships completely down the supply chain a long time ago. They reach them because we utilize first-tier suppliers like Siemens to manage those relationships. The days when they vertically integrated down to owning coalmines and steel mills are long over.

One note on the important, but difficult-to-measure, value of first-mover advantage: By leading customers and suppliers down a mutually beneficial trail, a company achieves the psychological benefit of becoming a quasi-consultant to everyone in the value chain, bolstering relationships and brand. This also calls for measurement of not just the technology or product's impact on a company's own costs, but also its impact on costs to suppliers and customers. Reducing the customer's cost of selling increases market share. Reducing suppliers' costs creates economies that flow throughout the chain, the same goal that Ford pursues by providing its purchasing power to its suppliers. Table 9-2 lists more examples of strategic investments in a variety of industries.

TABLE 9 - 2

A Wide Range of Strategic Investments

Strategic Objective	Investor and Venture	Result
Reduce cost structure	General Mills and MarketTools	Conduct consumer surveys online, saving money
	UPS and Savi	Use RFID technology to track shipments
Differentiate product or service offering	McDonalds and eMacDigital	Use software to improve customer experience in payment process
	Ford and Telcontar	Integrate superior telematics technology for vehicle navigation systems
Enter new markets	P&G and Magnifi	Enter the Fortune 1000 marketing software and hosting arena
	TRW and RF Micro Devices	Enter wireless semiconductor market

Source: Information on ventures and results is from the corporate Web sites of the companies listed.

Failure Redefined, and the Learning Cycle

One of the most difficult to quantify strategic measures is learning and its impact on performance. Yet it may be the most important for sustaining performance improvement. Every VBO must understand how to find the silver lining of learning in the dark clouds of a failed venture. Remembering that most new venture investments, internal or external, have a higher rate of "miss" than "hit," the VBO needs to have a process and plan in place for handling the issues associated with everything from legal to public relations to the corporate parent management. But burying failure and moving on—a traditional response of corporate management—is neither reasonable nor practical for the VBO. The VBO has to show that even ventures that don't succeed on their own can still bring value to the corporation—through the corporation's absorption of the venture's technologies or software or other products, learnings about a given marketplace and its infrastructure, critical access to new customers and insights into their requirements and behaviors, new partnering prospects via the venture's alliances, even access to new talent pools and networks . . . just to name a few.

Here's a specific illustration: A corporate venture we worked with was attempting to provide a new kind of financial investment service online to a specialized set of customers. The economic environment worsened, along with the customers' desire for the service. The venture could no longer support itself, and the parent pulled the plug. But that wasn't the end of the story. The parent company repurposed many of the elements of the venture, including key people, to build an online extension of a current service offering in-house. It absorbed the e-commerce platform the venture developed, along with much of its specialized financial instruments and online capabilities.

As to the venture "misses" themselves, the start-up world is all constant trial and error in uncharted territories. Build an assumption; test the assumption; refine the strategy based on the test results. Veterans of the start-up world have long contended that you learn a great deal more, much more quickly and cost-efficiently, from failure than from success. The idea is to reduce the risks and total amount of funds around those losses, not by constraining the number of the start-up "experiments" themselves, but by funneling lots of them through a progressive selection process, across all stages of development with a specific framework to guide weeding and feeding. Maintaining a detailed database comprising each portfolio company's progress, starting with the review of its first business plan and due diligence process, is critical to ongoing analysis and constant refinement of the VBO's operations and expertise.

VBOs that bring this level of critical self-examination to their ventures can educate themselves at three levels:

- *Learning about venturing.* What did the VBO staff learn about venturing that they didn't know before? Why did the venture fail? Were there problems in the team? Was the platform too ambitious? Was it a bad market, or a bad business model?

- *Learning about investing.* What did the VBO staff learn about their own investing prowess? Did they get in at the wrong time? Should they have got out earlier? Was the venture assigned a bad valuation?

- *Strategic learning.* Could the corporation learn anything about its own industry? Did it learn anything about demand for its other services? What insight did it obtain into its own customers and their needs? Did the company learn anything about its own business, including its processes? What can the company learn about its own strategic reasoning for venturing?

Use Venturing as a Catalyst for Corporate Transformation

This discussion is one of the most important in this book: How does a company transform itself using venturing as the catalyst? It's one thing to expect transformation; it's another to actually make it happen. This section deals with the techniques that VBOs use to catalyze corporate transformation:

- *Evolution, not revolution.* Transformation in large organizations is not likely to occur quickly—it is more likely to be the cumulative affect of many incremental changes.

- *Using early adopters.* External and internal customers and suppliers are vital to work alongside the VBO, with the new venture to shape and validate its offering.

- *Using acquisitions.* Once the new venture reaches a stable level of maturity, the corporate venture group, along with the relevant SBUs, need to make a decision about what to do next. Should they exit their investment, should they acquire the entire company, or should they continue as is indefinitely?

Transformation by Evolution, Not Revolution

To many, the notion of corporate transformation conjures up the image of a complete overhaul, as though the company turns around on a dime to embrace a new business model, a new line of products and services, or entirely different technologies and delivery channels. The reality is that a large business cannot quickly or radically change behavior built up over decades of experience among thousands or tens of thousands of people. A corporate revolution is more likely to be the end result of years of evolution. Like a journey of a thousand miles, it is made up of a series of small steps.

American Express, for example, bears little relationship today to the freight express service that began a century and a half ago. Its transformation into a financial services giant took decades, and it was achieved not through a strategic plan for radical change but through a series of small sustaining steps across surrounding business adjacencies in response to business challenges and opportunities.

American Express took the first step in the early 1880s, about thirty years after its founding. Facing a threat to its existing cash-shipping services business from newly introduced postal money orders, American Express introduced its own money order, leveraging its network of offices and its brand (which symbolized a sense of security to consumers).

Ten years later opportunity presented itself when the CEO took a European vacation. Finding it difficult to cash his letters of credit on the continent, he returned with a determination to broaden the company into a further adjacency. Soon the company introduced the American Express Traveler's Check. By contributing to the company's reputation for solving customer problems, the traveler's check provided a bridge to growth into the travel services business.[1]

American Express's decades-long transformational trek is representative of the way companies transform themselves—over time, in response to threats and opportunities, growing on the basis of accumulated expertise, technologies, brand, and delivery channels.

Internal corporate transformation is a conscious, strategic path that company leaders pursue. But it is also a necessary response to changes in the external environment. Companies, after all, are rooted in the needs of their markets, and market needs change. Companies that ignore the fact that even the most durable markets ultimately undergo change are never equipped to transform themselves. Like so many companies that once dominated an industry, they find themselves and their strategy suddenly obsolete.

Keuffel & Esser, for example, was a company that enjoyed a long and profitable life cycle, beginning in the 1880s, when it obtained the patent rights to Edwin Thatcher's slide rule. By the 1960s, Keuffel & Esser had established itself as the leading U.S. maker of slide rules. Determined to look to the future, in 1967 the firm commissioned a much-discussed report attempting to forecast America's future one hundred years out. The report, *Life in the Year 2067*, failed to predict one trend that was crucial to the company: the advent of the low-cost pocket calculator.[2]

Keuffel & Esser didn't have to wait a hundred years to see what would happen. By the mid-1970s, pocket calculators had turned the slide rule into a museum exhibit. And Keufell & Esser did not and could not respond, because the competencies necessary to compete were beyond the company. In 1976 the preeminent maker of slide rules slid out of business.

The same failure to advance its core capabilities doomed the venerable typewriter manufacturer Smith Corona, which found itself scrambling to introduce a personal computer in 1992 in a joint venture with Acer. Too late to the market, Smith Corona filed for Chapter 11 bankruptcy in 1995.[3]

The experiences of Smith Corona and Keuffel & Esser demonstrate why a corporation cannot expect to continue forever doing the same things in essentially the same way, any more than an individual can expect to live forever. But unlike people, a corporation has the opportunity to reignite its life cycle, by addressing new needs, developing new markets, and revamping the way it does business. To do that, a company cannot just get lucky. Nor can it simply use its financial resources to bet on a promising new technology. A corporation, especially one with a stable history, needs a plan—a strategic map—that plots out where a new corporate venture would actually complement the core business and extend its key capabilities. The goal, again, is not merely to see a return on investment. The corporation with the stagnant business strategy needs to re-energize itself. By developing an ongoing commitment to new ventures that expand the horizons of the corporation, transformation becomes possible.

Using Early Adopters as a Catalyst for Transformation

With the creation of a VBO (as described in chapter 4), the superstructure is in place to determine the company's venturing needs and opportunities, leverage its assets, launch specific ventures, and monitor performance. But in attempting to transform successful ventures into catalysts of corporate change, the VBO faces a unique challenge: the challenge of melding two worlds. Outside the corporation it must deal with the venture world, a world attuned to change, ambiguity, and risk taking. Inside, it must deal with a corporate world focused on stability, certainty, and risk mitigation. Outside, it must sell investors, partners, and the markets on the value of the corporation's ventures. Inside, it must sell business units, corporate service departments, management, and employees on the value of venturing.

An outside start-up trying to sell into a corporation is free to focus on finding an opening and selling into it. Once it has identified the right source point, an outside start-up surely has its own unique struggles in getting corporate attention and commitment. But it doesn't have to concern itself with the rest of the organization, or even with the corporation's overall goals. Its success depends on the effectiveness of the innovations it is developing, within tightly constrained parameters inside the corporation.

The VBO, however, is still a citizen of the corporation. It shares a concern about common issues—such as price per share, corporate politics, and relationships with people inside the organization—even as it must account for its own success. It must sell change in the language of the corporation.

To begin with, it faces the challenge of adoption values. The opportunity to introduce a new technology or innovation depends on the economics of changing from existing means of doing things. A business unit may be presented with a brand-new technology with bells that ring and whistles that roar, with new applications that can solve old problems. But to adopt the new technology, it must abandon an old one—one that may have a large installed base. Ralph Waldo Emerson opined that "he who builds a better mousetrap will soon find the world beating a path to his door." Emerson obviously never heard of the network effect or the lock-in factor. Linux is more stable than Windows, it offers many of the same popular applications, it's free, and all the source code is available for it. Yet few Fortune 500 companies have adopted it. An entrenched system with an installed base is a tough hurdle to overcome. Customers are understandably reluctant to be at the front of a parade toward something brand new, only to find no one joining in behind them. The annals of new venturing are littered with tales of better mousetraps—the pain of change simply overwhelms potential benefit.

As we pointed out earlier, customers locked into the status quo make up a large and formidable barrier to innovation. The lack of interest in

3.5-inch hard drives by IBM and other leading customers in the mid-1980s was one of the crucial factors that discouraged Seagate Technology from launching the new model, sacrificing its early lead in the personal computer industry.[4] Early adopters are needed outside the company, among customers and suppliers.

Of at least equal importance is the cultivation of early adopters inside the company, to address the other legacy problem—the cultural legacy problem. While technologies seem to expand the pace of change exponentially, people's ability to absorb those changes seems to advance arithmetically. It is even more difficult to induce change in a group of people than it is among individuals, and the larger the group the greater the challenge. And if people need to unlearn things before they learn new things, effecting change is as difficult as it can be.

To find early adopters within a company requires more than just the organization chart—it requires an intimate understanding of the personal dynamics within the organization that only an insider can provide. This is where the rubber meets the road for the VBO, in its role as interior corporate navigator and potent partner in identifying the best contact points, building the case for the venture's benefit in language and applications familiar to the corporation, and continuing to manage and guide those relationships over time. If the VBO fails in this responsibility, it will be unable to deliver on its key differentiator to the outside venture community and interior corporate world alike.

Addressing legacy products, culture, customers, and suppliers is beyond the scope of the VBO to pursue by itself. Even a CEO cannot do so by fiat. One that tries to will soon find that acceptance depends on collective buy-in.

A client of ours learned that in a very short space of time. One of the company's new ventures had successfully launched a technology platform useful to its core business. But when the CEO sought to mandate adoption of the new platform by five autonomous business units, he was reminded of the difficulties that might be involved in gaining acceptance for it throughout the ranks. His response was swift and certain: "This is not a damn democracy." Just a month later, having felt the negative whiplash, his response was resigned and fatalistic: "I'd rather not make any changes than screw up the implementation of a major change and just throw our money and time away." The lesson he needed to learn was not that big change is doomed to failure. Rather, it is that change demands buy-in at the middle of the organization and among stakeholders, and that it also requires consistent support at the top. And that takes the right environment and incentives.

Some people resist change no matter how compelling the value proposition. As the CEO learned, in some ways a corporation *does* resemble a "damn democracy." Employees vote with their performance; departments and business units vote with their agenda. Middle-level managers accept or avoid responsibility; marketing and sales departments promote or ignore new products; IT sits on technological implementation projects that compete for resources with established systems. If corporate venturing is to transform an organization, the products, services, and processes it spawns must achieve buy-in *throughout*.

The need for buy-in means that it is not enough simply to mandate business units to embrace the technologies, products, or services that corporate ventures generate. It is not enough to mandate support for the VBO. The advantages of any change have to be sold to the business units. Support for it must flow from the top, and back up through the middle.

Many assume that innovation, because it is so important, is something that requires management approval. In fact, given the competing demands on senior managers' time and attention, working from the top is the most difficult way to achieve change. Change is often introduced without senior management knowledge, much less approval, providing a small-scale test of wider applicability. An example of that (described by authors Larry Downes and Chunka Mui[5]) was a decision by BP's regional manager in Germany to create multimedia shopping kiosks at BP's gas stations in the country, significantly adding to the strategic value. Using discretionary marketing funds, a small team outfitted the kiosks with digital technology and created strategic alliances with name-brand merchants and credit card companies. In a country with tight restrictions on shopping hours, the service drew significant consumer interest. And the entire initiative was driven by regional management: BP headquarters didn't learn about it until more than a month into pilot deployment.

Like the "skunkworks" concept in R&D, there is an underground aspect to much business R&D. If top management sets a tone that reinforces a commitment to innovation, people throughout the organization will

274 the venture imperative

feel more comfortable pursuing skunkworks projects at the implementation level.

So how do you find the early adopters within a company, give them aid and encouragement, and widen their circle? Early adopters tend to be risk takers who by and large are cultivated out of big companies. The challenge is to keep them in, capture their value, and inculcate their thinking throughout the ranks. If the failure of a good idea (or even a bad idea) results in someone being chosen as a scapegoat, with his or her career track frozen, the organization will be permeated by "innovation chill." It will become part of company lore, and an abject lesson recounted to anyone who considers taking a risk. The water cooler question will be, "Remember what happened to Fred when he tried something like that?" If a failed idea becomes a source of learning and is recognized (even celebrated) as such, it too will become part of company lore. The question will become, "I wonder if I can gain the same stature Fred did by taking a chance and learning from it?" If the performance measurement for all employees includes metrics addressing the rate of adoption, it opens up the overall risk profile by setting expectations for taking measured risks.

3M shaped a culture of innovation largely by rewarding people for risk taking and innovative successes, rather than punishing them for failures. In fact, 3M sets a target of obtaining 40 percent of current-year revenues from products that were introduced during the previous five years. Nokia saw a full 20 percent of its revenue in 2000 come from innovative new products and services introduced over the previous several years.

Driving the growth of the early-adopter segment within the company sets in motion an adoption cycle. Basically, early adopters inside the company have to find and cultivate early adopters outside among customers, suppliers, and potential partners. They need to be able to isolate an element in a pilot to test, such as the value proposition or adoption barriers. It becomes an essential part of the VBO's role—to champion the offerings of its portfolio companies among critical internal early adopters, and advise if not cajole them on the need for measuring and validating performance. This is true whether the venture was built inside or invested in on the outside. The VBO's ability to provide assistance in "getting the job done," delivering this ability to "run interference" and "grease the skids" for valuable adoptions, will determine how well the VC community perceives it (e.g., as a "go-to" partner of value in the deal) and how the corporate parent measures strategic value, and the VBO as its initiator.

How do you overcome the natural disinclination to adopt early? First, the core issue of adoption values must be addressed by the VBO. Companies have good reason to be concerned about the implied risk of overturning an existing system in favor of a potential Betamax. The added value being offered through any innovative product or service has to be determined to significantly surpass the adoption barrier. To overcome a large installed base, for example, improvement must be more than incremental; it must offer step-function improvement that yields at least two or three times the value of the existing function for the same or less cost—or alternatively, two to three times lower costs—and that delivers the same performance.

How to address the latent concern about being "Betamaxed" out? For example, customers and suppliers who signed on with Eastman in its webMethods venture, described earlier, could well have found themselves effectively boxed out of an alternative technology, and boxed in to an expensive technology that didn't match the rest of the industry. It is just as important for a company to promote a willingness to live with ambiguity among early customers and suppliers as it is within the corporate organization.

Because customers and suppliers are being asked to take a risk in being an early adopter, they expect commensurate reward. Early customers expect premium treatment, in terms of price, service, delivery, problem solving, and access to ancillary expertise. More often than not, a promise of premium treatment is also an effective deal closer, the last incentive in the final terms and conditions that provides the needed push to sign on the dotted line.

Using Acquisitions as a Catalyst

Most corporations are familiar with two traditional approaches for transformation: acquisitions and strategic alliances. If the corporation is acquiring, it can either fold the acquisition under the existing organization, or else fold the existing organization under the acquisition. If the corporation is establishing a strategic alliance, what role will the partnership play relative to the core business? We'll explore all these possibilities.

THE VBO CONNECTION:

LINKING BUILDING TO INVESTING

Early-adopting customers and partners are crucial for any new venture, and the VBO can play a pivotal role in facilitating those relationships. A good example is the three-cornered relationship between the global delivery service DHL, its Latin America–focused spin-off Allogis, and the Internet-based automated global trade management service myCustoms (since renamed Open Harbor).

In the late 1990s, DHL was confronted by the bureaucratic and logistical morass of cross-border shipment prompted by the growth of international business-to-business orders over the Internet. Many companies were expanding into markets where they lacked their own established infrastructure. Such companies demanded tailored expertise and technology to ensure seamless global e-commerce, including trans-border logistics, customs clearance, VAT and duty calculation and compliance, and pinpoint-accurate calculation of landed cost—that is, the full cost of getting a shipment to the doorstep. Accurate calculation of landed cost is especially important to made-to-order manufacturers like Dell, who need to know total cost on a transaction-by-transaction basis.

DHL had already grown its expertise in the Latin American market developing a repair-and-return program for computer industry companies such as Sun Microsystems, which had achieved sudden sales growth in Latin America and faced a need to quickly ensure postsales support. The unique factors involved in transporting to and from Latin America—characterized by a wide range of customs requirements and corporate ownership regulations—prompted DHL's regional office in Fort Lauderdale, which oversees Latin American operations, to propose spinning out a company as a third-party logistics provider (3PL) focusing on the region. The company, Allogis, would be able to absorb the disproportionate start-up infrastructure costs against small margins, a combination that would have had significant impact on DHL's own ROI evaluation.

While Allogis moved through testing and identification of a beta customer, the founder of myCustoms approached DHL's CEO regarding a potential venture arrangement. There were potential synergies: the combination of DHL's global platform and brand, Allogis's Latin American expertise, and myCustoms's leading-edge technology. The two companies struck a deal: DHL would become a customer of myCustoms, making significant investments in its own infrastructure (such as open-system, IP-based, XML messaging) to ensure interoperability, in exchange for an equity stake in the Internet firm.

While the jury is still out on the long-term results of this venture, early signs are favorable. And the logic behind it and the process driving it illustrate the potential for building on early adopters both inside and outside an organization: By connecting the investing and incubating operations, DHL made it possible for each to learn from the other.

- The creation of the spin-off Allogis was prompted by a unit within the company, the Latin American operations marketing department, demonstrating support for early adopters.

- The move was largely in response to the needs of a specific segment: high-tech made-to-order manufacturers that provided an early-adopter customer base.

- The venture offered potential learning benefits for DHL's owner, Deutsche Post, by providing proof of concept for myCustoms as a potential global vendor.

To get a sense of how a company can use corporate venturing to transform itself, think back to Sony's spin-out and reacquisition of Verant. In reacquiring Verant, Sony brought back into the fold the popular online role-playing game EverQuest. In its first year on the market, the game was able to generate $70 million. But what was $70 million to Sony? Roughly 0.1 percent of its total revenue that year.

What EverQuest did for Sony was not simply add another trickle to an ocean of revenue. It changed Sony's view of how to generate revenue online. With broadband access becoming ubiquitous, and Internet connections getting faster and faster, EverQuest—a virtual game with 3-D graphics that can be played by thousands at a time—created a new model for online entertainment. It prompted a shift to subscription-based games, a major departure from the free offerings based on advertising support that had formed the basis for Sony's online entertainment strategy up to that point.

Sony basically rewrote its old business model. With the reacquisition, Sony Online closed its New York offices and transferred headquarters to

Verant's four-story office building in San Diego. Verant became the centerpiece of the new division. Its start-up culture and atmosphere—characterized by little bureaucracy and lots of flexibility—was maintained. EverQuest's profits were poured back into the design of new online games, based on the EverQuest model. We can almost ask, Did Sony reacquire Verant—or did Verant reacquire Sony? The answer is that Sony acquired Verant's strategy, business model, and culture. Those were the real advantages of spinning out and reacquiring Verant, and they exceeded the millions of dollars in revenue generated by the division's first game. Sony realized the importance of the venture to its existing operations.

The challenge facing all corporate ventures is to create change that will spill well beyond the venture's own borders and into the rest of the organization.

Cisco Systems is typically cited as a standard setter that handles venture acquisitions well. The company is known for the way it has used venturing as a front-end filter to identify and qualify acquisitions. Its net effect: a means of attaining growth, a substitute for significant amounts of R&D, and a means of accelerating its own rate of transformation. And most acquirees will tell you that Cisco is a dedicated learner, absorbing what works and what doesn't in one acquisition and applying that wisdom to the next. The higher-level process works essentially like this: The corporate venturing group learns from the SBUs what its target areas on new technologies and innovations are, as well as the direction of ventures in these spaces. The corporate venturing group then begins due diligence. A minority investment in one or several ventures in the targeted area may also result. When the company determines that acquisition is the desired next step, the M&A group gets involved, and with guidance from the corporate venturing group and SBU, they consummate a deal. Cisco knows that the acquisition is just the beginning in the challenges to realizing value: most acquisitions fall apart after the deal is made, owing to an inability to assimilate. Cisco wants to integrate the entity into its operation as quickly and productively as possible—without killing it or slowing down the incumbent organization.

Using the example of Cisco's acquisition of ArrowPoint, a maker of intelligent content router systems for the Internet, let's look at Cisco's approach:

- By the time the acquisition *closes*, ArrowPoint is fully integrated in all Cisco systems (e.g., phone system, Web sites, product names and part numbers).

- The core ArrowPoint team is left as intact as possible. Then there is a focus on leveraging the Cisco sales force, field organization, and channels to boost sales. (ArrowPoint becomes a unit within the Cisco organization, and the CEO becomes the head of that organization.)

- In the last phase, the long-term agenda starts to play out, merging product, service, and enabling technologies into the core Cisco organization.

ArrowPoint is clearly doing better as part of Cisco than it would have done independently. Further, while other little guys are suffering and going away, ArrowPoint has actually picked up some market share points, even though the market is relatively flat at the moment, which should translate into strong revenue and profit growth as the business climate improves. There is also solid progress being made in leveraging the content-networking technologies across the rest of Cisco.

Another example of a venture acquisition illustrates a slightly different approach to capturing strategic value. As a Yellow Pages advertising firm, TMP Worldwide saw the Internet as an opportunity to continue to build on its strategic base. Moving into executive search through its recruitment ad creation, multiple-market placement, and direct-marketing and customer relations services, by the late 1990s TMP was already a business in transformation. In 1999, it acquired the executive search firms LAI Worldwide and TASA Worldwide to become one of the top executive search firms, claiming more than 480 of the *Fortune 500* as clients.[6]

Seeking to bolster its sales channel in the job-search field, in 1999 TMP acquired and merged The Online Career Center, started in 1993, with The Monster Board, started in 1994. As a jobs and career site, Monster.com became a classic exploiter of the network effect. As 3M founder Robert Metcalfe has observed, networks dramatically increase in value with each additional user, so that its value is the square of the number of its users—whether the network is fax machines, telephones, Morse code, or the Internet. In the online career industry, the network with the largest selection of jobs attracts the most job seekers, which makes it more attractive to employers, which reignites the cycle of growth. Monster.com grabbed the network advantage early, consistently scoring the largest number of unique visitors and job postings. (It is important to keep in mind that in the online job market, employers can list a job simultaneously on more than one site.) One of the best measures of market share is the total time users spend at each site. According to Jupiter Media Metrix's data for March 2001, Monster.com captured just over 42 percent of the cumulative time spent on career-oriented sites—more than four times as much as its closest competitor.

One of the greatest values the Internet sales channel brought to TMP was customer base diversification. With no single corporate client accounting for more than 0.5 percent of Monster.com's revenues, the site achieved a degree of insulation from the risks of customer concentration.[7]

Expand the Reach of Corporate Venturing

In chapter four, we suggested that the VBO have a business plan that would include its expansion strategy. The first step in executing on the VBO expansion is to review its progress against the original plan to understand if expansion is justified by results to date. How is the VBO performing against it goals? Has it achieved key milestones on the path to those goals, as it forecast? Without evidence that the plan is being achieved successfully, the case for expansion will likely be difficult. The VBO needs a detailed inventory of the various types of strategic and financial measures we cite earlier in this chapter, as well as an ongoing assessment of individual venture valuation and stage of development. To summarize:

1. Aggregate status of valuations of its portfolio (hits, misses, holds) and follow-on funds required to maintain it (a standard VC practice).

2. Strategic investment map coverage with the current portfolio (what's covered, what's not, what's needed), and active alignment with the corporation's core strategy.

3. Degree of integration of portfolio company capabilities within core businesses (includes harvested strategic value from specific portfolio company "misses" or write-downs as well).

4. Degree of active and measurable integration and leverage with other growth units, such as M&A, R&D, licensing, and corporate development (e.g., citing specific projects as evidence).

5. Status of other VBO deliverables to the corporation, such as education and recruiting (e.g., screening of internally generated business plans, with *n* number returned for implementation to appropriate SBUs; indirect leverage and learning for IT or e-business functions; newly attracting "A" type recruits).

6. Stability of VBO operations and organization including operating plan and control; productive and qualified team; formalized systems and venture business processes at repeatable level of quality; established network infrastructures inside and outside the corporation.

Managing the Portfolio

Corporations investing in a venture are ultimately going to have to come to a decision point: to step up their investment, to step down from it, or to step away. A venture company is not a dividend stock; one can't capture value from it by just holding on forever. A venturing company is going to have to decide that the venture is so important that it has to own it and integrate its value throughout the organization or decide it has already captured all available strategic value, either unwinding or reducing its investment.

A portfolio management strategy demands a continual rank ordering of all investments in the portfolio, with a process for culling out those that are less valuable both strategically and financially. It's important to keep in mind that this process demands *relative* assessment and culling. Even portfolio companies that are performing well—generating good returns and strategic benefits—have to be compared against the average. In a world of finite resources, results have to be compared against potential results that the same capital and resources could generate or put to other uses. In any case, planning the exit from the venture becomes as important as any step in building it up.

In addition to maintaining a comparative ranking, the VBO must measure investments against a set of decision triggers to determine whether to increase the investment, put it in a holding pattern, absorb it into the core business, sell it to somebody else, spin it off, or simply kill it. These decision triggers must be examined on an ongoing basis against every company in the venture portfolio that has been invested in or incubated.

Ford Venture Capital Group, for example, measures all its investments periodically, at least once a quarter. Investments are broken down into three categories: Investments that are on track are designated green; those needing corrective action are yellow; and investments requiring turnaround or liquidation are red. What are the criteria for a red alert? It could be financial, but it could just as easily be that the company isn't achieving its original goal for utilizing the strategic relationship.

When it comes to continuing, stepping up, or stepping down an investment, the parent company's decision has to depend on an assessment of whether it has captured all the value it can, or whether further investment can yield more strategic benefits. Here's another way of putting it: Has the investing company fully absorbed the transformational impact of the investment, or can it harness even more? Or is a continued financial interest sufficient and necessary to accrue or extract strategic value?

How to proceed with a portfolio company depends on whether it offers further value. At Ford's venture group, they may continue to utilize a venture company as a supplier, but unless there is some strategic reason to maintain an equity presence in the company for some potential insight or leverage, they'll exit the investment and try to maximize financial return.

Same Venture, Two Different Strategic Decisions. It's possible to see this question examined from two different perspectives in the case of a start-up called Newgistics, developers of software for the management of reverse logistics—moving goods from retailers or consumers back to manufacturers, such as in the case of customer dissatisfaction or damaged goods or unsold inventory.

One of Newgistics's early investors was USF Processors, a division of USFreightways, which runs a disposition service for returned items that manufacturers do not want returned to stock. As the next investment round approached, USF Processors had to make a decision: Do we make another investment, or stand pat and accept dilution of our stake?

USF Processors's early investment could be considered a success-in-progress—Newgistics was still in business. And it had achieved its strategic goal, securing access to a growing company and developing a tight customer relationship that offered the potential of significant revenue. At this point, continued investment appeared to be a pure financial play with little or no additional strategic upside, unless it were necessary to keep Newgistics in business. But, absent these further strategic opportunities, USF had no compelling reason to increase its equity position.

At the same time, another first-round Newgistics investor—the logistics arm of R.R. Donnelley, the printing company—was assessing its own investment from a very different perspective. Unlike USF Processors, which disposes of returned goods that the manufacturer is not interested in, Donnelley Logistics aggregates returned goods and transports them back to the original manufacturers and distributors. It serves as a collection point from all the retailers at the edge of the distribution network. This both-way logistics capability enhanced Donnelley's value to customers who used Newgistics' logistical software.

R.R. Donnelley had another consideration: a business unit with strong relationships with catalogers, who move goods out through the distribution chain and must be able to arrange for returns when necessary. A catalog customer of Donnelley is a natural customer for Newgistics, and vice versa. By enriching the logistics software firm, Donnelley was able to enrich itself. Having made an investment in a company that actively generates additional business, Donnelley had a strong incentive to ensure growth. Given this relationship, the company took an active role in advising Newgistics. That included making a senior executive available to the Newgistics advisory board, an executive with close relationships with firms in the catalog business.

For USF Processors, the decision not to make a second-round investment in Newgistics came down to the absence of a further strategic upside. For R.R. Donnelley, the connection to the catalog industry and logistics business provided strategic synergies that determined its decision to join in the second round.

Exiting Ventures That Are No Longer Strategic. Sometimes the lack of strategic fit between a company and a venture dictates an exit. In 1999, the CEO of Telogy Inc., a fifteen-year-old privately held company in the custom measurement equipment rental business, took a look at the dot-com gold mine and decided it was time to spin out an Internet-based venture company aimed at serving as an exchange in a highly fragmented industry. First, the move would unlock the door for investment.

As a business with millions of dollars of assets on the books in the form of rental equipment but little liquidity, Telogy could not yield sufficient value in the markets. Second, it was anticipated that establishing an exchange in the measurement equipment rental business would open both more supply channels and more sales channels, and create a more efficient market.

Telogy partnered with three venture funds in Testmart.com, an Internet venture that had been set up three months earlier. With 80 percent of its rental assets on subrent from Telogy, and access to company resources and systems, the goal was for the new dot-com to complement Telogy. Telogy became the start-up company's outsource lab and service partner, equipment repair service, and logistics provider.

But the relationship had inherent problems and contradictions. Margins from Telogy's inventory did not provide sufficient margins to support costs. To increase margins, it would be necessary for Testmart to buy its own rental equipment inventory, and break out of the original business concept as an exchange to become a supplier of private marketplaces. Increasingly, Testmart was competing with, rather than complementing, Telogy. Moreover, the relationship was not providing brand support for the new company. The venture's owners and managers recognized that a change in strategy was necessary, shifting Testmart from an exchange to a virtual marketplace. Linkages to the core business were disappearing.

What advantages did the relationship yield for Telogy? Testmart did serve as a customer. It also generated concepts for the Telogy Web site. But without a venture business office or comparable structure, absent a venture portfolio, and with the shift from the original business concept, Telogy ultimately derived little or no strategic value from the relationship.

Planning for the Next Phase of Growth

The VBO, like any new venture it advises, should aspire to grow. Intel didn't start its corporate venturing group by investing a billion dollars in the first year—but it does now. Boeing started its internal venturing group with roughly $40 million in the first year, or less than 1 percent of revenue, along with good access to the R&D portfolio. We've seen other Fortune 500 companies begin their venture groups with as little as $5 million to $10 million.

For the VBO, the overall review of its initial operation is, in fact, similar to the kind of progress assessment and review that takes place in the Market Calibration and Expansion Stage for the new ventures it nurtures. Like any business, the VBO has to earn the right to expand. Given a successful calibration period, a refined platform, and a degree of stability that will be "scalable" with quality, the VBO can look ahead to executing on the next strategic phase of its growth. Possible areas for expansion could include the following:

- *Business unit coverage.* The venture could extend past the first early adopters/business units to other business units, incorporating their directions and priorities into next-phase investment outlooks.

- *Additional VBO offices.* The venture could expand geographic coverage to establish local presence in areas where concentrated venturing communities exist or are being formed (national/international, depending on business direction of parent). The most successful corporate VBOs have established multiple offices, typically with anchor coverage in Silicon Valley and New England. The idea is to build local infrastructures of influence, thus increasing alliances, access to investment partners, and deal flow.

- *Investment partner outreach.* The VBO could invest in other funds and/or venture capital firms, and it could engage in fundraising among other complementary corporations and value chain members. The net effect would be increased funds and deal flows.

- *Supply-chain coverage.* The parent can play a broader role: from marketing partner to supplier to customer of the venture, for example.

- *Increasing the number and mix of early- to late-stage investments.* VBOs should get their "sea legs" before taking on too many early-stage investments, for example. While not as costly in funding as downstream, later-stage investments, early-stage investments are more difficult and time-consuming to get right—and riskier in terms of the end result. Experience and expertise can mitigate these effects.

- *Increasing the mix of incubations versus investments, inside and outside the corporation.* For example, the VBO could move from later-stage investments, where better-risk scenarios have also led to effective learning with other VCs, to building ventures based on internal technology, or vice versa.

- *Additional content areas of venture interest and lengthening strategic horizons.* Given coverage and accomplishment across the first strategic investment map, the VBO further coordinates with corporate strategy, development, M&A, and R&D to determine new or otherwise different points of interest in "adjacencies" and outlying areas to the core. With this may come extension on the time horizon or hurdle for return, from near to longer-term (near-term could be two to three years, and longer-term could be five years).

When the VBO reconfirms its next-phase goals, establishes its strategy, and defines incremental milestones (with detail around the next year), it should once again refine the business plan appropriately. It continues to serve as the VBO's central control document, and it provides an integrated view of the VBO's thinking across its operations.

Conclusion
corporate venturing

a new context for value

Big organizations can change. Nokia, GE, Sony and many other corporations are examples. But like a supertanker, a large organization cannot turn on a dime. That is where venturing—and a venture business office—comes in. A corporate venturing program can serve as a nimble pioneer and scout—a powerful tugboat leading the tanker, charting a new course and navigating waves of change to establish a clear direction in the technology economy.

Every corporation that vigorously pursues new ventures will be most eager to determine how it will prove and measure success. Too often companies declare failure before venturing has been given a fair chance, or accept failure without understanding how they could have turned venturing into a success. Even if they have managed the venture process efficiently, many companies have not given enough thought to how venturing can be integral to their core strategies.

New ventures can be powerful sources of direct or indirect revenue growth for the corporation. But as we have argued throughout this book, corporate venturing must earn its ultimate returns via a broader, deeper, more strategic role, closely aligned with the corporation. To define that role, a company must carefully examine its own operations, history, talent, resources, and needs. It must look at its core capabilities and current markets to see what adjacent opportunities exist. It must cast a fresh eye on the traditional parameters of its business to see where new ventures, unconstrained by the orthodoxies of the existing industry, might open new opportunities. To advance down this path, a corporation must pursue a venturing strategy that is conducive to innovation and long-range transformation, not merely the rare, ad hoc investment success. That requires a corporate venturing effort with four key characteristics:

- *Identity.* Corporations must create a zone of irregularity under the corporate umbrella, a sphere within the company where the rules are tuned to venture development and portfolio management, and many traditional corporate rules are suspended. This unit, the venture business office, becomes the central venturing resource within the corporation.

- *Cooperation.* The VBO requires the development of support throughout the organization if it is to succeed. By itself, a VBO committed to transformation—no matter how enthusiastic or skilled in ventures—can generate nothing more than the sound of one hand clapping. Ultimately, a company's ability to implement change depends on the willingness of the corporate business units to discover and capture the strategic value that venturing can offer. That, in turn, depends on a CEO and senior management team that encourage and reward business units that do.

- *Consistency.* Venturing, just like M&A, R&D, or business development, must continue in bad times as well as good. The fruits of venturing are reaped not in the current business cycle but in the next one, and after a weak market may give way to a robust one.

- *Evaluation.* Venturing is a matter of continually bringing an out-of-focus picture into sharper focus, learning by doing and viewing mistakes as part of the learning process. Strategic value is gained from assessing the factors of success and failure so that the venture process and VBO itself become a unique engine of continual self-improvement.

With the venture business office as a vehicle, value comes in the form of exposing the corporation to new expertise, customers, and technologies that, on its own, would have been impossible to achieve. The greatest impediment to corporations who have sought to venture—mostly in vain—was the absence of any consistent means and method, in which ventures could be promoted on an ongoing basis and value could be achieved in nearly every instance, even when financial goals were not realized. We believe that the approach outlined in this book helps redefine value for the corporation so that it can approach corporate venturing with less trepidation and more purpose. The result will be a VBO closely tied to the larger strategic objectives of the corporation, working in concert with other strategic growth departments and core business units, offering it new pathways to regeneration.

afterword

Technology will undoubtedly continue to change the economic, political, and social fabric of our civilization as far into the future as we can imagine. Interestingly, those changes are occurring more rapidly as new generations of technology leverage and extend old generations. The challenge for management is to navigate these highly volatile and uncertain waters and channel this flow, while simultaneously driving value from the current business.

I believe important lessons can be derived from the technology industry that is responsible for all these changes. Technologists, since the advent of Moore's Law, understand the need for rapid and continual improvements in the price–performance ratio of their products (the number of transistors per square inch on integrated circuits has doubled every year and a half since their invention). They also understand that this price–performance curve gets steeper and requires tremendous investment and creativity to sustain. From this understanding, the concept of the technology platform developed. The idea is that a base set of technology provides the foundation for generations of product, all with improved price–performance ratios. Intel's microprocessor platforms and Microsoft's operating system platforms are quintessential examples in the technology industry of foundations for a continuing series of products.

Today, this law must be applied to *all* types of businesses. And, in fact, it is often the de facto standard in many industries primarily because every business relies more and more on technology as a core component of product and service offerings. Take an obvious example by looking at what Amazon has done to the book business. It used to take hours, if not days, to find less popular titles by combing through bookstores, and then you'd likely pay a full retail price. Today, you can buy that book in seconds, at the best retail discount, and have it delivered to your door. In addition, you'll likely be able to find reviews on the book and recommendations for similar books at no additional cost, with very little additional time. These examples can be found in every business—with the most profound impact being in businesses that have deployed technology the most extensively.

Let us now extend the concept of the technology platform to non-technology businesses. The "business" platform is the foundation on which multiple product families or even separate businesses can be launched. It is the set of standards, skills, modules, and processes that form the differentiating and base intellectual capital of an organization and allow it to produce new offerings continuously. Sometimes the key element of this platform can be technology. Look at what FedEx is doing to virtually every corner of the transportation industry: using its technology to make near real-time track-and-trace the ante for playing. Or what ExxonMobil's Speedpass product is doing to expedite payment processing for any business (e.g., gas, fast food) where fast payment is important.

But be forewarned—platforms can fail. The road is littered with poor technology platforms, such as 8-track tapes, Betamaxes, and Newtons. And the lesson is important here: Bad platforms kill, good platforms launch. And by this very nature, a platform entails choices—after all, you can't be everything to everyone. These choices—standards, skills, modules, and processes—will enable or disable your platform. Fortunately, tools—some of which are presented in this book—are now available to calibrate the strengths and weaknesses of existing and proposed corporate platforms. Nevertheless, making the right choices is an extensive effort requiring the brightest folks inside, and often outside, your organization.

Enter corporate venturing. It is my belief that corporate venturing is a core element of innovation, which itself is a core element of the corporate platform. Innovation is the element of the platform that enables a company to renew itself. Corporate venturing by its definition is focused on the company "futures": taking options on new products or services or businesses that offer the promise of competitive advantage.

Of course, corporate venturing interacts deeply with other innovation elements, such as research and development and corporate development. Similar to a technology platform, the key to making this element of the corporate or business platform work is the architecture—as exemplified by its standards, interoperability, and openness. Numerous case studies in this book illustrate how real companies are beginning to do this right.

Finally, we must overlay the growing importance of new technology onto the survival of every business. Given that technology is key to an organization's competitive survival; given that most organizations have difficulty attracting and retaining the best technologists; given that most innovation occurs outside big, established companies; given that the magnitude and speed of change continues to increase in every industry, just as it has in technology for decades—with all these givens, it is imperative that corporations use ventures as one, if not *the*, core tool for innovation in the years to come.

Gordon Bell
Los Altos, California

appendix a

VBO business plan elements

- Five-year business plan *with emphasis on the next twelve to twenty-four months* within fifteen to twenty pages (not including appendixes).

- Executive summary, including charter and goals, vision, and value propositions.

- VBO platform uniqueness as basis for sustainable operation (e.g., venturing uniqueness with brand, key leverage points, and competitive advantages of parent, such as pilot access).

- Platform requirements and dependencies on parent corporation: strategic alignment and integration, compensation structures, governance, management oversight and support, make-buy-partner latitude, and so on.

- Venture building and venture investing scope with critical areas to explore, weak spots to shore up, and competitive scene (e.g., venture business processes, deal flow, investments, builds, inside/outside "pipeline," internal/external infrastructures, venturing competency and support to SBUs, competitive scene is quality and execution hurdle, other VC groups, other in-house efforts, etc.).

- Summary of investment focus areas (with strategic investment map) and financial/strategic priorities, with a simple "market map" to identify the channels by which to reach (e.g., including the Web). Possibly include some consideration to international.

- Overview of marketing and business development plans both within the corporation and in the outside venturing and industry communities.

- VBO performance road map and key milestones: VBO operations quality and market development, deal flow generation, portfolio development, value return and time horizon (*note:* emphasis on twelve-month plan with six-month milestones).

- Financial plan, including funding strategy and pace of disbursements (building versus investing), VBO compensation structures (i.e., if different from parent-partnership with carried interest), and operating expenses—with first twelve months in detail by quarter.

- Management team (citing board of advisors, corporate "governors," and other critical sources of support).

appendix b

the VBO board of advisors agreement

(Company Name) considers itself very fortunate to be able to draw on the senior-level experience and expertise of a group of Advisors to help the company set its course and guide its development. The company intends to build a broad base of Advisors with expertise in a variety of areas relevant to the company's business and vision.

The board is intended as a haven for discussions and seeking counsel on issues pertinent to the Venture Business Office. The members will offer guidance and perspective, and help identify and anticipate problems. They are objective in their views, but clearly committed to the overall success of the (VBO) and the innovation and discovery it serves up to (parent corporation). Service on the board is not a legal, fiduciary, or operational responsibility for board members.

The Nature of the Advisor's Role

An Advisor can be tapped for assistance and counsel on topics pertinent to all aspects of the VBO's operation, including but not limited to issues in portfolio and business strategy, portfolio company selection and management, building and investing, technology and product development, marketing and sales, partnering, operations, management of growth, and financing strategy.

An Advisor may be asked to aid in recruiting and interviewing new hires. An Advisor may also be called upon to provide high-level introductions to potential partners, key accounts, and influencers.

Frequency of Meetings

(Company name) is keenly aware of the value of an Advisor's time, and will be judicious in its contact. The majority of individual contact will be handled by phone or e-mail, with specific meetings as appropriate.

(Company name) will hold a meeting for all Advisors on a quarterly basis, to provide a relaxed environment in which Advisors can meet, talk with one another and the (company name) team, and be brought up to date on the VBO's progress. Advisors will receive periodic communications from the VBO, as well, in an effort to keep them current with news and other events pertinent to the company.

Disclosure of Advisor's Role

(Company name) asks that an Advisor's name with a short summary of the Advisor's background be made available for inclusion in company material such as the business plan, Web site, corporate backgrounder, press releases, and other marketing/sales collateral.

In some instances, the VBO may call on an Advisor to be available to talk with press or analysts on the company's behalf.

Conflict of Interest

Occasionally, conflict of interest issues arise. In the case of a conflict, (company name) asks that the Advisor alert the company, mutually assess the impact of the conflict, and refer the company to another person who may be able to assist with the particular topic.

Duration of Agreement

(Company name) asks for a minimum of a one-year commitment.

Compensation

Advisors will be compensated according to agreed-upon retainer rates. If there is mutual agreement between the company and Advisor, equity compensation is associated with the advisory role.

(Add specifics here re: details of arrangement with advisor, such as size of equity compensation, vesting schedule, etc.)

appendix c

nanyang ventures's use of the bell-mason venture development framework

The Bell-Mason Venture Development Framework and Diagnostic was created by Gordon Bell, legendary technologist and father of DEC's VAX family of computers, and Heidi Mason, veteran Silicon Valley start-up specialist. The Bell-Mason tool set is a first of kind venture development system and diagnostic, offering an objective means by which to evaluate early-stage ventures, comparing strengths and progress against benchmark standards and providing focused, prescriptive guidance. The Bell-Mason tool set, used commercially for over fifteen years, has been specifically adapted (since 1995) for Internet ventures and corporate ventures, and is continually updated. It has been licensed around the globe, most recently to DiamondCluster International, a business strategy and solutions firm, which delivers value to clients worldwide by developing and implementing digital strategies that capitalize on the opportunities presented by new technologies. Bell and Mason are also DiamondCluster International Fellows. For additional information, please contact Diamond-Cluster International (www.diamondcluster.com).

The Bell-Mason approach is a heuristics and rule-based system, documenting and embedding new-venture "best practices" in its framework. The architecture has four key elements:

1. *Twelve dimensions or categories of analysis*, which be used to characterize virtually any venture (platform, product/service, delivery, business plan, marketing, business development/sales, CEO, team, board, cash, financing, control/operations)

2. *Four well-defined stages of development* that chronicle the evolution of the venture (as a whole and per dimension) over time (Concept Validation, Venture Prototyping, Venture Testing, Market Development/Tuning and Scaling)

3. *Quantification of progress* via key milestones and specific *yes/no, evidence-oriented questions* derived from *industry best practices* (*note:* there are over 1,000 in the independent venture diagnostic, and roughly 1,600 in the corporate venture version)

4. *Relational graphs* that depict the ideal state of venture evolution across the four stages and provide a means to compare the real venture against the ideal

The Bell-Mason Venture Development Framework and Diagnostic has been used by CEOs and start-up teams, a broad base of investors and corporate venture groups alike. What follows is an excerpt of a survey of the tool's effectiveness completed by venture firm licensee Nanyang Management. A listing of additional readings pertinent to the Bell-Mason VDF and Nanyang reports completes this appendix.

The Bell-Mason Diagnostic as an Investment Evaluation Screening Tool

Ian Neal, Managing Director, Nanyang Management P/L

Introduction

In April 1995 Nanyang Management became the Australian licensee of the Bell-Mason Diagnostic and since then we have conducted 29 diagnostics. This paper explores Nanyang's experience with the diagnostic as an investment screening tool by examining performance of enterprises in the diagnostic with subsequent business and investment performance of enterprise.

Background

On the basis of years of experience combined with the analysis of over 600 companies, Bell and Mason jointly established a well-defined process for successful business development. They found that this process can be modeled to measure the state of a venture's progress, and to predict the outcome for the enterprise on the basis of actions to be completed.

Their proven system, the Bell-Mason diagnostic, is a tool for assessing the health of a growth enterprise at four well-defined stages of development:

1. Concept

2. Seed

3. Product Development

4. Market Development

If you asked practiced investors and entrepreneurs what is the key to business success one will generally get a set of rules of thumb such as:

"Cash is king."

"I look for the vision above all else."

"People, product, plan."

"A big wave carries a lot of surfboards."

Where the Bell-Mason Diagnostic is different is that it provides a systematic, multidimensional graphical evaluation of a venture across twelve dimensions:

1. Technology

2. Product

3. Manufacturing

4. Business plan

5. Marketing

6. Sales

7. CEO

8. Team

9. Board

10. Cash

11. Financing

12. Control/operations

The Bell-Mason approach codifies start-up evaluations by transforming the founders' combined fifty years of experience with over 600 companies into rules and guidelines for each of the twelve core dimensions. From that database it has generated a list of rules relating to successful company operations, and from that analysis over 1,000 questions have been developed which require yes or no answers from staff. Appropriate questions from that pool are then asked of the company, and the answers plugged into the Bell-Mason diagnostic model. Golis (1996) presents a more in-depth explanation of the Bell-Mason Diagnostic process.

St. George Bank appointed Nanyang Management as the manager of its Venture Capitalfund, St. George Development Capital Limited, in April 1996 and has publicly stated that a key reason for its decision was that Nanyang Management held the Australian–New Zealand master license for the Bell–Mason Diagnostic.

With three years of live experience using the Diagnostic in Australia the question then is how has the BMD behaved as a predictor of business success or failure? This study answers that central question.

Method

We have taken the results of each diagnostic and reduced each to a percentage score. This was achieved by taking the raw percentage number for each of the twelve vectors and averaging the scores to come to the final percentage. The companies have then been ranked by percentage and comments about their subsequent performance have been added.

Results

The table following shows the results of the study.

Venture ID Number	Score (%)	Comments
1	29	Restructured, struggling
2	36	New CEO, poor market rating
3	48	Struggling
4	49	Struggling
5	51	CEO replaced
6	51	Performing well, having implemented recommendations
7	51	Not commercialized
8	56	Taken over cheaply
9	58	Failed to raise capital
10	59	Receivership after raising $2M
11	59	Now starting to perform well
12	61	Struggling
13	63	Profitable, low growth
14	64	Struggling
15	67	Struggling
16	68	No capital raised, struggling
17	70	Taken over at fair value
18	70	Venture failed
19	72	Taken over cheaply
20	74	Taken over, investors made substantial returns
21	76	Buyout agreed with angels
22	76	Sound but slow profit growth
23	77	Successful capital raising
24	80	Sound performance
25	82	New investment
26	83	Taken over, exceptional value
27	83	Performing well
28	90	Excellent performance, price up
29	95	Excellent profit growth

Also (available through Nanyang) are copies of the Bell-Mason graphs, with scores and comments attached to give the reader a better feel for the results and correlation of performance versus performance in the diagnostic.

This study clearly shows a correlation between performance of businesses and results of the Bell-Mason Diagnostic. Any useful investment-screening tool must pick winners and reject losers. Errors are of two types. Type 1 errors are investments picked as winners that become losers. Type 2 errors are investments rejected as possible losers that become winners.

On the evidence to date the Type 1 performance is exceptional. If one invested in businesses with scores of 75 or over the investor would be showing a success rate of over 95%. This is well above the success rates of venture capitalists where success rates of over 50% are rarely achieved and typically at least one-third of the portfolio is written off.

On the other hand the Type 2 error is also minimal. Of the businesses scoring 74 or less there are only two companies of the 20 that could be viewed as potential investment successes after 3 years. Note that these 20 possible investments had already been picked out of a deal flow of over 500 deals by three venture capitalists with a combined experience of 40 years and 60 transactions as having significant potential for returns. Subsequently 90% of those possible investments have performed poorly.

Every analysis of venture capital returns has shown that there is a significant variance in performance between the average and the outperformer. For example, a recent study by Macquarie Bank has shown the average performance by Australian Venture Capital Managers to be 3% over the All Ordinaries Accumulation Index. The above median performance was in excess of 33% over the AOAI.

This study demonstrates clearly that the Bell-Mason Diagnostic is a tool that will deliver that outperformance.

Nanyang Ventures Epilogue

As of July 1999, the IRR for Nanyang I was 45 percent, post management fees and performance incentives. By March 2001, in the midst of a global economic recession and disadvantaged venture capital environment, Nanyang's IRR was holding at 24 percent, very respectable performance; in a market where many firms were going out of business or retrenching, they were able to close yet another fund. Partners cite the BMD as instrumental in helping them achieve and make sustainable their returns.

Additional Readings

Bell, G., and John McNamara. *High Tech Ventures: The Guide for Entrepreneurial Success.* Reading, MA: Addison-Wesley, 1991. (Chapter 10, "The Bell-Mason Diagnostic," describes the original architecture and stages of venture development. Cases are included.)

Golis, C. 1996. "Warning Bells—or Sounds of Success." *JASSA* (July–September).

Golis, Christopher, and Ian Neal, Nanyang Ventures. "The Bell-Mason Diagnostic as an Aid to Venture Capital Decision Making." June 2000. Available through Nanyang Ventures.

Gupta, A. K., and H. J. Sapienza. "Determinants of Venture Capital Firms' Preferences Regarding the Industry Diversity and Geographic Scope of Their Investments." *Journal of Business Venturing* 7 (1992): 347–362.

Mason, H., and G. Bell. "New Tools for Entrepreneurs." *Context* (September–October 1998).

Mason, H., G. Bell, and S. Joni. "Innovations from the Inside." *Management Review* (September 1997).

Mason, Heidi, and Timothy J. Rohner. "Nothing Ventured . . . ," *Context* (July–August 1999).

Zacharakis, A. L., and G. D. Meyer. "A Lack of Insight: Do Venture Capitalists Really Understand Their Own Decision Process?" *Journal of Business* Venturing 13, 1 (1998): 57–76.

_____. "The Potential of Actuarial Decision Models: Can They Improve the Venture Capital Investment Decision?" *Journal of Business Venturing* 15, 4 (2000): 323–346.

Zacharakis, A. L., and D. A. Shepherd. "The Nature of Information and Venture Capitalists' Overconfidence." *Journal of Business Venturing* 16, 4 (2001): 311–332.

appendix d

venture business office diagnostic

The VBO Diagnostic is a set of questions to calibrate progress and prescribe actions for implementing a venture business office, as we've outlined in this book. The structure of this diagnostic is similar to the Bell-Mason Venture Development Framework, which is outlined at a very high level in chapters 5 through 8 and referenced in additional detail in appendix C. The notable difference is that these questions and top-level categories are tailored to the formation and operation of the corporate venture group, whereas the Bell-Mason framework is generically applicable across the breadth of ventures that the VBO pursues. Also included in this appendix is an overview of the three phases of venture business office development (see figure D-1).

The VBO Diagnostic, like the Bell-Mason framework, is one important component in a larger tool kit; many of these tools can be found in this book or on our Web site at www.theventureimperative.com. Also, while this diagnostic should be useful to the layperson, a fair amount of training in both the delivery of the questions and interpretation of the responses is necessary to extract the full potential. And, as with the Bell-Mason framework, we use spider graphs to communicate the results of the diagnostic.

1. Platform

1.1 Is there a clear, documented strategy for the corporate venturing program that utilizes the parent corporation's existing business, core

Creating the Corporate Venturing Engine

Translate Corporate Strategy[a] (2–3 months)

- Corporate platform: Create inventory of core capabilities
- Assess growth areas
- Finalize Strategic Roadmap

- Investment Map for corporate venturing program
- Assess cv synergies and linkage: Corporate development, M&A, R&D, SBU

Create and Integrate Venture Business Office (3–6 months)

- People — Team, BOA
- Practices — Incubate, Invest
- Portfolio
- Funding
- Governance
- VBO Business Plan

- Outside/Inside infrastructure and links
- Strategic pipeline, deal flow
- Rigorous venturing management and decision process
- >2 deals done
- Control points with parent

Operationalize for VBO Sustainability (24+ months)

- Refined operation/funding
- Diversified portfolio
- SBU/corp integration
- System of critical and incremental measures
- Continue to expand internal/external network

- Venturing track record
- Venturing source point (inside)
- ~10 deals done
- Measurable results (incremental, financial, and strategic) for VBO and parent

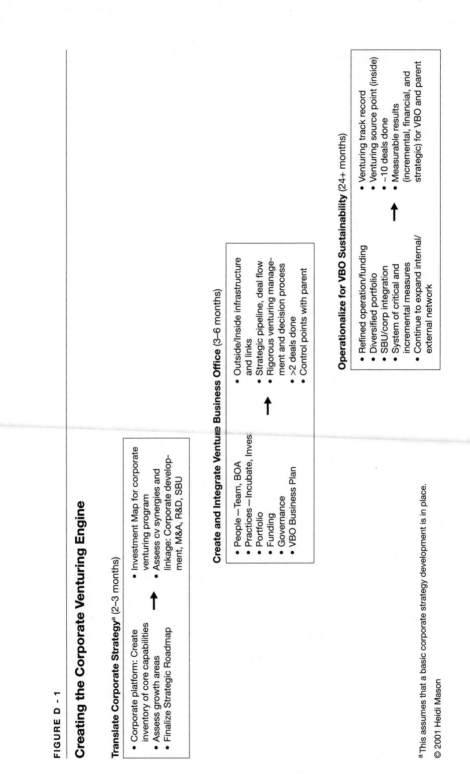

[a]This assumes that a basic corporate strategy development is in place.

© 2001 Heidi Mason

capabilities, brand, and other resources to build its unique position, as an "inside-outside" channel for innovation and new venture development engine

- within the venture community?
- within the parent corporation?
- within the parent's industry and infrastructures?

1.2 Have corporate assets and competency maps been developed that serve as a building block for the VBO, and ensure that the VBO investment strategy relates back to the parent organization and its strategy?

1.3 Have the VBO and parent specified a platform that will enable the sustained conversion of innovative ideas to new venture builds and investments, as well as create a source point for venturing expertise and education within the corporation? Does its platform include specifications for the following?

- *Element 1:* Governance. Investment and operational decision-making roles and responsibilities; ongoing interface with parent (executive committee and SBU)
- *Element 2:* VBO team. Core team, managing director, VEO and CEO, advisors, partners
- *Element 3:* Portfolio strategy. Creation of a focused investment opportunity map and collection of venture investments and builds for diversification and risk balance
- *Element 4:* VBO Practices. Expert methodologies and business process for venture development and delivery, such as IP and VC quality business processes for deal flow, screening and due diligence, venture builds and investments, portfolio management, corporate business process connect points and integration, strategic and financial performance measurement and tracking

1.4 Does the VBO leverage the operations of R&D, M&A/finance, partnering and joint ventures/corporate development and other growth engines within the parent? Are there ongoing, working relationships with each group?

1.5 Are top-performing individuals from the various disciplines (e.g., finance, technology, marketing, venture investing, and building) being sourced inside and outside the corporation, and identified and hired by the VBO? Does a clear plan to continue talent acquisition exist, with industry- and venture-competitive compensation structures?

2. Portfolio of Options

2.1 Has the VBO developed a strategic investment map that lays out areas of focus and the VBO's vision of its investment landscape, with targets and relative priority order for individual deals?

2.2 Are the approximate number, types, stages, and sizes of investments described, especially for year 1 of VBO operation? In particular, are venture investments and venture builds called out separately?

2.3 Are the strategic and functional relationships between the VBO's portfolio/venture investments and the corporation's products/services defined? Have performance targets been set with the VBO to guide individual investments/builds?

2.4 Given that the VBO meets expectations in the first phase of its operation (nine to twelve months), have areas for expansion been indicated in its plan? (e.g., geographic expansion via additional offices in strategic locales, domestic and international; expansion of investment areas of focus into additional, strategically relevant technology and business adjacencies)

3. Option Investing and Building
(Quality Venture Delivery Process)

3.1 Has the VBO modeled, documented, and made operational its front-to-back business processes and systems for venture delivery (VC-quality deal flow, investments, and builds; facilitation of shared venturing info and communication linking "outside and inside"; internal venturing competencies and outside partnering/networking as support to SBUs)? Has it been rationalized and approved by the corporate parent?

3.2 Has the VBO done make/buy/partner analysis, made trade-offs, and implemented decisions with appropriate corporate approval? (e.g., venture-relevant software purchases, methodology licenses, subscriptions and memberships, outsources)

3.3 Are corporate execution capabilities (e.g., development and manufacturing, product introductions, sales) leveraged where appropriate? If they are not appropriate or are insufficient to meet the VBO's needs, is there an agreed-upon decision process with the parent corporation that allows the VBO to go outside?

3.4 Is the same true regarding existing corporate partnerships and business alliances? Are they leveraged where appropriate? If not, is the VBO free to look elsewhere?

3.5 Has the VBO designed, standardized, and formalized its proposal submissions, screening process, and due diligence for investments and builds? Do they integrate best venture practices with proprietary corporate information and corporate process (e.g., financial and strategic analysis)?

3.6 Has the VBO identified its inside and outside network of critical individuals and organizations (by both explicit and implicit agreement) to generate quality venture proposals and fill its pipeline?

3.7 Has the VBO identified its e-business/IT systems needs, and specified/designed these systems with strategic linkages and appropriate access to the parent's IT infrastructure and team? (e.g., proprietary linkages to existing marketing information and customer databases, technology/IP/patent histories, HR functions, internal Web access/e-mail, creation of VBO investment and build databases)

3.8 Has the VBO obtained critical SBU linkages for the purposes of screening and due diligence, early testing, piloting, customer endorsement, and continuing business relationships with portfolio ventures?

4. Business Plan

4.1 Has the five-year business plan *with emphasis on the next twelve to twenty-four months* (about fifteen pages, not including appendixes) been formalized and validated? Does the business plan include the following?

- Executive summary with a vision, mission, and value proposition
- A description of the VBO platform uniqueness as a basis for sustainable operation (e.g., venturing uniqueness with brand,

key leverage points, and competitive advantages of parent, such as pilot access)

- Platform requirements and dependencies on the parent corporation: strategic alignment and integration, compensation structures, governance, management oversight and support, make-buy-partner latitude, and so on
- Venture build and venture investment scope with critical areas to explore and competitive scene (e.g., venture business processes, deal flow, investments, builds, inside/outside "pipeline," internal/external infrastructures, venturing competency and support to SBUs, competitive scene is quality and execution hurdle, other VC groups, other in-house efforts, etc.)
- Summary of investment focus areas (with strategic investment map) and financial/strategic priorities, with a simple "market map" to identify the channels by which to reach (e.g., including the Web), including some consideration to international
- VBO performance road map and key milestones: VBO operations and market development, deal flow generation, portfolio development, value return, and time horizon
- Financial plan, including funding strategy and pace of disbursements (building versus investing), VBO compensation structures (i.e., if different from parent-partnership with carried interest), and operating expenses, with first twelve months in detail by quarter
- List of management team (with board of advisors, VEO, corporate "governors" and investment committee, and other critical sources of support cited)

4.2 Has the VBO business plan been approved, and have key executives (in corporate and the VBO) been aligned?

4.3 Have key decision trigger points in the VBO's development been defined based on venture practice and corporate governance structure?

5. Marketing

5.1 Has the issue of market branding for the VBO, and its impact on the corporation, been addressed? Has the impact of the VBO marketing on other corporate products and businesses been articulated and resolved? (e.g., internal/external, IR, public relations, branding.)

5.2 Has the VBO outlined a marketing plan? That is, has the VBO made a list of what to do to create demand for its venturing skills, fill its pipeline, populate its portfolio, and deliver back-end value return to portfolio companies and the corporate parent?

- Corporate VBO positioning platform with context setting and market strategy, for "inside" corporation, inside and outside portfolio companies, and the "outside" venture community and parent's industry
- Simple descriptive VBO "customer" profiles with "buyer" motivations, biases, and requirements cited (venture communities, corporate communities, new venture teams with the VBO as an active investor and/or build-team builder). Include an overlay of investment focus areas and cite any specialized requirements.
- Corporate, venture community, and industry infrastructure maps refined, with an outline of marketing requirements and alternatives
- Global cost of tactics to build its position and reach its targets, both inside the corporation and outside in the venture community (including strategic PR, promotion, and seminars, etc.)

5.3 Have the "customers" for the VBO been sampled, and do they validate the VBO's fundamental value propositions and strategy for development? Have insights and/or changes been factored into the VBO's strategy and implementation plan?

5.4 Is the VBO's business plan updated quarterly based on real experience and new information?

5.5 Has the VBO designed and launched its Web site (independent and/or addition to parent's and affiliates' Web sites) and spelled out its charter, goals, investment focus, and process? Is the proposal submission questionnaire (with key information required to streamline handling) included on the Web site, and are submissions integrated with the VBO's back-end systems and databases?

5.6 Has the VBO developed a targeted strategic communications plan, designed to build awareness and endorsement in its communities of interest? Is it separate from, but consistent with, the corporation's PR programs?

6. Business Development and Partnering

6.1 Has the VBO developed a preliminary "sales" plan sketch, delineating channels, geographies, organization, sales cycle, and "model"? (This is a prioritized plan outlining for whom the VBO must "close" in order to generate deal flow, efficiently screen and perform due diligence, make investments and builds, pilot, etc. The venture process itself becomes the guideline for business development and portfolio creation and maintenance.)

6.2 Have the VBO's infrastructure and partnering development plans, and specific venture investment and build deals, been rationalized against the parent's corporate development program and sales models?

6.3 Has the VBO's "sales" plan been compared to "best-practice" and like-kind top performers (on the corporate venturing side, the private venturing side, etc.)? Does the plan specify timelines, targets, strategy, tactics, and goals?

6.4 Is the VBO building awareness, creating evangelists and active supporters as targeted in the plan:

- within the corporation, especially at the SBU level?
- within the venture community (a cross-section of those who have influence on new ventures, from VCs to entrepreneurs/start-up teams to venture service providers and analysts)?
- within the industry (i.e., prospective corporate partners, alliances, sources of talent and deal flow)?

7. VBO Managing Director

7.1 Has the VBO's leader (managing director/general manager) been instrumental in creating:

- the linkage to corporate strategic map?
- the definition of the VBO, driving assessment of corporate potential, articulating value to senior management, building the VBO plan, defining critical requirements like governance and compensation, and leading its financing?

7.2 Does the VBO's managing director show missionary zeal and leadership ability? Does he or she have sufficient history and stature in the parent corporation to build a broad coalition of support throughout the organization (with the assistance of the board/investment committee, VEO, and advisors)?

7.3 Has the managing director driven "change efforts" within the corporation? start-up efforts within existing corporate organizations?

7.4 Has the managing director shown clarity about organizational expectations of the VBO (strategies, transformational goals, immediate objectives for venture investments and builds, compensation structures, corporate tolerance for three- to five-year hurdles on return)?

7.5 Has the VBO managing director created an operating state that is appropriate to venturing, including the following?

- Straight talk regarding concerns and issues
- Management focus on results
- Clear accountabilities
- Managing by objectives, measuring against plan

7.6 Does the managing director have venture development and investment experience and expertise? If not, does he or she augment his or her own skills with relevant experience in management team, directors, or advisors?

7.7 Is the VBO managing director's compensation package (e.g., equity as a percentage of carried interest in the VBO portfolio/salary as management fee) within the range of others with similar risk/reward profiles who are leading comparable endeavors on the outside?

8. VBO Team

8.1 Is the VBO core team in place or soon to be hired? Does it comprise people with appropriate depth and breadth of experience for the deal generation, investment and build, piloting and business development roles (sourced from inside and outside the corporation)?

8.2 If not, are skills gaps being filled by outsiders such as consultants or advisory board members, such as the following?

- For VC investor: venture investment experience and expertise, strong financial background, business development/strategic partnering skills, domain knowledge, network access, ability to "manage and do" in newly created environment, high risk/reward profile
- For venture build: early-stage start-up/build experience and expertise, cross-functional management understanding and competency, network access, domain knowledge, ability to "manage and do" in newly created/resource constrained environment, high risk/reward profile

8.3 Have industry and corporate criteria been established for VBO recruiting, based on roles in such areas as operations and best-practice standards? Is a systematic method in place for ensuring that recruiting occurs in an effective, high-quality, and timely way from inside and outside the parent organization?

8.4 Are compensation structures and incentive plans in place for the investment and build teams (e.g., a competitive percentage of equity in portfolio/cash compensation)? Are they competitive based on other outside, comparable endeavors and risk/reward profiles?

8.5 Are all VBO team members aligned with the vision, position, goals and strategy, and milestones for implementation?

9. VBO Board

9.1 Has the VBO named a venture executive officer? Is the VEO on board for a minimum of one year? Has he or she had a primary role in shaping the vision of the corporate venturing effort?

9.2 Is the VEO a C-level or equivalent high-level executive within the corporation, who has management authority and clout? Is he or she a vocal supporter and high-level champion for the VBO, both inside and outside the corporation?

9.3 Does the VEO run interference on the VBO's behalf when a bottleneck occurs?

9.4 Does the VBO governing body include the corporation's CEO and a limited number of top executives from the parent's management team? Does it include key outsiders who bring critical areas of venture/industry experience and expertise, to provide appropriate guidance and support to the VBO? (e.g., recruiting, strategic partnering, and business development for the VBO and its various initiatives)

9.5 Is there a small, "lean and mean" investment committee to provide corporate review and approval of the VBO's investments and builds?

9.6 Has the board approved the VBO's plan within the context of the corporate business and financial strategy? Does the plan also outline the investment decision-making process and criteria for decision making?

9.7 Has the governance structure between VBO and corporate parent been formalized? Is it working effectively to insulate the VBO from the day-to-day processes and operations of the parent corporation, while guiding exceptional decisions, conflict resolution with the parent corporation, corporate policy and access, trigger points on venture investment and development, and so on?

9.8 Has an advisory board been assembled for the VBO and its investing and venture build groups? Does it include key, senior-level outsiders with venture expertise/experience?

9.9 Do the VBO's structure and compensation plan for the team, advisors, and directors compare favorably with those in similar endeavors? Is such compensation adjusted to be in the "strike zone" by the end of the first year of operation? (e.g., equity partnership structures, equity participation, per diem cash compensation)

10. Portfolio and Option Funding

10.1 Is current funding for the VBO committed and protected within the corporate financial plans?

10.2 Does the corporation release funds in a timely and efficient manner (within the tolerances set by venture capital practice)?

11. Financial and Operational Performance

11.1 Has the venture plan been correlated with the corporate five-year plan (or equivalent) for anticipated capital and human requirements and bottom-line impact? Has the parent's chief financial officer approved it?

11.2 Have the financial projections for the VBO been "reality checked" with comparable endeavors and validated by an outside expert?

11.3 Are the market value and liquidation/exit strategy of actual investments tracking to plan with variances understood and addressed?

11.4 Does actual cash flow (in and out) map to expectations? Does the VBO understand variances and address them, with actual results reflected back in original plan?

12. Controls and Processes

12.1 Is there agreement with the VBO team on critical deliverables and milestones?

12.2 Has a results management process been established to evaluate progress against key milestones, institute individual and team accountability for delivery, and provide for contingency plans in case of changed expectations?

12.3 Has the corporation provided the VBO with the authority to exert control over budgeting, recruiting, and spending processes to manage present and next-stage cash and to control the VBO's spending?

12.4 Is the VBO performing satisfactorily against milestones and forecasts? If milestones have been missed, were senior management expectations successfully recast?

12.5 Have the VBO and the parent defined, approved, and used explicit investment decision-making criteria? Has the governance structure between the VBO and parent proved effective, rather than burdensome, in supporting the VBO's progress?

appendix e

customer/application profile template

Description of Application

Brief description of tasks being performed and for what purpose. General view of need.

User Title and Job Function, Institution or Company Description, and Market Segment

Who is the user? What is his/her job function, title, and number of direct reports? What is the organizational structure (dept. or division of which user is a part), and to whom does the user report?

Estimate size of company (employees/revenues) and typical budget cycle. Include overview of the purchase decision cycle typical to the company. How many people are involved in making the decision? What are their titles/departments and roles in determining product purchase? Who signs the check? What are the key influences in priority order, necessary references, and other user profile information (e.g., from everything the user reads to where the user goes for referral information)?

Be specific. Define the access to funds and budgeting. Note the typical lead time to adoption of new product or inclusion of additional product in systems planning budgeting cycle. How/when/by whom are these decisions made? What are the levels/who are the people you must positively influence, by what means, in order to make the sale? Is there an evaluation or benchmark you must provide or participate in? Is the criteria for product acceptance formal or informal?

How does the user/company typically learn about new products? From colleagues (inside and/or outside the company)? To what degree is the Web used? From whom does the company typically buy products of this nature, with what attendant level of support? Whose opinions do they trust? Which luminaries do they follow and respect? How do they weight testimonials, case performance data, and customer lists? What do they read? To what professional societies or organizations do they belong and how do they rate them as a vehicle by which to learn about new things and important issues? What conferences and industry shows do they attend, and for what purpose? Any online or direct mail solicitations that are deemed successful?

Description of Application Environment

Includes the "topography" of the user's application operation: What is the workflow, output or results, and how many others are involved, doing what functions? Where are sensitivities/problem areas? What are key pressures and performance expectations? To what degree/for what purpose is the Internet/Intranet/Extranet used in this application?

This is specific to the customer site: e.g., in what kind of specific site or settings would your product be used? Is this a centralized function? Departmental? Single user? Random access driven? Servicing how many people or operations, with what frequency? Size of operation?

Is this an "island" or mainstream application? In development, pilot, or production?

Description of the Systems and Software Environment

Includes the "topography" of the user/company's current systems' environment into which any new product solution must fit. What are the configurations? Which platforms, rdbms, applications? Off-the-shelf vs. homegrown? What's the net infrastructure set-up? Are there mandated standards? Are the mandates informal but still present?

How are the components of this environment supported?

How Is the Application Currently Being Addressed, and with What?

Characterize the current solution, be it with a directly competitive product, or with an alternative approach or product. If another product, estimate unit price and aggregate dollars for typical configuration (i.e., price per seat/total number of seats), meantime to/complexity of installation and follow-on support. If alternative approach, estimate price, benefit, installation, and support.

Determine (from user info and your knowledge) where the present solution falls short: What user needs are not being adequately or optimally met with the current solution? Include application and customer support requirements in this analysis.

For example, if there are already alternative solutions in place, what was the rationale and what did the customer pay for them (or get list if customer price not available). Was benefit or performance measured? If so, how? How well-entrenched are the current solution providers? Is there any dissatisfaction with the status quo? Is the support adequate? Are present solutions measurable and meeting the customer's stated objectives?

What is the customer's level of urgency and motivation in terms of affecting a change or addition?

How Does Our New Product Specifically Solve This Problem?

How do the key product features/functions/benefits (top five FFBs) line up with the particular customer/application needs and systems requirements to address the problem in a way that hasn't been possible before?

What's the ultimate payoff (business case/benefit), and how does Company X with Product Y make that uniquely achievable and practical?

What are specific impediments to the sale that must be overcome?

This goes straight to the heart of your corporate and product positioning and performance, unique selling propositions per segment and customer, and the customer's level of resistance to the sale. How, specifically, will adoption of your products meet the customer's stated needs and prove measurably better than the competitors' products? Is this "goodness" compelling enough to motivate action or change on the customer's part? What barriers to the sale are in and out of your control? What "evidence" of your corporate and product capabilities must be in place to persuade the customer that action is warranted?

Clearly understand whether you are: a direct replacement for a known product, a substitution, a new component of an existing solution, a new complete solution, etc.

appendix f

segmentation analysis guide

Stage of Venture Development	Segmentation Focus	Segmentation Goals	Research Requirements
Early Stage (Concept-Seed Round)	High-level market and customer segmentation and characterization	Develop initial market segmentation strategy. • Validate initial market vision and positioning • Validate technology and business model • Identify strawman customer segments (2–3) with assumptions regarding critical need, leverage ability, and barriers • Define strawman customer segment–specific total product requirements • Map potential competitor landscape	• Facilitated internal brainstorming • 3–5 existing/ potential customer interviews (more interviews may be required for broader markets and for corporate ventures) • 2–3 interviews with relevant analysts or other market influencers • Identification and scan of available research and trade journals

Stage of Venture Development	Segmentation Focus	Segmentation Goals	Research Requirements
Product Development Stage (A-B Funding Rounds)	Prioritized and profiled market entry customer segments	Develop market segment leadership roadmap. • Refine market vision and positioning • Identify, size, and prioritize market entry customer segments (1–2) • Define customer segment–specific total product requirements and roadmap • Develop detailed characterization of market entry customer segments • Create representative customer segment application profiles (company and individual) • Develop plan for market entry customer segment penetration including beta and strategic customer development • Map customer segment–specific competitor landscape	• Facilitated internal brainstorming • 15–20 current/ potential customer interviews • 5–10 interviews with current/ potential channel partners or total product partners • 3–5 interviews with relevant analysts or other market influencers • Identification and scan of available research and trade journals

Stage of Venture Development	Segmentation Focus	Segmentation Goals	Research Requirements
Market Development Stage (Liquidity Event Preparation)	Market segment development plan and programs	Create market development strategy and plan to build on and leverage successes to date. • Refine market vision and positioning • Identify and prioritize follow-on customer segments (2–3) • Define customer segment–specific total product requirements and roadmap • Develop detailed characterization of follow-on customer segments • Create representative customer segment application profiles (company and individual) • Develop plan for follow-on customer segment penetration including strategic customer development • Map customer segment–specific competitor landscape • Define channel strategy and program implications • Define marketing strategy and program implications	• Facilitated internal brainstorming • 30–40 current/ potential customer interviews • 5–10 interviews with current/ potential channel partners • 3–5 interviews with relevant analysts or other market influencers, including financial analysts • Identification and scan of available research and trade journals

Source: Liz Arrington, Affiliate, Sevin Rosen Funds and Bell-Mason Group.

appendix g

partner profile template

Target Corporation/Institution Vital Statistics:

Name:

Size: (in people, revs)

Principal business:

Industry segment/ranking within:

Primary competitors:

Primary contact(s): (w/ phone, e-mail, address, etc.)

Type of partnership desired:

Nature of Relationship:

_____ Joint venture partner

_____ Strategic partner

_____ Strategic alliance

Primary Area(s) of Value to Venture:

_____ Technology/platform development

_____ Web delivery

_____ Content

_____ Channel/sales

_____ Power brand

_____ Funding

Support Desired:

_____ Corporate investor

_____ Board member or advisory role

_____ Internal business unit sponsorship and project codevelopment (e.g., internal resources such as people, divisional dollars budgeted for project, access to customer base, access to IT support/existing platform, access to and support from marketing, sales, customer care, etc.)

_____ Brand/communications support (including references, testimonials, missionary work)

_____ Domain expertise

Brief Statement of Desired Partnering Relationship

Include simple, but specific, description of partner's contribution to the working relationship (e.g., who does what, with what desired result). Outline performance metrics for both sides.

How does the venture's operation map compare to that of the partner? Include other linkages within partner corporation, as required.

For example, the operational seat of the new venture might reside in the Internet Services Group within the partner organization, but venture also needs access to and timely cooperation of the partner's marketing, sales, and IT/e-business operations. Who are the contact points likely to be, and are they on board?

Description of Partner Value Proposition

What's the business case, simply stated for the venture?

What's the strategic business value to be delivered by the venture to the participating partner (short term, long term)?

Does this proposed value proposition directly line up with the partner's corporate/business priorities over the next twelve to eighteen months? Specifically, how?

Is there direct, measurable competitive value? Does this allow the partner to "catch up" with a competitor's offering? Beat another competitor or set of competitors to market? Provide a first-mover advantage?

What is the current financial health of the prospective partner? For example, if public, how has its stock performed over the last few quarters?

Is there enough perceived urgency on the part of the partner for this solution to propel the agreement forward?

Can you make the economic case for the partnership? Is it compelling enough to warrant action?

Description of Information Needed to Construct the Partner Business Model/Value Proposition. What Do You Need that You Don't Have to Make the Case?

Example: On average, what does corporation allocate as:

- dollars per current customer for retention (tied to churn rate)?
- dollars per prospective customer for acquisition?
- dollars for new product/service/platform development?

Example: What new product/service programs/budgets have recently been approved (internal to corporation or outside with partner)? (look for analogies and precedents)

Example: If the partner regularly invests in innovative new products/service development, or new business lines, what are corporate requirements for ROI, in what period of time? (look for partner expectations to meet/beat)

Description of Target Partner's Typical Agreement/Decision Cycle

Outline the prospective partner's typical relationship decision process to determine how long and who to close. Identify number and names/titles of people involved (as decision makers or decision influencers or postdecision supporters, and what specific roles they play in partnering negotiation and agreement inking).

Determine key requirements and incremental milestones in the process. For example:

- Proof of concept and operating prototype to be completed by venture
- Technical evaluation by IT
- Development of inside champion and sponsorship by business division (*note:* indicate whether sponsorship requires that division kick in funds, as well as time, attention, and other resources)
- Business plan/model review at partner corporation's executive committee level
- Joint pilot or "island application" as evaluation milestone and prerequisite

Partner Funds

Determine access path to funds and identify the appropriate funding agents (and signatory authority, if possible) within the target partner organization (e.g., divisional budget versus corporate strategy "slush fund" versus corporate VC; division head, executive vice president of corporate strategy or CFO; corporate VC and CFO)

How Much Funding Does this Prospective Partner Typically Allocate for the Following?

Venture capital investment

Venture partnering and launch

Innovative new product and service development

Will Funding Be Part of a Corporate Budgeting Cycle?

Are You Competing with Other Internal Development Efforts or Competitive Projects for Scarce Resources?

Partner's Organizational Map of Influence for Partner Agreement

"Aerial" view of who you need to get to: simple graphic organizational chart with names, titles, roles and indicators of who's required, whom you've converted, who's outstanding, etc.

Is there an e-business group or Internet services division?

Is there a formal corporate venture capital group?

Which divisions are known as the innovators? as leaders in taking on partnered projects?

Which people are the most likely champions?

Do the executive committee, CFO, and/or CEO ultimately have to approve the relationship?

What Are the Primary Barriers to a Partner Agreement?

The more specific you can be, the better: It will help you itemize, rank order problems, and devise specific strategies to counteract any barriers. For example:

Are you competing with internal development for limited resources? Are there competitive projects or alternative programs to yours being considered, and with which you must compete?

Is one of the key decision makers a nonbeliever who can stall the deal? Are there too many people in the decision loop, including the most senior level to whom you are not granted audience or access?

Are there onerous terms or conditions? (typically around exclusivity, access and ownership of customer information, venture valuation)

Is the technology base (or lack thereof) a significant drawback?

Partnering History

Does the target partner have any history of making strategic relationships with early-stage ventures? If so, with whom?

Have they participated in pilots or other such "tests"?

Did they fund these, in part, or in whole?

Did any of the relationships become mature? have market impact?

Did the participants deem these experiences successful or unsuccessful? Why or why not?

Describe Partner's IT and e-Commerce Environment

Includes the "topography" of the partner corporation's current IT environment and e-commerce platforms into which the venture's products/services must fit.

To what degree has the prospective partner Web-enabled its current operations and business process? Does it have online customer accounts? Does it manage sales and transactions on line? Has it had experience linking up with other ASPs, web-hosting services?

What are the platforms, databases, transaction environments, and/ or interfaces with which the venture operation must interact?

Are there any obvious challenges or problems with this front- to back-end integration?

Do they have existing partnerships for whom these technical linkages have been perfected?

What are the mechanisms for info exchange? Are there formally mandated and/or informal corporate IT or e-business standards?

What are the primary technical issues and concerns to be resolved for the partnership?

If it's pertinent to the partnership, describe the strategy for and degree of integration required for the partner and the venture environments to achieve product/service delivery.

What level of support and expertise is available/committed at the partner site to support this development effort?

notes

Preface

1. Peter Drucker, "The Way Ahead—A Survey of the Near Future," *The Economist*, 3 November 2001, 19.

Chapter 1

1. Fred Wiersema, *The New Market Leaders: Who's Winning and How in the Battle for Customers* (New York: The Free Press, 2001).

2. Clayton M. Christensen and Michael Overdorf, "Meeting the Challenge of Disruptive Change," *Harvard Business Review* 78, no. 2 (March–April 2000): 66–76.

3. Joseph L. Bower and Clayton M. Christensen, "Disruptive Technologies: Catching the Wave," *Harvard Business Review* 73, no. 1 (January–February 1995): 43–53.

4. A. L. Zacharakis and D.A. Shepherd, "The Nature of Information and Venture Capitalists' Overconfidence," *Journal of Business Venturing* 16, no. 4 (2001): 311–332.

5. Michael Lewis, *The New, New Thing: A Silicon Valley Story* (New York: W.W. Norton & Company, 1999).

Chapter 2

1. Joseph L. Bower and Clayton M. Christensen, "Disruptive Technologies: Catching the Wave," *Harvard Business Review* 73, no. 1 (January–February 1995): 43–53.

2. Christopher T. Heun, "Corporate Venture Capitalists Undeterred by Economy," *Information Week,* 23 April 2001. See <http://www.informationweek.com/834/vc.htm> (accessed 18 December 2001).

3. Ibid.

4. Kevin McLaughlin, "Agilent Sets Venture Unit," *CNN*, 7 February 2001. See <http://www.cnn.com/2001/BUSINESS/02/07/biz.agilent/> (accessed 18 December 2001).

5. Matt Hicks, "Venturing Onward," *eWeek*, 28 May 2001. See <http://www.eweek.com.>

6. Samuel Kortum and Josh Lerner, "Does Venture Capital Spur Innovation?" National Bureau of Economic Research, Working Paper No. W6846, December 1998.

7. Ben Worthen, "Nothing Ventured, Nothing Gained," *CIO*, 15 May 2001. See <http://www.cio.com/archive/051501/venture.html> (accessed 18 December 2001).

8. Tom Stein, "VC Whispers: Pharma's Insider Information," *Red Herring*, 1 April 2001. See <http://www.redherring.com/mag/issue95/1930018993.html> (accessed 18 December 2001).

9. Worthen, "Nothing Ventured, Nothing Gained."

10. Pete Yoo, "Innovate, Don't Downsize," *Wall Street Journal*, 23 April 2001.

11. Michael J. Mandel, *The Coming Internet Depression* (New York: Basic Books, 2000).

Chapter 3

1. Clayton Christensen, *The Innovator's Dilemma: When New Technologies Cause Great Firms to Fail* (Boston: Harvard Business School Press, 1997).

2. Michael Lewis, *The New, New Thing* (New York: W.W. Norton, 1999).

3. David Batstone, "Boo.com's Blunder Should Spook European Entrepreneurs," *eCompany Now*, 24 May 2000.

Chapter 4

1. Chris Zook and James Allen, *Profit from the Core: Growth Strategy in an Era of Turbulence* (Boston: Harvard Business School Press, 2001); and Fred Wiersema, *The New Market Leaders: Who's Winning and How in the Battle for Customers* (New York: The Free Press, 2001).

2. Jonathan D. Day, Paul Y. Mang, Ansgar Richter, and John Roberts, "The Innovation Organization," *The McKinsey Quarterly* 2 (2001).

Chapter 9

1. James C. Collins and Jerry I. Porras, *Built to Last: Successful Habits of Visionary Companies* (New York: HarperBusiness, 1997).

2. Alex Philippidis, "Revco, Physicians Online among Nominees for Smithsonian Awards," *Westchester County Business Journal*, 10 April 1995.

3. Melissa A. Schilling, "Technological Lockout: An Integrative Model of the Economic and Strategic Factors Driving Technology Success and Failure," *Academy of Management Review*, April 1998.

4. Joseph L. Bower and Clayton M. Christensen, "Disruptive Technologies: Catching the Wave," *Harvard Business Review* 73, no. 1 (January–February 1995): 43–53.

5. Larry Downes and Chunka Mui, *Unleashing the Killer App: Digital Strategies for Market Dominance* (Boston: Harvard Business School Press, 1998).

6. Information from the TMP Worldwide Inc. "Company Capsule" on Hoover's Online. See <http://www.hoovers.com/co/capsule/7/0,2163,41617,00.html> (accessed 20 December 2001).

7. Jane Black, "Job Sites Are Doing a Heck of a Job," *Business Week*, 9 March 2001.

selected bibliography

The Study of Corporate Venturing

The study of venturing and corporate investment in promising ideas is not new, of course. More than twenty years ago, in July 1981, the *Harvard Business Review* published "New Ventures for Corporate Growth" by Edward B. Roberts. Like many early studies of corporate venturing, the article focuses on joint ventures and partnering, which defined the bulk of corporate activity in new businesses through the 1980s. But Roberts's article also takes note of the incubation process at 3M. Although the endeavor was located within the company's R&D division, Roberts points out that its commitment to new products and its entrepreneurial quality made it different from the business development office in most other companies.

Roberts was unable to detect any clear methodology for corporate venturing. Indeed, he conceded that studies of such internal ventures were rare. But over the next two decades, there would be a considerable accumulation of experience in both private and corporate venturing from which lessons could be drawn.

A potent example is Gordon Bell's 1991 study, *High-Tech Ventures*, a book that was ahead of its time in many ways. Our book builds on the framework and perspective that Bell discussed in that publication. The initial Bell-Mason Diagnostic forms the basis for Bell's chapter 10. In *High-Tech Ventures*, Bell lays out a structure for how independent new ventures are created. We build on and further develop that methodology and understanding to show how corporations and corporate venturing are different. Bell wrote when the world was still on the brink of the great technology upheaval of the 1990s. We have extended these ideas now that the IT revolution has proved to be both a necessity to growth and a threat to exhausted business models.

We were also deeply influenced by Larry Downes and Chunka Mui's best-selling book, *Unleashing the Killer App*. Although they were not writing a book on corporate venturing in the strictest sense, the authors understand how traditional planning is inadequate to the task of nurturing new ideas. They provide a very structured method for how to integrate New Economy ideas into Old Economy management.

Books such as Rita Gunther McGrath and Ian C. MacMillan's *The Entrepreneurial Mindset* or Gifford Pinchot and Ron Pellman's *Intrapreneuring in Action* echo many of the same important themes, including the necessity of developing a separate set of entrepreneurial rules with a corporate structure. This lesson is critical to the success of corporate venturing, which invariably requires incentives, a work environment, a compensation plan, and management experience that is different, if not at odds, with an otherwise successful corporate culture.

Paul Gompers and Josh Lerner authored the 1999 study *The Venture Capital Cycle*, one of the most detailed examinations of how the venture capital process works. Their book also includes a comparison of venture capital activity with corporate venturing and notes some key differences. But the most important point in their study for our purposes is the recognition that successful venture capital is a cycle with several key and carefully timed stages. In this book, we emphasize how corporate venturing is a process that moves from the concept stage to the launch of the business, each stage having its own set of milestones to meet.

The 1995 book *Corporate Venturing: Creating New Businesses Within the Firm* popularized the concept of managing new, high-risk ventures from within a corporation, rather than through a venture capital firm. The authors, Zenas Block and Ian MacMillan, emphasize the potential cultural clashes between traditional corporate management and a new venture, and stress the importance of creating an entrepreneurial environment where innovative ideas can flourish. Suffice it to say that many great books on subjects directly and indirectly related to venturing exist. We are not challenging those works; in fact, we are integrating many of them. Here is a list of some of our favorites:

Alterowitz, Ralph, and Jon Zonderman. *New Corporate Ventures: How to Make Them Work.* New York: Wiley, 1988.

Block, Zenas, and Ian C. MacMillan. *Corporate Venturing: Creating New Businesses Within the Firm.* Boston: Harvard Business School Press, 1995.

Burgelman, Robert A., Modesto A. Maidique, and Steven C. Wheelwright: *Strategic Management of Technology and Innovation.* New York: McGraw-Hill Higher Education, 2000.

Christensen, Clayton M. *The Innovator's Dilemma: When New Technologies Cause Great Firms to Fail.* Boston: Harvard Business School Press, 1997.

Corporate Strategy Board. *Staffing Corporate Venture Groups: Enabling Effective Venture Investing and Incubation.* Washington, DC: Corporate Executive Board, 2001.

Corporate Strategy Board. *Corporate Venture Capital: Managing Equity Investments for Strategic Returns.* Washington, DC: Corporate Executive Board, 2000.

Corporate Strategy Board. *The New Venture Division: Attributes of an Effective New Business Incubation Structure.* Washington, DC: Corporate Executive Board, 2000.

Dörner, Dietrich. *The Logic of Failure: Recognizing and Avoiding Error in Complex Situations.* Cambridge, MA: Perseus Publishing, 1996.

Downes, Larry, and Chunka Mui. *Unleashing the Killer App: Digital Strategies for Market Dominance.* Boston: Harvard Business School Press, 1998.

Drucker, Peter. *Innovation and Entrepreneurship: Practices and Principles.* New York: HarperBusiness, 1993.

Evans, Philip, and Thomas S. Wurster. *Blown to Bits: How the New Economics of Information Transforms Strategy.* Boston: Harvard Business School Press, 1999.

Foster, Richard. *Innovation: The Attacker's Advantage.* New York: Summit Books, 1986.

Gompers, Paul, and Josh Lerner. *The Venture Capital Cycle.* Cambridge, MA: MIT Press, 1999.

Hagel, John, and Marc Singer. *Net Worth: Shaping Markets When Customers Make the Rules.* Boston: Harvard Business School Press, 1999.

Hanan, Mack. *Consultative Selling: The Hanan Formula for High Margin Sales at High Levels,* 6th edition. New York: AMACOM Books, 1999.

Kanter, Rosabeth Moss. *When Giants Learn to Dance.* New York: Simon and Schuster, 1989.

Kawasaki, Guy. *Rules for Revolutionaries: The Capitalist Manifesto for Creating and Marketing New Products and Services.* New York: HarperBusiness, 2000.

McGrath, Rita Gunther, and Ian C. McMillan. *The Entrepreneurial Mindset: Strategies for Continuously Creating Opportunity in an Age of Uncertainty.* Boston: Harvard Business School Press, 2000.

McGrath, Michael E. *Product Strategy for High-Technology Companies.* New York: McGraw-Hill Professional Publishing, 2000.

McKenna, Regis. *Relationship Marketing: Successful Strategies in the Age of the Customer.* Cambridge, MA: Perseus Publishing, 1993.

Moore, Geoffrey. *Crossing the Chasm: Marketing and Selling High Tech Products to Mainstream Customers.* New York: HarperBusiness, 1999.

Moore, Geoffrey. *Living on the Fault Line: Managing for Shareholder Value in the Age of the Internet.* New York: HarperBusiness, 2000.

Pinchot, Gifford, Ron Pellman. *Intrapreneuring in Action: A Handbook for Business Innovation.* San Francisco: Berrett-Koehler Publishers, 1999.

Porter, Michael. *Competitive Strategy: Techniques for Analyzing Industries and Competitors.* New York: The Free Press, 1980.

Sawhney, Mohanbir. The *Seven Steps to Nirvana: Strategic Insights into eBusiness Transformation.* New York: McGraw-Hill Professional Publishing, 2001.

Shapiro, Carl, and Hal R. Varian. *Information Rules: A Strategic Guide to the Networked Economy.* Boston: Harvard Business School Press, 1998.

Slywotsky, Adrian. *Value Migration: How to Think Several Moves ahead of the Competition.* Boston: Harvard Business School Press, 1996.

Von Hippel, Eric. *The Sources of Innovation.* Oxford: Oxford University Press, 1988.

Wiersema, Fred. *The New Market Leaders: Who's Winning and How in the Battle for Customers.* New York: The Free Press, 2001.

Zook, Chris, and James Allen. *Profit from the Core: Growth Strategy in an Era of Turbulence.* Boston: Harvard Business School Press, 2001.

index

about the authors

Heidi Mason, a Fellow with DiamondCluster International, is Managing Director of the Bell-Mason Group, which provides strategy and consulting to independent and corporate e-ventures. She is also co-creator, with partner Gordon Bell, of a first–of–kind venture development system and diagnostic, The Bell-Mason Diagnostic (BMD), which pioneered an objective means by which to evaluate early stage ventures. She has been immersed in new ventures in Silicon Valley for twenty years.

Prior to the establishment of the Bell-Mason Group, Mason, an entrepreneur who has cofounded and run multiple ventures of her own, was Cofounder and CEO of Acuity Inc., a Silicon Valley technology marketing and communications consultancy.

In addition to her work over the years with independent start-ups and the venture community, Mason has also advised a spectrum of global 1000 corporations, including Mitsubishi International, CNA Insurance, and Eastman Chemical, on corporate venturing. She holds a B.A., Phi Beta Kappa, from the University of Pennsylvania. She resides in Palo Alto, California.

Tim Rohner is a Partner with DiamondCluster International, a management consulting firm, where he is a leader in the firm's digital strategy and new ventures consulting practices. He assists clients in creating technology-driven business strategies and then executing those strategies to deliver measurable value.

Rohner has served clients in high technology, retail, financial services, transportation, publishing, distribution, and health care. He's addressed senior management issues in the areas of market and product strategy, operations, procurement, logistics, real estate, information technology, and customer care.

Currently, Rohner is focused on helping established companies innovate and grow through the use of new ventures. Prior to that, while at McKinsey & Company, he counseled top management on strategic and operational issues that had strong technology components. And prior to that, while at Arthur Andersen & Company (now Accenture), he led portions of large custom software development projects.

Rohner holds a B.S. in Finance from the University of Illinois and is a certified public accountant. He resides in San Diego, California.